STALEMATE

STALEMATE

Causes and Consequences
of Legislative Gridlock

SARAH A. BINDER

BROOKINGS INSTITUTION PRESS
Washington, D.C.

Copyright © 2003
THE BROOKINGS INSTITUTION
1775 Massachusetts Avenue, N.W., Washington, D.C. 20036
www.brookings.edu

Library of Congress Cataloging-in-Publication data
Binder, Sarah A.
   Stalemate: causes and consequences of legislative gridlock /
Sarah A.Binder.
   p.   cm.
Includes bibliographical references and index.
   ISBN 0-8157-0910-2 (cloth : alk. paper)—
   ISBN 0-8157-0911-0 (pbk.:alk. paper)
   1. United States. Congress—History.   2. United States.
Congress—Voting—History.   I. Title.
JK1021.B56 2003
328.73'077—dc21   2002154556

9 8 7 6 5 4 3 2 1

The paper used in this publication meets minimum requirements of the
American National Standard for Information Sciences—Permanence of Paper
for Printed Library Materials, ANSI Z39.48-1992.

Typeset in Sabon

Composition by R. Lynn Rivenbark
Macon, Georgia

Printed by R. R. Donnelley
Harrisonburg, Virginia

For Forrest, Noa, and Mica

Contents

Figures

Foreword

O ne of Brookings's three research programs is now called Governance Studies. No issue of governance is more timely, at the beginning of a new Congress, than how to make that institution and its processes more efficient. Why is Congress remarkably productive at some times and mired in stalemate at others? Today, after years of complaints about legislative gridlock in Washington, this question is especially pertinent. Although in recent years Congress and the president have reached agreement on such major issues as education, welfare, and campaign finance reform, other problems often seem impervious to reform. In *Stalemate*, Sarah Binder, a senior fellow in Governance Studies, reviews more than fifty years of legislative history, measures the frequency of deadlock during that time, and offers new insight into the variation in Congress's performance.

Conventional wisdom holds that unified party control of Congress and the White House is essential to breaking deadlock. Building on recent work that challenges the centrality of that premise, Sarah proposes and empirically tests another explanation. She finds that party control is important, but that it alone cannot explain the variation in Congress's performance. Instead she argues that two sets of tension—bicameral differences and partisan polarization—are two principal common denominators of legislative stalemate. At the same time she finds that unified party control of Congress and the White House is not a magic bullet for resolving legislative deadlock since bipartisan coalitions are almost always needed to break deadlock. She also argues that the "disappearing political center," the subject of much debate, is real, and it affects Congress's ability to reach legislative agreements that will stick. Finally, bicameral differences play a large part in shaping Congress's capacity for policy change. Although political differences among the branches and the parties typically garner the most attention in Washington, differences between the chambers are equally pivotal in shaping the prospects for major policy change.

Sarah warns, however, that legislators have little incentive to alter their rules and practices because there are few electoral consequences of Congress's frequent bouts with deadlock. More frequent gridlock does, however, measurably affect the public standing of Congress and the president, suggesting that failure to legislate may weaken the legitimacy of both branches. She concludes her study by proposing a number of innovations to increase Congress's legislative capacity. Introducing special negotiating procedures in committee and in bicameral settings, she suggests, might improve Congress's legislative performance and its standing in the public's eye. In a post–September 11 world ensuring legislative capacity should certainly be a priority.

Brookings gratefully acknowledges financial support for this project from the Dillon Fund.

Strobe Talbott
President

January 2003
Washington, D.C

Acknowledgments

I owe a great deal to innumerable colleagues and friends in Washington and beyond, several of whom read and commented on the entire manuscript. For their advice and assistance, I am especially grateful to Stan Bach, Mike Bailey, Neal Beck, Chuck Cameron, Joe Cooper, Chris Deering, E. J. Dionne, Dick Fenno, Mo Fiorina, John Kingdon, Keith Krehbiel, Eric Lawrence, Frances Lee, Forrest Maltzman, Tom Mann, David Mayhew, Elizabeth Rybicki Merry, Eric Patashnik, Keith Poole, Wendy Schiller, Lee Sigelman, Barbara Sinclair, Steve Smith, Jim Stimson, Paul Wahlbeck, and Kent Weaver. I am also indebted to Matthew Atlas, who spent over a year burrowed in the microfilm closet at Brookings and various libraries around town; his superb assistance in developing a measure of legislative gridlock made the project possible. Superb research assistance by Kara Chessman, Grace Cho, and Larissa Davis (who also verified the manuscript) was invaluable as well. I also appreciate the assistance of Brookings interns Jason Friedman, Mattias Geise, Russell Lippmann, Jess Melanson, Sheela Portonovo, Benjamin Robbins, and

Rohit Shah. Elizabeth McAlpine and Susan Stewart provided administrative support, Theresa Walker edited the manuscript, Inge Lockwood proofread it, and Enid Zafran prepared the index.

My greatest debt remains to Forrest Maltzman, at once my most favored colleague and companion. I could not have completed, let alone started, this book without him. Finally, to Forrest, Noa, and Mica, I dedicate this book. No coalition brings me greater joy.

STALEMATE

1 | Stalemate in Legislative Politics

We think both parties misread the temper as well as the intelligence of the American electorate if they think it is "good politics" to stall and delay on important issues and eventually come up with nothing.

New York Times EDITORIAL, JUNE 24, 1956

Gridlock is not a modern legislative condition. Although the term is said to have entered the American political lexicon after the 1980 elections, Alexander Hamilton complained more than two centuries ago about stalemate, at the time rooted in the design of the Continental Congress.[1] In the very first *Federalist*, Hamilton bemoaned the "unequivocal experience of the inefficacy of the subsisting federal government" under the Articles of Confederation.[2]

More than two hundred years later, innumerable critics of American politics still call for more responsive and effective government. The predominance of divided party government in recent decades disheartens many critics. They charge that divided government brings "conflict, delay, and indecision" and frequently leads to "deadlock, inadequate and ineffective policies, or no policies at all."[3] The short period of unified party control under the Democrats after the 1992 elections failed to abate criticism of Washington. As the *Washington Post* observed in reviewing the legislative record of the unified 103d Congress (1993–94), "It's

1

back to gridlock, or so it has seemed lately—but of a nasty internecine kind."[4] Even the bipartisan cooperation between Congress and the president that emerged after the terrorist attacks of September 11, 2001, lasted only a short while before the parties returned to sparring over economic and social issues.

In many ways, stalemate, a frequent consequence of separated institutions sharing and competing for power, seems endemic to American politics. Periods of lawmaking prowess are the exception, rather than the norm. When they occur, we give them enduring political labels, like the New Deal and the Great Society. Outside of these episodes of significant policy change, the frequency of gridlock varies considerably, variation that has attracted the attention of political observers and political scientists. In this book, I probe these trends in legislative performance, asking questions about the dynamics of lawmaking. How often does gridlock occur? What explains the historical ups and downs in policy stalemate? What are the consequences of Congress's uneven performance over time? How does legislative performance shape the ambitions of members of Congress, their electoral fortunes, and the reputation of the institution in which they serve?

There is a history to these questions. For years, political observers, participants, and scholars have fingered unified party control of Congress and the White House as essential for breaking deadlock: when one party is in control of both branches, the majority party's common electoral and policy interests help to bridge the Constitution's separation of powers and thus foster major lawmaking.[5] Some scholars have questioned the impact of divided government on lawmaking, and I build from their work in several ways.[6] First, I revisit the notion of "framers' intent," investigating whether gridlock was the preferred outcome of those who designed the American system of separated powers. Second, I explore the ways in which elections and institutions together shape the capacity of Congress and the president to make public law. And third, I offer a new empirical approach for testing accounts of policy stalemate during the decades since World War II. My aims are to encourage scholars, political observers, and lawmakers to rethink the causes and consequences of legislative stalemate and to consider reforms that might bolster Congress's capacity to resolve major policy and political differences.

"A Way of Life and Law"

In surveying scholarship on American politics, political scientist Charles O. Jones has observed that scholars rarely study lawmaking in itself. Although the American experience represents "a way of life and law," Jones notes that legislative scholars are more apt to study institutional arrangements and legislative behavior than they are to ponder broader patterns that structure the making of law.[7] Such a focus is curious, Jones contends, in light of the centrality of lawmaking to democratic governance: lawmaking is the "core decision-making process of a democratic state" and as such justifies our attention.[8] When we draw our research topics too narrowly, Jones warns, we fail to explain the most basic feature of democratic life.

Why study policy gridlock? Normatively, exploring the causes of stalemate is important, regardless of one's party or ideology. Lawmaking is the process by which governments "legitimize substantive and procedural actions to reshape public problems, perhaps to resolve them."[9] If we care about whether and when our political system is able to respond to problems both new and endemic to our common social, economic, and political lives, then explaining the conditions that underscore policy change and stability is a valuable and worthwhile endeavor.

Some might object that interest in gridlock implies a normative preference for legislative activism and liberal policy change. As Jefferson's maxim implies, "that government is best which governs least."[10] If Jefferson was always right, then gridlock might always be a welcome feature of legislative politics. But views about gridlock tend to vary with one's political circumstance. Former Senate majority leader Bob Dole put it best: "If you're against something, you'd better hope there is a little gridlock."[11] Because legislative activism can move the law in either a conservative or liberal direction, calls to end gridlock are not the exclusive province of liberal interests. In some respects, the confusion lies in the choice of words, as we often use the terms *gridlock, stalemate,* and *deadlock* to describe legislative inaction. In this book, I too refer to stalemate and gridlock, but more precisely I am exploring Congress's relative ability over time and issues to broach and secure policy compromise on issues high on the national agenda. Framed in this way, a study of legislative performance should interest any keen observer, participant, or student of national performance, regardless of her party or ideology.

A study of policy gridlock also promises to advance our understanding of the dynamics underlying legislative politics. Legislative scholars have traditionally concentrated on segments of the institution and its members—pursuing single-chamber studies, roll call analysis, committee politics, party operations, and so on. The broader politics and patterns of lawmaking have garnered less attention than the various features and practices of the institution. By exploring empirical patterns in legislative performance over time, this book should help us to disentangle the forces that shape Congress's ability to secure policy compromise. In particular, although we know much about the politics of conflict between the branches, we know far less about intrabranch dynamics. Probing the effects of two such frictions—bicameral relations and partisan polarization—may yield important new insights to explain patterns of lawmaking and stalemate in the contemporary Congress.

Finally, although scholars often shy away from the practical implications of their work, this book potentially offers something useful to lawmakers and others engaged in national policymaking: concrete advice about how they might improve the institutional capacity of Congress. To be sure, policymakers naturally disagree about the desirability of institutional reform, often (although not exclusively) along party lines. Those seeking to improve Congress's capacity to compromise on major policy issues may still learn something from this study. Given the impact of bicameral differences and partisan polarization on the ability of lawmakers to reach agreement on major policy change, I suggest some institutional innovations might make bargaining over policy differences more productive and thus make policy compromise more likely. Given the enormity of the challenges facing Washington after September 11—particularly with the return of budget constraints—creative reform of legislative practice ought to be desirable across partisan and institutional divides.

Stalemate in a Madisonian System

It is fairly easy to address skeptics who question the study of gridlock on normative grounds. It is harder to disarm constitutional skeptics. Such skeptics argue that stalemate is a constant of American political life. They suggest that James Madison bequeathed us a political system designed not to work, a government of sharply limited powers. According to this view, the framers appreciated and preferred stalemate, intentionally designing the Constitution to guarantee gridlock. Efforts to disentangle causes of gridlock ultimately run into a constitutional bulwark against effective lawmaking: stalemate, they would argue, is a natural, intended, and constant consequence of the Constitution. It makes little sense to study its causes or variation over time.

Constitutional arguments are also used both to defend and bemoan legislative inaction. For defenders, gridlock signals the health of the Madisonian system of separated institutions sharing powers. Former member of the House of Representatives Bill Frenzel put it best when he argued that gridlock is the "best thing since indoor plumbing."[12] Why? Frenzel offers a constitutional defense: the tendency toward gridlock is "a natural gift the Framers of our Constitution gave us so that the country would not be subjected to policy swings resulting from the whimsy of the public."[13] But for critics of inaction, gridlock is a symptom of disease: The Madisonian system thwarts well-intended efforts to enact policy change. As veteran *Los Angeles Times* correspondent Robert Shogan diagnosed it, "At the root of the problem . . . is a political and governing system that was designed not to work."[14]

Political scientists offer constitutional diagnoses as well. Writing in the 1960s to urge revitalization of the Democratic Party and its leadership, James MacGregor Burns argued that we "underestimate the extent to which our system was designed for deadlock and inaction."[15] Burns placed the blame squarely in the hands of James Madison, whom Burns accused of "believ[ing] in a government of sharply limited powers. His efforts in Philadelphia . . . were intended more to thwart popular majorities in the states from passing laws for their own ends than to empower national majorities to pass laws for *their* ends."[16]

A competing interpretation suggests an alternative way of interpreting framers' intent. As Charles Jones has observed, "It is worth remembering that the Founders were seeking to devise a working government. They did, of course, have fears about tyranny and thereby sought protection through competing legitimacies. But the point was not solely to stop the bad from happening; it was to permit the good, or even the middling, to occur as well."[17] This alternative view suggests that the founders sought a strong national government that could govern—though one that would be partially insulated from the passions of popular majorities. The result was an "intricate balance between limiting government and infusing it with energy."[18] This disagreement over framers' intent is important. If the framers did not intend to create a system that was prone to deadlock, then we cannot simply dismiss episodes of stalemate in American politics as a desirable and untouchable gift from the framers. Frequent policy gridlock might instead be an unintended consequence of constitutional design. Distinguishing between the origins and effects of institutions may shed a different light on the framers, the Constitution, and their views of government inaction.

Foremost in the minds of the framers in designing a new constitution were the inadequacies of the Articles of Confederation and the political instability engendered in the states under a variety of constitutions.[19] James Madison and Alexander Hamilton saw the impotence of the Continental Congress as an enormous threat to the future of the new union, using the first half of the *Federalist* papers to explain the flaws of the existing government. Because supermajority or unanimous support was required to enact many types of policy or constitutional change, and because it failed to raise adequate revenues, command state support, protect commercial interests, support troops, and secure western expansion, the Continental Congress proved inadequate to the tasks of governing.[20]

Delegates to the Constitutional Convention, with well-noted exceptions, largely agreed with Madison and Hamilton's goal of a more centralized government.[21] They agreed in principle that the new union would require a much stronger national government, what Hamilton called "an enlightened zeal for the energy and efficiency of government."[22] Or as Madison summarized later in *Federalist* 37, both stability and energy were critical to good government.

Although conventional accounts suggest considerable opposition by delegates to a strong national government, more recent accounts cast doubt on the degree and intensity of such differences across state delegations. The New Jersey plan—traditionally portrayed as buoying the power of states vis-à-vis the new central government—in fact "did not signal any sincere ideological opposition to Madison's centralizing goals.[23] As Frances Lee and Bruce Oppenheimer have recently argued, small states were simply staking out the costs for agreeing to Madison's centralizing plan: equal state vote in the Senate was the small states' condition for supporting a new, stronger national government.[24] As Roger Sherman from Connecticut made clear during the Constitutional Convention, "everything . . . depended on this."[25] There was far more agreement at the convention on the merits of a stronger, more active government than the received wisdom suggests.

Skeptics might point to the doctrine at the heart of the Constitution, the separation of powers, as evidence that the framers sought to hamstring the new government. To be sure, the division of power between legislative, executive, and judicial branches is typically portrayed as a mechanism chosen by the framers to check or limit federal power. The separation of powers is said to restrain the making of policy and thus to encourage stalemate instead of policy change. "It has not been an easy constitution with which to make policy quickly and to govern efficiently," scholar Clinton Rossiter observed in the 1960s, "which is exactly the kind of constitution the framers intended it to be. The gaps that separate the executive from the legislature . . . have often been as discouraging to men of good will as to men of corrupt intent."[26] Even Madison defended the separation of powers during the ratification campaign as a device "necessary to control the abuses of government."[27]

A competing interpretation of the separation of powers is worth considering. As Gordon Wood observed in studying the origins of the Constitution, the separation of powers had a unique meaning for the new nation: "When Americans in 1776 spoke of keeping the several parts of the government separate and distinct, they were primarily thinking of insulating the judiciary and particularly the legislature from executive manipulation."[28] Rather than seeking to limit legislative capacity, the framers saw the separation of powers as a mechanism for protecting the autonomy of the judicial and legislative branches. The experience of royal governors intervening in the affairs of the colonial legislatures shaped such early American views about the separation of powers. Interestingly, after independence a decade later, the problem was reversed. Now, limiting legislative encroachment over executive responsibilities was central to the framers' views about the separation of powers. Creating and protecting an executive separate from the legislature was critical to ensuring legislative and administrative capacity in the new government.[29]

The costs of failing to separate governing powers were visible in the unicameral Congress established under the Articles, a chamber that legislated as well as executed the duties and details of government. As Hamilton complained, "Congress have kept the power too much into their own hands and have meddled too much with details of every sort. Congress is properly a deliberative corps and it forgets itself when it attempts to play the executive." Thomas Jefferson had earlier voiced similar misgivings about the Continental Congress: "Nothing is so embarrassing nor so mischievous, in a great assembly, as the details of execution."[30] In this context, the separation of powers makes perfect sense as an instrument for pursuing effective governance. By dividing lawmaking, administrative, and judicial functions of government, each would be protected from the encroachments of the others. Creating distinctive branches of government would simultaneously check political power, enhance executive energy, and incubate legislative capacity.

Given competing interpretations of the separation of powers, we should consider the principle a malleable doctrine. As one scholar has observed, even at the Constitutional Convention "everyone sought to associate his favorite constitutional reform proposal with this design principle."[31] The division of legislative, executive, and judicial functions could be claimed to ensure an energetic executive (according to Alexander Hamilton) or to inhibit lawmaking (according to Roger Mason and other defenders of states' rights). Madison himself had a strong strategic incentive to adjust his defense of the separation of powers as the convention proceeded. As Samuel Kernell has suggested, Madison originally defended the Virginia Plan (which would have created a strong national government dominated by the legislature) on the basis that it separated powers.[32] Compared with the dismal experiment of the Continental Congress, the separation of powers under the Virginia Plan would enhance government efficiency. When Madison's Virginia Plan was defeated, he simply adjusted his defense of the separation of powers. Instead of fostering efficient governing, the separation of powers became a crucial tool of checks and balances against unrestrained governmental power. In other words, the framers' embrace of the separation of powers and its checks and balances is not sufficient grounds for establishing that they sought to design a constitution that would make deadlock the most common outcome.[33]

Finally, remember that the framers refused to engage in rulemaking for the newly created House and Senate chambers. Conspicuously absent from the two new chambers of Congress were the supermajority rules that so often caused stalemate in the Continental Congress. Nor did the members of the first House or Senate create rules that strongly limited the power of simple majorities to pass legislation.[34] Why did the framers not impose legislative rules on the new Congress? One plausible interpretation is that the framers did intend to design a system prone to gridlock, but they believed additional procedural restraints on legislative power were unnecessary. They had already staggered the elections of senators, established different electoral bases, and set different terms for members of the House and Senate. What further constraints on lawmaking could be necessary? Under this view, meddling with the internal organization of the new Congress was simply unnecessary.

An alternative and equally plausible interpretation is that the framers wanted to create a stronger and more efficient national legislature, and thus they purposefully avoided hamstringing the new Congress with the types of rules that encumbered the Continental Congress under the Articles of Confederation. To be sure, we can never be sure why something did *not* happen. But we know for sure that Hamilton and Madison opposed the system of supermajority requirements for passing bills used by the Continental Congress. Both wrote explicitly about the dangers of limiting the powers of simple majorities. As Madison argued in *Federalist 58*,

> It has been said that more than a majority ought to have been required for a quorum, and in particular cases, if not in all, more than a majority of a quorum for a decision. That some advantages might have resulted from such a precaution, cannot be denied. . . . But these considerations are outweighed by the inconveniences in the opposite scale. In all cases where justice or the general good might require new laws to be passed, or active measures to be pursued, the fundamental principle of free government would be reversed. It would be no longer the majority that would rule; the power would be transferred to the minority.[35]

Madison clearly felt compelled to defend the framers' decision *not* to impose supermajority requirements. The passage suggests that the framers' silence in the Constitution about internal legislative procedures cannot simply be interpreted as a sign that the framers believed procedural restraints unnecessary.

Hamilton also attacked the structure of the Continental Congress, criticizing its rules that required a two-thirds vote of the states to pass legislation regarding revenue, spending, or military matters:

> The necessity of unanimity in public bodies, or of something approaching towards it, has been founded upon a supposition that it would contribute to security. But its real operation is to embarrass the administration, to destroy the energy of government, and to substitute the pleasure, caprice or artifices of an insignificant, turbulent

or corrupt junto, to the regular deliberations and decisions of a respectable majority.[36]

Madison and Hamilton, in short, rejected writing for the new Constitution those institutional rules that had fostered stalemate in the old Congress—suggesting that the framers at least sought to avoid some of the procedural traps that so often led to deadlock under the Articles of Confederation.

Revisiting the political context in which the constitutional delegates worked suggests that we temper our conventional interpretation of framers' intent. In well-known ways, draftsmen of the Constitution sought to check and thus restrain governmental power, seeking to prevent the new government from sliding into tyranny. At the same time, the framers faced rigorous opposition from Anti-Federalists in the campaign to convince the states to ratify the new Constitution. These pressures gave the Federalists a strategic incentive to emphasize the ways in which power would be restrained—not enhanced—under the new Constitution.[37] Regardless of the ratification campaign, the framers' experiences with the Continental Congress limited their willingness to hamstring governmental capacity. They favored checking popular powers, but they were clearly motivated by the failures of the Continental Congress to design a government more capable of responding to national crises and problems. As I explore in chapter 2, gridlock may be an unintended consequence of the institutions they chose, but it is unlikely that it reflected the sincere preferences of the men who drafted the Constitution. We simply cannot explain away contemporary policy gridlock as a matter of framers' original intent.

Plan of the Book

I present my account of legislative stalemate in chapter 2. I start with the notion that political institutions are prone to evolve over time. When institutions and their environments change over time, we often find that institutions come to have consequences that were unintended by their designers. Congress, as a political body in a constitutional system of separated powers, clearly fits this notion of an evolving institution. In chapter 2, I examine two facets of its institutional evolution: the emergence of the Senate as a coequal legislative partner of the House and the insertion of political parties into a legislative arena originally devoid of parties. Both of these factors—bicameralism and partisan politics—form the basis of my conjectures about forces that encourage more frequent legislative stalemate.

To test my ideas about these causal mechanisms, I develop a measure of legislative performance in chapter 3 that taps the frequency of policy gridlock. I show why counts of legislative output ought to be measured in proportion to the number of issues on the legislative agenda and introduce a methodology for determining the size and content of Congress's agenda and the frequency of gridlock. I then analyze patterns in legislative performance during the second half of the twentieth century, showing the frequency of policy deadlock and the legislative stages at which it has most often emerged in the postwar period.

In chapters 4 and 5, I use the new measure of stalemate to explain empirical patterns in the frequency of gridlock. The results weave together the effects of institutions and elections and place in perspective the impact of divided government on legislative performance. I show that intrabranch and intraparty conflict—perhaps more so than interbranch rivalry—are central in shaping deadlock in postwar politics. I also explore the effects of these factors on the fate of salient legislative measures considered during the 103d (1993–94) and 104th (1995–96) congresses, illustrating how variation in bicameral and partisan differences have helped to shape the incidence of stalemate in recent years.

I conclude in chapter 6 by addressing the consequences of legislative stalemate, assessing whether and to what degree deadlock might affect electoral fortunes, political ambitions, and institutional reputations of legislators and presidents. The results suggest that recurring episodes of stalemate pose a dilemma for legislators and others who care about the institutional standing and capacity of Congress: despite ample evidence of gridlock's institutional consequences, legislators lack sufficient electoral incentive to do much about it. I conclude by exploring some modest reforms intended to bolster Congress's capacity to secure policy compromise. Such reforms might have limited effect on legislators' electoral fortunes, but they could have strong and salutary effects on the institutional standing and legitimacy of Congress and the president.Without a sufficient motivation for legislators to overcome the dilemma of stalemate and redress the excesses of gridlock, however, deadlock is likely to be a recurring and enduring feature of national politics and policymaking.

2 | Unintended Consequences of Constitutional Design

The framers of the Constitution are often blamed for purposefully designing a political system loaded with barriers against lawmaking. Recall Clinton Rossiter's lament about the separation of powers: "It has not been an easy constitution with which to make policy quickly and to govern efficiently."[1] Rossiter and leagues of other critics are certainly on the mark when they argue that the framers' design made it very difficult for majorities to pass legislation in a swift and timely manner. By separating institutions and forcing the executive and legislative branches to share several key powers, the framers raised the bar against minorities seeking to impose their views on the majority and against the easy formation of majorities seeking to tyrannize the minority. Not surprisingly, the framers are often blamed for designing a system made "not to work."[2]

It is possible, however, that the Constitution makes it difficult to legislate, even if that was not the express intention of the framers. Institutions can have consequences that were unforeseen and unintended by their designer. A mismatch between the design of an institution and the effects of that institution can occur for two reasons. First, political players do not always get what they want. The framers may have preferred a political system that could easily allow majority sentiment to become policy, but compromises made during the Constitutional Convention may have eliminated the possibility of such an outcome. If the framers had rigidly pursued their preferences, that might have yielded no new constitution at all, a status quo unacceptable to the framers. Because the framers were not monolithic in their views about the desired features of a new Constitution, a mismatch between institutional preferences and outcomes might have emerged. Compromises at the Constitutional Convention, in other words, may have obscured the framers' true preferences, assuming consensus ever existed.

A second reason a mismatch might occur is that the choice of an institution (and thus the reasons for its choice) may have little relationship to the effects of that institution after it is created. Here we enter the realm of unintended consequences. Why might such unintended effects emerge? One possibility is that the framers of an institution simply miscalculate how an institution's features will work. Another possibility is that as new forces come into play within and outside an institution, its features develop unintended consequences. The emergence of the Senate filibuster is a nice example of such unintended consequences. Unlimited debate was made possible in the Senate in 1806 when senators eliminated a chamber rule that would have allowed a majority to cut off debate. The rule was dropped not because senators sought to lift restraints on their rights of debate but because they were cleaning up a messy rulebook and did not foresee the implications of removing the rule.[3] When partisan conflict appeared three decades later, senators discovered that there was no way to cut off a minority determined to talk a bill to death. Clearly, the consequence of the procedural choice in 1806 was neither intended nor anticipated by senators in altering their institution.

My account of legislative gridlock draws from both of these sources of mismatch between an institution's design and its consequences. First, as shown in chapter 1, there is little evidence that the framers' sincere preferences dictated that they choose a Constitution that under most conditions would produce policy deadlock. A plausible alternative is that the framers wanted a Constitution that would allow legislators to secure policy compromises in face of pressing demands, a Constitution that could both "stop the bad from happening . . . [and] . . . permit the good . . . to occur as well."[4] To the extent that separated institutions sharing powers enhanced the probability of stopping the bad and diminished the chance of securing the good, those institutional choices did not mirror the sincere preferences of the framers. Compromises in crafting the Constitution could easily help account for the mismatch between institutional design and consequence.

In this chapter, I focus on the second source of mismatch: that institutions may develop consequences unintended by their designers. That institutions are not fixed in stone is a long-held tenet applied to political structures. Decades ago, Edward Sait observed, "Institutions rise out of experience. . . . A borrowed institution will change in character to the extent that the new environment differs from the old."[5] Indeed, questions about institutional change have been at the heart of much recent work on the U.S. Congress. Even a small sampling of work on the development of Congress suggests extensive change in the institutional character of the House and Senate. For instance, we know that the institution became more routinized, professionalized, and bounded as the nineteenth century unfolded; that committees—originally given only temporary powers to recommend bills—gradually developed procedural rights that bolstered their powers relative to the chambers'; that committee members accrued turf rights to seats on particular committees; and that majorities gradually acquired procedural rights that significantly reduced the legislative role of the minority party in the House.[6] There is no reason to expect that these institutional changes were anticipated by the delegates at the Constitutional Convention, let alone by the first members of the House and Senate in the late eighteenth century. Even if we find that legislative institutions help shape the frequency of gridlock, we need not conclude that the framers explicitly designed Congress to ensure that stalemate was the most likely and frequent outcome.

In this chapter, I focus on two institutional developments of the early nineteenth century that I argue are critical in shaping legislative outcomes in the contemporary Congress. These are the emergence of the Senate out of the shadow of the House and the integration of political parties into the politics of the chambers. The transformation of the Senate altered the relevance of bicameralism in the legislative process and raised the centrality of bargaining between the chambers. The emergence of parties was consequential because it introduced the possibility that considerations beyond policy would influence the legislative strategies of legislators and presidents. The framers were unlikely to have anticipated either development, but both sets of changes helped to mold Congress as an institution and thus both, I conjecture, have contributed to shaping patterns of legislative politics in the contemporary Congress.

Consequences of Senate Change

If there is one central constitutional "principle" underlying the American political system it is undoubtedly the doctrine of the separation of powers—what historian Gordon Wood called "the dominant principle of the American political system."[7] Most agree that the notion of separation of powers had near universal appeal among the framers. As explored in chapter 1, the separation of powers might have had different, even *evolving*, meanings for the various strategists in Philadelphia. But delegates never seriously contested the concept at the Constitutional Convention.[8]

Given the canonical status of the separation of powers, division of authority between executive and legislative branches figures prominently in discussion of institutional constraints on lawmaking. Whether models of policy gridlock are inductive or deductive, they invariably pit the executive against the legislature, treating lawmaking as a function of a single executive opposed to the preferences of a unicameral legislature. Indeed, several recent works on Congress have shown how the separation of powers creates structural incentives for presidents and legislators as they interact in the process of making and executing the law.[9]

Although scholars understandably focus on the impact of separated powers, it was not the only doctrine with near universal support at the Constitutional Convention. Equally shared among the framers was a belief in the importance of bicameralism.[10] At the time, bicameralism was the norm, present in every state legislature except two. Just as a separation of government powers was paramount in the eyes of the framers, bicameralism was also accepted as a guiding constitutional principle. Because, as James March and Johan Olsen have argued, institutions come to "define the framework within which politics takes place," it is important to probe how bicameralism—as well as the separation of powers—affects the making of public law.[11]

The "Original" Bicameralism

The framers selected a bicameral legislature as a mechanism for checking legislative power, understanding that bicameralism would affect the dynamics of lawmaking. Toward that end, they designed two very different legislative bodies. With the chambers so different, Madison argued that collusion between the branches would be unlikely. "I will barely remark," Madison explained in *Federalist* 62, "that as the improbability of sinister combinations will be in proportion to the dissimilarity in the genius of the two bodies; it must be politic to distinguish them from each other by every circumstance which will consist with a due harmony in all proper measures, and with the genuine principles of republican government."[12]

In designing contrasting chambers, the framers argued that the Senate would serve as a necessary check on the workings of the House. In *Federalists* 62 and 63, Madison defended the Senate as a tool for correcting the "defects" of the House. By the qualifications of its members and their numbers, the mode and timing of elections and the length of terms, and its equality of representation, the Senate was designed to temper the excesses of the House. Madison made the argument explicit at the convention: the purpose of the Senate is to "consist in its proceeding with more coolness, with more system, and with more wisdom than the popular branch."[13]

Beyond a doubt, the Senate was intended to be a tool for checking the passions of the House. What is less certain is whether the framers foresaw that the House could be a tool for checking the biases of the Senate.[14] No justification of the House as a check on the Senate was ever considered in debating the structure of Congress. Since the purpose of the additional chamber was to constrain the rash impulses of a lower chamber so closely connected to local constituencies, it would have made little sense for the framers to think of the House as a check on the actions of the Senate.[15] Nor does there seem to have been any precedents in the state legislatures for viewing the House as a restraint on the Senate.

Consistent with this interpretation of the roles of the House and Senate is the pattern of legislative activity that emerged in the first decades under the new Constitution. The legislative activity of the House far outpaced that of the Senate.[16] For example, during the first eight Congresses, House legislative activity exceeded the Senate's activity by on average three to one.[17] These data suggest that the Senate routinely deferred to the House in originating legislative measures. The House eclipsed the Senate in several other ways. Senate debates were closed to reporters for its first eight years. It took more than a decade before senators allowed reporters to sit on the floor to record its debates, and thus, not surprisingly, House debates received far more news coverage than Senate debates in the Senate's formative years.[18] In sum, the House was the more active and visible of the two chambers. This suggests that the Senate rarely initiated controversial measures, and thus the House had few chances to check the actions of the upper body. By virtue of its greater legislative activity and tendency to act first, the House was clearly the agenda setter of Congress, diminishing the Senate's ability to set the terms of debate and thus shape the scope and direction of policy change.

A "New" Bicameralism

Had the Senate remained frozen in time after its creation in 1787, the distinction in the roles of the House and Senate might not matter. We might still have a Senate that corrects "defects" of the House, and yet rarely would the Senate be checked by the House. The framers did of course succeed in locking in the basic constitutional design, having set such a high threshold for its amendment. But they were unable to prevent or restrain the evolution of the Senate. Although the Constitution proved immutable to most change, the rules and norms of legislating unleashed by the Constitution were amenable to change. The framers' vision of the Senate hardly constrained the early development of the Senate. Contrary to their intentions, the upper chamber quickly emerged in the early nineteenth century as a prominent legislative chamber with its own proactive agenda.[19] The Senate swiftly evolved beyond the expectations of the framers, developing a new public visibility, a reputation for legislative initiative, independence from the executive, and a new relationship with states and electorates back home.

Evolution of the Senate had direct consequences for the character of bicameralism. By emerging as a legislative rival to the House, the Senate no longer served simply to rein in the majoritarian impulse of the House. Instead, as Elaine Swift has argued, "The bicameral separation of powers between the Senate and the House of Representatives was redefined along more democratic lines."[20] Why is this change so important? Under the original bicameralism, the Senate could certainly block or amend policy change advocated by the House. But it was the House that generally set the policy agenda and terms of debate, since the Senate rarely initiated legislative measures. Under the new bicameralism, both chambers had equal incentive to incubate and formulate policy, and the two chambers theoretically had an equal capacity to influence the direction, scope, and likelihood of legislative change. Not only did the level of legislating expand with the increased activism of the Senate, but the tenor of bills being exchanged between the two chambers likely changed as well, given the Senate's proclivity for overweighting the interests of small states at the expense of the large states.[21] With the House now more often confronted with measures biased by Senate rules and apportionment, the need for interchamber negotiation to secure major policy change probably increased too. The emergence of the Senate, in short, probably made *interchamber bargaining* over the terms of policy change a more central and frequent component of the legislative process.

The framers certainly understood that the original form of bicameralism would restrain the legislative excesses of a population-based lower chamber. But it is unlikely that they would have anticipated the emergence of the new and more democratic bicameralism and its effects, given that it took several decades for the Senate to emerge as an equal legislative partner to the House. For this reason, we can think of the effects of bicameralism as unintended consequences of the original bicameral design. Because institutions do not remain fixed in stone once created, the choice of an institutional structure does not necessarily predict its effects later in time. The early transformation of the Senate seems to fit this notion neatly. As senators began to set the legislative agenda and terms of debate, the character of interbranch bargaining surely changed. The House no longer had a monopoly on setting the agenda, and both chambers developed a need for bicameral resolution whenever they sought major policy change.[22]

Why should we care so much about the emergence of the Senate and the development of a more "democratic" bicameralism if models of legislative politics suffice nicely when they depict Congress as a unitary actor facing off against the president? Theoretical work on the impact of bicameralism encourages caution in assuming a unicameral legislature in a separation of powers system. Works by George Tsebelis, Jeannette Money, and others have shown that policy outcomes in a bicameral system are shaped by the distribution of policy views between the two legislative chambers.[23] The preferences of both chambers matter in shaping final legislative outcomes. Because I am interested in explaining the frequency of legislative gridlock, we need to explore the possibility that interchamber dynamics affect the prospects for policy change in a systematic and predictable fashion.

Bicameralism has recently attracted the attention of a number of scholars interested in mathematical models of politics. Their approaches provide an analytical framework for exploring the impact of bicameralism on legislative outcomes. In a formal sense, such work suggests that as the critical players (usually the median member of each chamber) in a bicameral game move away from one another, the "win set" of the status quo contracts.[24] This means that the set of policy proposals that can defeat the policy status quo shrinks. Less formally, the concept is straightforward. When the views of the two chambers (represented by the median legislator in each chamber) grow more dissimilar, the win set gets smaller. That is, it is harder to reach bicameral agreement because the number of policy proposals acceptable to pivotal players in the two bodies goes down. But when the policy views of the median legislators grow more alike, it should be easier to reach legislative compromise acceptable to both chambers. The likelihood of policy change (and its inverse, policy stability) thus varies directly with the degree of policy differences between the two chambers.

Theoretical work on the impact of bicameralism leads us to a simple hypothesis about bicameral effects: *the greater the policy differences between the House and Senate, the higher the frequency of legislative stalemate.* In chapters 3 and 4, I offer an empirical approach for testing this conjecture. If we find that bicameral differences directly shape the incidence of gridlock, then we can say that the emergence of a Senate coequal to the House produced unintended consequences, at least from the perspective of the framers. The original bicameralism was intended to restrain populist-flavored policy outcomes. Support for the impact of the "new" bicameralism would suggest that bicameralism affects the frequency of policy change across the policy spectrum and that its effects are conditional on the degree of policy differences between the two chambers. Thus, even if we find that the frequency of stalemate is rooted in the structure of legislative institutions, that does not mean that gridlock flows naturally from the framers' original intent and design.

Consequences of Political Parties

The emergence of the Senate in the early years of the nineteenth century was not the only institutional development that came to affect the character of congressional policymaking. Contemporaneous with change in the Senate was the development of political parties in the lower and upper chambers. As others have observed, the arrival of legislative and electoral parties within the first few decades under the Constitution was ironic, given the framers' well-known distaste for the arts of political management (and as they saw, political manipulation).[25] Despite the framers' apparent dislike of factions, however, parties during the nineteenth century became integrated into the lives of legislators and their leaders. By the end of the 1800s, parties had taken on the tasks of setting chamber agendas, managing the House and Senate floors, and appointing chairs and members to committees, besides tending to their electoral responsibilities.[26]

The emergence of parties was consequential because it introduced the possibility that considerations beyond policy would influence the legislative strategies of legislators and presidents. In designing the separation of powers *without* political parties, the framers had impeded the easy formation of majority coalitions. Without a shared electoral tie linking legislators and the president, large coalitions could only be formed on the basis of shared policy views. But consensus based on policy grounds alone was unlikely to emerge easily or often given the ways in which the separation of powers was fortified by staggered elections, differing constituencies across chambers and branches, and so forth. That of course was the goal of the framers: to make major policy change possible (compared with its difficulty under the Articles of Confederation) but not necessarily easy.

In contrast, once parties had been introduced and integrated into legislative politics, a means of bridging the separation of powers was created. Members of a party—whether serving in the House, Senate, or White House—now shared both electoral and policy interests that would theoretically provide a better means and incentive for legislators and presidents to secure major policy change. In sum, political parties in principle altered legislative dynamics, doing so without regard to the expectations or intentions of the framers. Once again, if we can show that partisan dynamics did affect the likelihood of gridlock, then we have further evidence that stalemate is aptly considered an unintended consequence of the framers' original design.

Effects of Divided Government

The question of whether and how political parties affect legislative performance recurs throughout past and present research on Congress. For decades, split party control of Congress and the president was most often indicted as the central cause of deadlock. That indictment was rooted in what we might call a long-lived love affair of political scientists with political parties. The affair stretches back to the early twentieth century, to the origins of American political science as a profession. For Woodrow Wilson, Henry Jones Ford, Frank Goodnow, and others, political parties were seen as critical instruments for achieving unity of purpose and action in American governance. As Wilson argued,

> The degree of separation now maintained between the executive and legislative branches of our government cannot long be preserved without very serious inconvenience resulting. . . . What we need is harmonious, consistent, responsible party government, instead of a wide dispersion of function and responsibility; and we can get it only by connecting the President as closely as may be with his party in Congress.[27]

By the mid-1940s, this view of parties had been enshrined as the "doctrine of responsible parties," a view holding parties essential to democratic life. Classically stated by E. E. Schattschneider in his 1942 work, *Party Government*, "The political parties created democracy and . . . modern democracy is unthinkable save in terms of the parties."[28] Only parties—by virtue of their goal of assembling majorities to win elections—could claim authority and legitimacy to rule in a democracy. Pressure groups were an obvious alternative, but they had narrow policy aims, no intentions of building electoral majorities, and hence no legitimate claim on power.

Responsible party advocates, writing in the 1940s, worked in a climate of unified government, with divided government occurring only three times between 1900 and 1946. In explaining the dynamics of lawmaking, prevailing theories "identified the political party as the indispensable instrument that brought cohesion and unity, and hence effectiveness, to the government as a whole by linking the executive and legislative branches in a bond of common interest."[29] Democracy was unthinkable except in terms of parties. *American* democracy—with its separated institutions—was unthinkable except in terms of unified party government. Some means of ensuring common electoral and policy purpose across separated institutions was necessary, and unified party control of government was deemed the natural solution. Although its presence was never considered sufficient, it was viewed as necessary for ensuring responsive government.[30] V. O. Key, writing in the 1960s, offered the now classic view: "Common partisan control of executive and legislature does not assure energetic government, but division of party control precludes it."[31]

The conventional wisdom about the unifying force of party yields a simple hypothesis about patterns of gridlock: *divided party control of government increases the frequency of gridlock, while unified control decreases it.* The logic underpinning this conjecture is simple. Under a system of separated powers, unified party control of government fuses the electoral and policy goals of the president and congressional majority. Legislative leaders in Congress thus have an incentive under unified government to use their (limited) tools and resources to enact a larger share of legislative initiatives. In contrast, divided party government reinforces policy and electoral disagreement that is endemic under the separation of powers and thus makes it difficult to assemble policy majorities necessary to forge significant change.[32] Unified government, it follows, boosts the prospects for legislative success; divided government weakens them.

Strangely enough, despite its canonical status among political scientists, no rigorous test of the impact of divided government occurred until David Mayhew's 1991 work, *Divided We Govern*. Mayhew's theoretical focus was the effect of a particular independent variable: divided government. Toward that end, he identified landmark laws in a two-stage process.[33] In the first stage (Sweep One), Mayhew used annual end-of-session wrap-up articles from the *New York Times* and *Washington Post* to survey contemporary judgments about the significance of Congress's work each session. In the second stage (Sweep Two), Mayhew relied on policy specialists' retrospective judgments about the importance of legislation. Using the results of Sweep One to inform his selection of laws in Sweep Two, he generated a comprehensive list of landmark laws enacted each Congress between 1946 and 1990.[34] He then tested whether the presence of divided government reduced the number of major laws enacted each Congress.

The strongest imprint of *Divided We Govern* is a null result for the impact of divided government. Mayhew finds that unified party control of Congress and the president fails to produce significantly higher levels of lawmaking in Washington. It matters little whether a single party controls the White House and Congress: not much more gets done than under divided party control. Absolving divided government as a cause of legislative inaction, Mayhew disentangles several other influences on legislative performance. Some factors, such as legislators' electoral incentives, point toward constancy in the lawmaking record. Others, such as shifting public moods, presidential cycles, and issue coalitions that cut across the left-right ideological divide, figure as sources of alternative variation.

Mayhew concludes that analysts have overestimated the capacity and intentions of American political parties.[35] When parties are viewed as "governing instruments," we expect them to yield substantial dividends during unified government, an unrealistic expectation. Mayhew instead counsels a less commanding view of parties as "policy factions," coalitions that can muster results regardless of the regime of party control.[36] Demanding more from parties, Mayhew reasons, runs up against the pluralist component of the American system: the agile response of parties to cross-cutting currents within the American polity. Mayhew suggests more is demanded from parties than they are able to deliver in our system of separated powers. Are Mayhew's conclusions robust to alternative measures of legislative performance? I return to this question in chapter 3.

The Impact of Pluralist Parties

Regardless of what we conclude about the impact of divided government, it would be wise to heed Mayhew's conclusions about the pluralist character of American politics. Such pluralism is perhaps most visible in the array of policy views that make up each of the two major parties. We can think of two stylized alignments of legislators' policy views by party. At times the preferences of the two major parties will be polarized, with legislators from each party standing at opposite ends of an underlying ideological spectrum. Today, the House and Senate parties are markedly polarized: Democrats cluster on the far left of the ideological spectrum, Republicans occupy the far right. Few legislators fill the political center. At other times, partisan moderation dominates, with a greater number of legislators standing close to the ideological center between the parties. Legislators from either or both of the parties would be spread across the ideological spectrum, with many legislators sharing central space between the parties.

Figures 2-1 and 2-2 illustrate both conditions, using a scoring system based on roll call votes to place legislators along a liberal-conservative spectrum.[37] Figure 2-1 shows the alignment of House members in the 91st Congress (1969–70) along the conventional left-right spectrum. In this first term of the Nixon administration, both parties exhibit partisan moderation, with substantial overlap between Democrats' and Republicans' right- and left-most members, respectively. Figure 2-2 shows the ideological distribution of House members by party during the 106th Congress (1999–2000) at the end of the Clinton administration. Thirty

Figure 2-1. *Ideological Distribution of the Parties in the U.S. House, 1969–70*

Kernel density

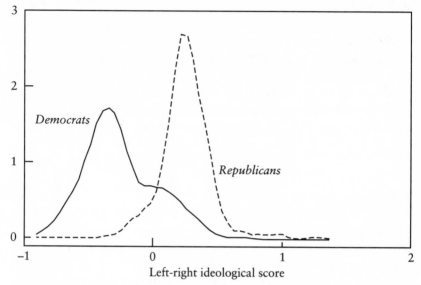

Left-right ideological score

Source: Ideological scores are first-dimension DW-NOMINATE scores. See Nolan M. McCarty, Keith T. Poole, and Howard Rosenthal, *Income Redistribution and the Realignment of American Politics*, AEI Studies on Understanding Economic Inequality (Washington: AEI Press, 1997). Graph shows density plot of House members' ideological scores by party.

years later, there is virtually no ideological common ground shared by the two parties, clearly a condition of polarized parties. Only four Democrats stand to the right of the left-most Republican, Connie Morella (R-Md).[38] A large ideological middle dominates the House in the late 1960s; thirty years later, the two parties are strongly polarized.

The number of moderate legislators is important, because it likely affects the ease of crafting and finalizing policy compromises. As John Gilmour suggests, legislators often prefer disagreement to compromise, especially if electoral incentives encourage the two parties to differentiate themselves.[39] Such incentives are more likely to be present as each party's core electoral and activist constituencies become more dissimilar and homogeneous.[40] When constituencies polarize, the two parties have an increased incentive to distinguish their records and positions and a lower

Figure 2-2. *Ideological Distribution of the Parties in the U.S. House, 1999–2000*

Kernel density

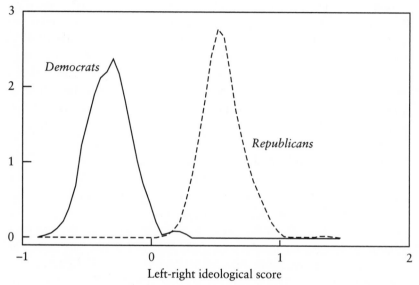

Left-right ideological score

Source: Ideological scores are first dimension DW-NOMINATE scores. See McCarty, Poole, and Rosenthal, *Income Redistribution and the Realignment of American Politics.* Graph shows density plot of House members' ideological scores by party.

incentive to bargain and compromise. As Democrat Barney Frank of Massachusetts observed in 1999 during a particularly polarized Congress, "Right now, the differences between the two parties are so great, it doesn't make sense for us to compromise. We'll show where we stand, and let the people decide."[41] Given a political system that favors oversized legislative coalitions, it is likely easier to build a broad—and usually bipartisan—enacting coalition when a block of legislators from both parties hold similar policy views.[42] If the presence of moderate legislators affects the ease of compromise, we should observe the following relationship: *the greater the polarization of partisan elite, the greater the frequency of legislative gridlock.*

Taken at face value, this polarization hypothesis seems to run counter to a key assumption of the "responsible party" school. Party government school theorists were attentive, by and large, to the characteristic weaknesses of American political parties.[43] But they held as a matter of faith that reformed parties—unified, disciplined, and coherent—were essential to effective government. Party homogeneity was a necessary condition for responsible party government, with each party's members standing together on matters of serious policy. Only then could collective responsibility by parties replace individual responsibility. In other words, polarization of parties under the responsible party model should enhance prospects for accountability. The parties would stand coherently for different policy prescriptions, voters would choose between stark alternatives, and the winning party would receive a mandate to carry out that program and take responsibility for the government's action or inaction in the next election.

The alternative hypothesis, if true, suggests that polarization might be counterproductive to securing policy responsiveness of political parties, turning the argument of the responsible party school on its head. Given the institutional structure of Congress and the separation of powers that distributes vetoes across the system, party polarization might ironically make major policy change less, rather than more, likely. Moreover, the emergence of ideologically polarized parties may have the paradoxical effect of deepening support for divided government: "The more divergent the parties' modal ideological positions, the more reason the remaining centrist voters have to welcome the moderating effect of divided government."[44] Given that in recent times greater polarization has occurred among party leaders and activists than party followers, elite polarization may raise more problems than it solves.

Electoral Mandates

Parties may also shape legislative outcomes when they interpret elections as mandates for major policy change. When a party has been in the minority for a long time, it most likely has a greater incentive to legislate when it regains control of Congress. The *New York Times* summarized the argument well in a 1948 editorial at the close of the first Republican Congress since before the New Deal:

The Republicans took control of Congress on the basis of an obvious popular revulsion against some of the policies of the Roosevelt-Truman administrations. There was no landslide but there was a perceptible movement of the political terrain. The new legislators certainly had a mandate to liquidate some war measures, to loosen some New Deal controls, to check some New Deal projects and to effect practicable economies.[45]

Republican capture of the House and Senate in the 1994 elections after forty years as the House minority party is another prime example. House Republicans claimed a mandate to pursue more conservative economic and social policies, arguing that voters' disgust with long-term Democratic control of the House would support a sharp reversal in the ideological tenor of policymaking. Such elections create mandates, even if they provide a party majority with only a temporary surge in power.

Although Republicans tended to justify their conservative legislative agenda in terms of voter demand, there was also pent-up supply of conservative policy ideas. The length of time a new majority is out of power thus probably fuels the fervor of their pitch for new policy. The longer a new majority served in the minority, the more dissatisfied it is likely to be with the policy status quo, and the greater its incentive to produce legislative change upon gaining control of both chambers. There is also a strong electoral incentive for a new majority to prove that it can govern, further increasing the chances for major policy change.[46] The relationship between electoral shocks and policy outcomes suggests the following hypothesis about party mandate: *the longer a legislative party has been in the minority, the lower the frequency of gridlock when it regains control of both chambers.*

Although many claim that the Constitution preordained that the political system would tend toward deadlock, the emergence of political parties came to affect the lawmaking process. Divided government may garner the most attention, but elections and parties affect legislative performance for reasons other than control of the branches of government. Accounting for the many ways in which elections and institutions together shape lawmaking builds a stronger explanation of patterns in legislative stalemate.

External Influences on Congress

In crafting the institution of Congress, the framers also understood that political trends and influences outside of the national government could be volatile. A bicameral Congress apportioned on different bases was intended in large part to check the legislative powers of the House. Having designed the lower chamber to be particularly sensitive to local, popular constituencies, the framers insulated the Senate in many ways from such shifts in public opinion. As argued earlier, the Senate's evolution into a proactive chamber (eventually with its own direct tie to the electorate) undermined the framers' design. In altering the impact of bicameralism, the Senate's evolution meant that it became permeable to the same sorts of outside influences already embracing the House.

In the modern Congress, important features of the political environment affecting lawmaking are the budgetary climate and salient national trends. Recent studies have not reached a uniform conclusion about the effect of these factors on legislative performance, but there is some support for the claims that sunny budgetary climates and liberal public moods yield more productive seasons of lawmaking.

Budget Constraints

The logic underpinning the effect of the budgetary environment is straightforward. The greater the surplus relative to outlays, the easier it should be to accomplish legislative goals. When legislative proponents seek to expand or create a new federal program, ample fiscal resources should eliminate one common objection to new federal initiatives: the country cannot afford them. When a coalition seeks to cut taxes, opponents will find it harder to argue that cutting taxes will bankrupt the Treasury.

The arrival in 1998 of the first budget surplus in nearly thirty years illustrates the logic. Democrats characteristically responded with a raft of proposals to expand Medicare and other social programs, as well as a program of targeted tax cuts. Republicans hoisted up a perennial favorite of across-the-board tax cuts and more limited expansion of Medicare.[47] Both parties assumed that expanding benefits (whether through spending or tax cuts) would be easier than cutting them and that doing so would be easier during better fiscal times. The onset of budget deficits in the 1980s is another helpful example, as some claim that the liberalism of the 1970s was reversed in the 1980s by an "environment of constraint."[48]

Are we overestimating the positive political effect of budgets in surplus? The argument is implicitly about politics: ample federal coffers provide the side payments necessary to build and maintain successful legislative coalitions. A little oil greases the skids. The question is whether excess resources are sufficient to overcome every stumbling block to compromise or whether significant hurdles remain even in times of surplus. In short, it remains to be seen whether the budgetary situation has a predictable effect on the magnitude and direction of gridlock. Thus, I explore the following hypothesis: *the greater the federal budget surplus relative to outlays, the lower the frequency of gridlock.*

National Moods

Claims about the impact of national moods on policy agendas and action are based primarily on empirical observation. Liberal climates of opinion seem to underlie extended periods of activist government.[49] When a wave of citizen support for liberal governmental action ebbs, the national government seems to retrench. Arthur Schlesinger and Samuel Huntington called these periods of "public purpose" or "creedal passion"—times of public engagement that bring an extended phase of dramatic legislative accomplishment.[50] They point to three periods in the twentieth century as exemplary public moods: the Progressive era early in the century, the New Deal in the 1930s, and the period from Kennedy through Nixon starting in the 1960s and lasting into the 1970s.

Such moods are ascribed causal importance. A public mood emerges, generates a wave of citizen action, and smoothes the way for a prolonged period of legislative motion, a raft of ideologically coherent legislative accomplishments. But getting a grasp on the concept of a mood is difficult. As Mayhew observes, a mood "seems to be one of those phenomena that drive political scientists to despair by being at once important and elusive."[51] Their boundaries are fuzzy, causes unclear, and effects difficult to peg. They are rooted in mass public opinion and affected by electoral returns but are strictly synonymous with neither. John Kingdon puts it best:

> The idea goes by different names—the national mood, the climate in the country, changes in public opinion, or broad social movements. But common to all of these labels is the notion that a rather large number of people out in the country are thinking along certain common lines, that this national mood changes from one time to another in discernible ways, and that these changes in mood or climate have important impacts on policy agendas and policy outcomes.[52]

An alternative is to cast mood in explicitly ideological terms. James A. Stimson suggests we interpret moods as capturing the general direction of American public opinion, a means of measuring "the public's sense of whether the political 'temperature' is too hot or too cold."[53] Intuitively, moods represent a prevailing consensus of what is appropriate and necessary for the government to do, what might be called commonly held "global attitudes toward the role of government in society."[54]

It makes sense that surges of liberal opinion would lead to higher levels of legislative output. After all, we think of an era as *activist* because of its ideological tenor and volume of legislative motion. The question is whether shared public consensus over the role of government also dampens the frequency of gridlock. Is a general agreement on the aims of government sufficient to overcome institutional and electoral obstacles that protect the status quo from change? If so, looking beyond the confines of Washington becomes necessary for explaining what happens within. A final hypothesis follows: *the greater the level of public support for governmental action, the lower the frequency of deadlock.*

Some Other Alternatives

Modeling some real-world phenomena invariably raises the question of viable alternative explanations. What about interest groups? Particular presidents? Not every possibility of course can be studied. Models simplify the world as we know it. They place a few themes in relief, excluding countless others. The model of gridlock proposed here is no exception. Not every possible correlate of gridlock is considered; only those that seem most relevant to legislators' ability to compromise among themselves and with the president. As such, I have tried to emphasize general themes of electoral and institutional forces common in some recent work on gridlock. But I have also tried to put these general explanations to hard work, asking about the *multiple* ways in which elections and institutions shape outcomes in Congress.

With this approach, some suspects are excluded. The impact of interest groups is a prime example. Some would argue that the rapid expansion of the interest group community in Washington after the 1960s must have contributed to stalemate in Washington. Jonathan Rauch wages this argument most visibly, giving the disease its own name: *demosclerosis.*[55] According to Rauch, just as arterial sclerosis clogs vital arteries of the body, interest groups clog the arteries of politics. Too many groups pursuing their own narrow policy aims collide and make legislating impossible. More groups mean more conflict among groups, and most members are left on the sidelines loathe to take sides. Interest groups and gridlock are thus intimately tied: greater numbers of interest groups make compromise impossible and deadlock more likely.

Although the argument is intuitively appealing, there are strong theoretical and empirical reasons to question the link between the activity of groups and overall performance of government.[56] The increased number and diversity of interest groups might enhance, not dampen, chances for serious policy change. One possibility is that groups provide enormous information to legislators, informing politicians of the electoral and policy consequences of their legislative choices.[57] Groups, in this view, facilitate lawmaking by reducing electoral, legislative, and policy uncertainties endemic to the policy process. Competitive pressure fostered by the existence of opposing groups also keeps groups honest, raising the costs for misrepresenting information to members and staff. Another possibility is that the increase in the number of active groups has produced stiff competition among lobbies, thereby diminishing the clout of any single group. With the blocking power of lobbies broken up, legislators can resolve policy problems without interference from groups.

Empirically, the most exhaustive effort to date has failed to detect any strong relationship between the density of groups and the frequency of gridlock.[58] Examining a sample of 205 issues over three Congresses, Jeffrey Berry detected no evidence that the number of interest groups active in lobbying on an issue is related to the likelihood that legislation is enacted in that Congress. Nor do any group effects show up after controlling for the different types of groups involved. Even when business groups face no opposition from liberal citizen groups on an issue, there is still no difference in the likelihood of passage. In sum, there is little systematic evidence that interest groups increase or decrease the chances for gridlock. Given the conflicting theoretical possibilities and the lack of any empirical basis for them, interest group dynamics are one possible cause of gridlock that I leave untouched for others to investigate.

What about the president? Are some presidents, by dint of reputation or political talent, better at getting what they want from Congress? Accounts of Lyndon B. Johnson's legendary political prowess make LBJ a strong candidate. A big problem, however, permeates the "great man" theory of deadlock. It is extremely difficult, perhaps impossible, to separate presidential reputations from presidential performance. LBJ is considered a strong presidential leader because in retrospect his legislative legacy can be readily summarized. George H. W. Bush, in contrast, is considered a weak leader because in hindsight it is easy to see that he accomplished relatively little and that he was replaced by the first Democratic president in twelve years. This chicken-and-egg problem muddies the water, making impractical estimation of whether particular presidents might be especially good legislative leaders. Moreover, the causal argument for a presidential role presumes we are interested in the president's ability to get his own agenda enacted into law. If both Congress and the president contribute to setting the agenda, then the impact of any one president is incidental to the causes of policy gridlock.[59]

Summary

The relevance of institutions to legislative gridlock is hardly a new insight. When James MacGregor Burns bemoaned the "deadlock of democracy" in 1963, he pointedly condemned the Constitution as the prime culprit. The system of checks and balances, he argued, "exacts the heavy price of delay and devitalization."[60] My point, however, is institutions can limit or enable policymakers, depending on the array of legislators' policy views empowered under such institutions. Both institutions and elections matter, in other words, since elections affect the array of ideological views across national institutions.

Political scientists have tended to focus on only one of these important intersections between institutions and elections: whether or not elections yield unified or divided party control of the separated branches of government. My conjectures in this chapter are intended to broaden our theoretical focus, with an eye toward generating a plausible and robust account of the many forces that shape the frequency of stalemate in national politics.

In returning to the importance of institutions, my argument is not that today's deadlock is a direct consequence of framers' design. First, uncertainty in legislative politics is too great to believe that the framers could have rationally engineered an institution to guarantee gridlock over two succeeding centuries.[61] Second, and related, institutions evolve in a historical context, and they are unlikely to be immune to changes in their environment.[62] Institutions chosen by delegates to the Constitutional Convention have evolved beyond their designers' intent, making it difficult to attribute contemporary effects to original intent. Bicameralism and the emergence of parties are prime examples. The framers no doubt did not anticipate that the Senate would develop into a proactive legislative body and that parties would become integrated into daily legislative politics—making it impossible for them to proscribe their effects today on the dynamics of lawmaking. Such cautions suggest that history matters, especially today as one tries to discern the historical roots of contemporary stalemate.

If my conjectures about gridlock ring true for the experience of the past half-century, there are several implications for how we think about politics, parties, and stalemate more generally:

—First, divided government might only be one of several ways in which parties affect legislative performance. And it may be a less important cause of stalemate than perennially assumed.

—Second, if polarization of political parties increases the frequency of gridlock, some essential assumptions about the importance of strong political parties are turned on their head. Scholars advocating strong, responsible political parties have argued for decades that cohesive parties—offering distinctive choices to the electorate—are critical for ensuring accountable and responsive government under our political system. Contrary to their assumptions, it may be that polarization of party leaders and legislators creates incentives for deadlock, not action.

—Third, treating bicameral legislatures as if they were unicameral risks underestimating institutional constraints on policy change. Elections distribute policy views not only among the branches but also between the chambers, which helps to account for the phenomenon of "unified gridlock," stalemate that occurs under unified party control of government.

Much rides on disentangling the many roots of stalemate. Despite the centrality of lawmaking to the democratic experience, basic questions about its dynamics remain unanswered.

3 Measuring the Frequency of Stalemate

C asual observers of Washington politics can usually tell the difference between a Congress that produces a lot and a Congress that does little. A prime example of extreme gridlock is the slim legislative record of the Democratic 102d Congress (1991–92) under Republican president George Bush, gridlock that was bemoaned by candidates Ross Perot and Bill Clinton during the 1992 elections. Efforts to enact lobbying and campaign finance reform, to enact parental leave, banking, and voter registration legislation, and to cut the capital gains tax—to name a few salient issues facing Congress—all ended in deadlock. The most productive Congresses are also easily tagged, with the Great Society Congress under Lyndon B. Johnson in 1965 and 1966 named the most exemplary. Landmark health care, environment, civil rights, transportation, and education statutes, among many others, were enacted by that Congress—a total of twenty-two major laws, a record met only one other time during the past twenty-seven Congresses.[1]

We can judge gridlock at extremes, knowing intuitively that some Congresses are more or less productive than others. Many, for example, can rattle off the accomplishments of the Kennedy-Johnson years in the early to mid-1960s. But probably fewer people can recall the record of the Republican 83d Congress (1953–54) under Dwight D. Eisenhower, which banned the Communist party, enacted landmark housing and farm laws, and created the Department of Health, Education, and Welfare. We lack a yardstick for measuring the reach of gridlock, a measure that would allow us to assess variation in legislative performance over time. We can speculate about the dimensions and causes of gridlock without such a measure, but we cannot pinpoint them with confidence. In this chapter, I develop such a yardstick and use it to map Washington's legislative performance during the past half-century.

Defining and Measuring Gridlock

How we define gridlock largely shapes how we measure it. I follow political scientist Charles O. Jones, who encourages us to evaluate the "success of that system in treating public problems."[2] When an issue ends in stalemate, we mean that legislators and the president have been unable to reach a compromise that alters the policy status quo. As David Mayhew defined the challenge in *Divided We Govern*, we are interested in "some actually-did-pass numerator over some all-that-were-possibilities-for-passage denominator."[3] Framed this way, gridlock is best viewed as the share of salient issues on the nation's agenda that is left in limbo at the close of a Congress.

Scholars have typically thought about gridlock in terms of numerators: how much of importance did government get done? Accordingly, legislative performance has been assessed by counting up the number of important laws enacted each Congress. When output is low, we say that gridlock is high, and vice versa. But measuring output without respect to the underlying policy agenda risks misstating the true frequency of gridlock. A Congress might produce little legislation because it is truly gridlocked. Or it might generate few laws because it faces a limited agenda. With little on its legislative plate, surely a Congress should not be blamed for meager results. We can evaluate Congress's performance only if we have some idea of the size of the underlying policy agenda. As the *New York Times* editorialized in 1969, we should be cautious of admiring Congress "in proportion to the volume of bills it grinds out. The only sane criterion is a comparison of its record with the problems before it."[4]

Using both a numerator and denominator thus puts legislative activity into perspective, providing a barometer for gauging legislative performance. Although Mayhew recognized the importance of a denominator, he also understood the difficulty of getting it right: "It is very difficult to see what a denominator for a Congress—an agenda of potential enactments—might be. 'As demanded by the needs of the time,' perhaps? . . . That would be hopeless to administer."[5] Mayhew's solution was to focus only on numerators, leading Morris P. Fiorina to conclude in *Divided Government* that "an irreducible ambiguity in Mayhew's findings . . . remain[s]. Essentially, he has studied the *supply* of federal legislation and found that the supply is more or less the same during modern unified and divided government periods. But we have no information about the *demand* for legislation."[6]

Admittedly numerators are easier to build than denominators. Although reconstructing the legislative record over a half-century is no easy task, the raw material (enacted legislation) is tallied in many places. One devises criteria to help select from the hundreds of laws enacted each year and then applies the criteria in searching the historical record. Mayhew pioneered this method in his analysis of the consequences of divided government.

Denominators are another story. Here, we are interested in things that *did not* happen—bills that failed to become law, issues that never made it into the legislative hopper. My approach to building a denominator draws on concepts from the study of agenda setting. The political or policy agenda can be thought of as "the list of subjects or problems to which governmental officials, and people outside of government closely associated with those officials, are paying some serious attention at any given time."[7] It is a concept similar to the idea of the "systemic agenda" offered by Roger Cobb and Charles Elder. They define the systemic agenda as "all issues that are commonly perceived by members of the political community as meriting public attention."[8] Issues that are "possibilities for passage" in other words are issues on the systemic agenda, the range of policy ideas plausibly on the radar screens of policymaking elite and active electorates.[9]

The main task is to determine what constitutes the systemic agenda. Because the agenda includes both issues addressed by Congress and issues not taken up, relying on records of legislative activities would not fully capture the systemic agenda. Instead, I need a source that covers the minutiae of Congress but also steps back to observe what Congress fails to get done. Newspaper editorials are an ideal source for such opinionated coverage. Thus I use daily (unsigned) editorials appearing in the *New York Times* between 1947 and 2000 to recreate the political agenda for each Congress.[10]

Why editorials and why the *Times*? The choices are linked. The choice rests on the assumption that the nation's paper of record responds to issues under consideration in Washington and highlights public problems that deserve attention.[11] As former *Washington Post* editorial board member E. J. Dionne expressed it, an editorial writer's job is "to tack a notice up on the board . . . to put an issue on people's radar screen."[12] Current and former members of the *Times* editorial board concur. Their goal, they say, is to "get out in front of the news . . . jump out in front of an issue before it gets covered in the news," although they still recognize that they are often "driven by the news and react to the news."[13] Editorials, in short, capture issues at the "much talked about stage" and issues that might be considered the "agenda of potential enactments."[14] "I concern myself with the things my neighbors don't have time to think about," one former *Times* editorial writer observed, with issues that are "very important to our common life together."[15]

From the editorial pages of the *New York Times*, I extract the issues that plausibly constitute the systemic agenda. I code the legislative content of each editorial that mentions Congress, the House, or the Senate, and then use the issues mentioned in those editorials to compile a list of agenda items for each Congress. I consider any policy issue discussed in a *Times* editorial a "potential enactment." I also tally the number of editorials the *Times* wrote on each issue in each Congress. For example, the *Times* editorialized sixty-five times about the successful Civil Rights Act of 1964 (which it favored), forty-eight times about the Tax Reform Act of 1986 (which it also favored), and eight times about the failed constitutional amendment to require a balanced budget (which it opposed) in the 97th Congress (1981–82). The number of editorials per issue provides a proxy for the public or political salience of the issue, a proxy that can be used to divide the agenda into progressive levels of significance.

I then research the final disposition of each issue: whether it died in committee, on the Senate floor, in conference, and so on, or whether it was eventually enacted into law in that Congress. I then calculate a *gridlock score* for each Congress, which consists of the percentage of agenda items that failed to be enacted into law by the end of the Congress. For readers interested in the details of the coding process, a discussion of the methodology appears in appendix A.

The Denominator: Size of the Policy Agenda

Thus measured, the congressional agenda was smallest in the 86th Congress (1959–60) when it bottomed at 70 issues, and largest in the 99th Congress (1985–86) when it peaked at 160 issues.[16] Most recently in the 106th Congress (1999–2000), it totaled 137 issues, a jump up from the 116 issues on the agenda in the previous Congress. As shown in figure 3-1, the size of the agenda has increased over time. The sharpest change occurred at the start of the so-called activist era that ushered in unified Democratic control in 1961. By the end of the 87th Congress (1961–62), the size of the agenda had nearly doubled from its size in the previous Congress.

One might think that the size of the agenda would expand during times of unified party control when prospects for enacting bills into law might seem higher. But party control of government does not seem to drive the size of the agenda. For example, the agenda under unified government in 1993–94 (94 issues) was slightly smaller than the agenda that followed under divided government in 1995–96 (118 issues). More generally, between 1947 and 2000, there is no significant difference in the size of the agenda under unified and divided control: unified governments have faced on average 107 issues, divided governments 123.

Because the agendas developed from the editorials include issues that the *Times* supported as well as those it opposed, the agendas are not a record of liberal initiatives supported by the *Times*. Nor did the *Times* overselect issues that ended in stalemate, rather than enactment: of the 3,152 agenda items discussed during the fifty-four years between 1947 and 2000, just under half were enacted.[17] Nor did the *Times* write more often about issues mired in gridlock than issues clearly headed to passage, as the correlation between the number of editorials written per issue and the final outcome of the issue is only .1. The *Times* did write significantly more often about issues that made Mayhew's list of landmark laws. The *Times* editorialized nine times about the 294 issues that became landmark laws between 1947 and 2000, but under three times on all other issues—suggesting the validity of the number of editorials per issue as an indicator of policy importance.

Figure 3-1. *Size of the Policy Agenda, 1947–2000*

Number of issues on agenda

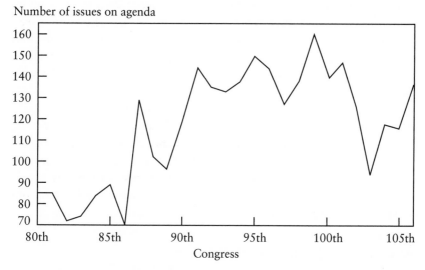

Source: See text for all figures in this chapter.

Using editorials to recreate agenda seems to avoid some of the vulnerabilities that Mayhew notes about his reliance on journalists' news summaries of important legislation. First, Mayhew notes that his compilation of contemporary judgments ("Sweep One") "singles out one kind of legislative action and ignores others. It looks for the major, direct innovative thrust . . . but it overlooks the practices and logics of the appropriations process, imaginatively placed amendments, and incrementalism by way of many small bills."[18] Because I use daily editorials, rather than year-end wrap-up articles, my method tends to capture these smaller legislative moments quite well. For instance, my method uncovers the issue of childhood vaccinations (enacted in the 103d) and repeal of the oleomargarine tax in the 81st (after stalemating in the 80th), seemingly small, yet important, issues of the day left out of year-end reviews.

Second, the editorial measure does not favor certain policy areas over others, as Mayhew notes is a weakness of his approach. For example, the method does not slight defense weapons buildups, a policy area that tends to be overlooked by Mayhew's method: the editorial method detects an alphabet soup of fights over weapons production: the A-12 Avenger, the B-1 and B-2 bombers, the MX and Midgetman missiles, and so on.[19]

Third, the editorial measure is not weakened by the problem of omnibus bills in the 1980s. Because the agenda for each Congress is based on particular issues—rather than final legislative packages—increased reliance on omnibus bills by the Reagan and Bush administrations does not affect the measure. If, say, three different legislative issues are combined into a single legislative package, each of the three issues still counts as a component of the agenda.

Finally, the editorial measure reduces the subjectivity problem raised by some other methods. George Edwards and his coauthors, for example, note that identifying the potential significance of bills that, if passed, would have been important remains "a series of judgments rather than straightforward codifications."[20] Because I rely instead on the judgment of the nation's paper of record to identify salient policy issues, the problem of subjectivity is reduced (though not eliminated).

Patterns of Legislative Gridlock

With a numerator (number of failed agenda issues each Congress) and denominator (total number of agenda issues each Congress), a gridlock score can easily be calculated as the percentage of agenda items that fail short of enactment. The resulting gridlock series appears in figure 3-2. Most important, the editorial measure generates gridlock scores that comport with the received wisdom about levels of policy stalemate. Using my method, the most productive Congress was the 89th (1965–66), the unified Democratic "Great Society" Congress under Lyndon Johnson. That Congress stalemated on just a third of its agenda. In contrast, the least productive Congress was the 105th (1997–98), as a Republican Congress faced off against Democrat Bill Clinton—an assessment confirmed by the editorial page of the *Washington Post*. "The barrenness of the legislative record," the *Post* editorialized in 1998, "is unmatched in recent memory."[21] The 106th (1999–2000) and 102d (1991–92) Congresses—also periods of divided control—ended in stalemate nearly as often, failing to enact 63 percent and 61 percent of their agendas, respectively.[22]

Another way of viewing the legislative record is to limit our focus to the more salient issues on the agenda. If we include only those issues on which the *Times* wrote four or more editorials, a similar trend emerges (figure 3-3).[23] This time, the 89th Congress is again remarkably productive, stalemating on just 29 percent of its agenda. The 80th and 88th were

Figure 3-2. *Frequency of Policy Gridlock, 1947–2000*

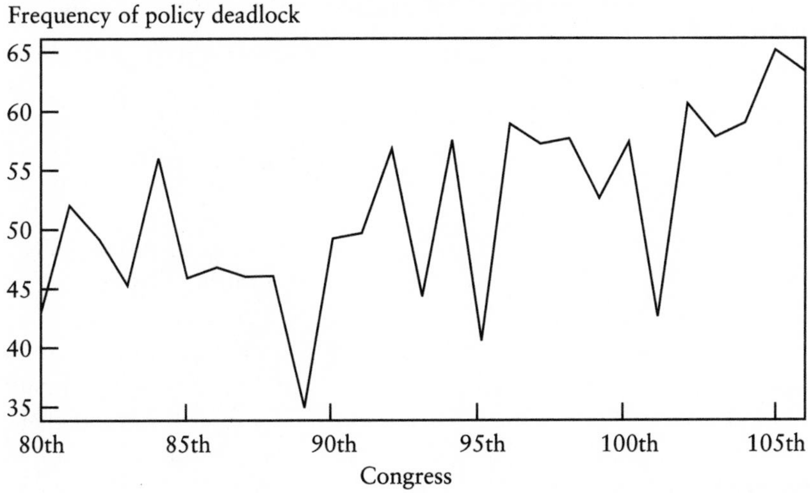

Frequency of policy deadlock

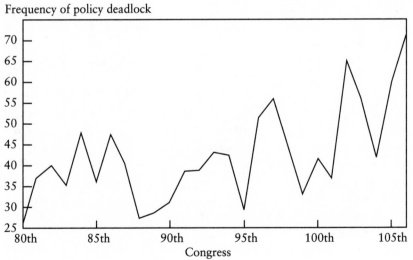

Figure 3-3. *Frequency of Policy Gridlock on Salient Issues, 1947-2000*

Frequency of policy deadlock

equally productive, with a gridlock frequency of 26 percent and 27 percent respectively.[24] The three least productive Congresses are again the 102d, 105th, and 106th, with the 106th stalemating on more than 70 percent of its agenda.

We can observe some general patterns in the frequency of gridlock during the past half-century. Clearly the frequency of gridlock varies markedly. Is Congress particularly gridlocked today? Critics of Congress who claim so are partially right. Gridlock has trended upward over the period, with the frequency of gridlock on the most salient issues in the 1990s double what it was in the 1940s. Even with the brief appearance of unified government under Bill Clinton and congressional Democrats after the 1992 elections, gridlock remained at a historic high, as more than half of its agenda remained in limbo when the 103d Congress adjourned.

But the level of gridlock does not simply trend upward. After its then-unprecedented high in the 103d Congress, gridlock on the most salient issues dropped fourteen points in the 104th Congress (1995–96), reflecting election-year compromises on reforming welfare, health care, immigration, and telecommunication laws and increasing the minimum wage. Still, no recent Congress has matched the performance of the Great Society, four years of legislative prowess in which presidents John F. Kennedy and Lyndon B. Johnson and their Democratic Congresses stalemated on only fourteen of the fifty most salient issues of those four years.

The value of including a denominator can be seen by comparing Mayhew's count of legislative landmarks to the editorial-based measure of legislative performance developed here. Mayhew's measure is strictly a numerator-based measure, showing the number of landmark laws enacted in each Congress. In contrast, the editorial-based measure includes a numerator (salient agenda items enacted) divided by a denominator (number of salient issues on the agenda).[25] Several trends are immediately obvious (figure 3-4). Most important, the two series display starkly different trends, correlating at just .44. Closer examination of the differences across the two series helps account for the divergent trends.

Note that Congress can pass just a few landmark laws and yet appear very productive. As shown in the early years of the series, relatively few landmark laws were passed, and yet Congress was at its most productive (see, for example, the 80th Congress). At other times, Congress can pass many landmark laws and again appear highly productive (see, for example, the 89th Congress). The difference of course is the size of the denominator, as the agenda expanded greatly between the 80th and 89th

Figure 3-4. *Alternative Measures of Legislative Performance*

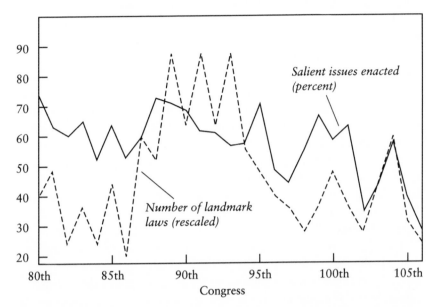

Source: For number of landmark laws enacted between the 80th and 101st Congresses, see David Mayhew, *Divided We Govern* (Yale University Press, 1991); for 102d–106th Congresses, see http://pantheon.yale.edu/~dmayhew/data3.html (May 23, 2002). For percent salient issues enacted into law, see text.

Congresses. Without a denominator, we would conclude from the few laws enacted that the 80th Congress was not terribly productive; with a denominator, we see that it was one of the most productive of the past half-century. At other times, the two series run almost perfectly in tandem, for example, across the decade of the 1990s. In these cases, Congress again passed very few landmark laws, but now it appears very *un*productive. This is a consequence of course of the size of the underlying policy agenda, which remained high throughout the period: very few laws enacted relative to a large number of issues on the legislative agenda. In sum, numerator-only measures provide a careful accounting of Congress's performance, but a denominator is necessary to put such accomplishments into perspective.

The gridlock scores also help to solve a puzzle noted by Mayhew when he compared the records of Johnson's Great Society Congress and Nixon's last (the 93d Congress in 1973–74). Both produced twenty-two landmark laws (making them the most productive of Mayhew's count), but the 93d failed to earn "much of a reputation for legislative achievement."[26] Mayhew reasons that because of the presence of divided government under Nixon and Ford, "Journalists . . . deprived of an opportunity for a carry-out-the-mandate script, tended to reach for a deadlock-between-institutions counter-script that probably under-reported real legislative motion."[27] But the 89th and 93d also differed in another important way: the legislative agenda of the 93d Congress was 40 percent larger than that of the 89th, yielding a gridlock score of 43 percent for the 93d and only 29 percent for the 89th. Journalists likely were inclined to stress legislative conflict in the divided years of the 1970s, but they also probably emphasized deadlock in the 93d because so much of the extensive agenda ended in stalemate. Accounting for numerators and denominators alters our interpretation of legislative performance.

The importance of including a denominator is most clear when we reassess the impact of divided government on legislative performance. Mayhew's critical achievement of course was to establish the near parity of divided and unified governments in terms of their legislative prowess: Mayhew detected no significant difference in the number of landmark laws enacted under each regime. As shown in table 3-1, for the twenty-seven Congresses between 1947 and 2000, Mayhew found on average thirteen laws enacted during periods of unified control and eleven laws enacted during divided control—a difference with neither substantive nor statistical significance. But does divided government affect legislative performance once we control for the size of the agenda? Sure enough, gridlock is significantly more likely in periods of divided government compared with unified control. Over the twenty-seven Congresses between 1947 and 2000, during divided governments, gridlock averaged 54 percent; during unified government, gridlock dropped to 48 percent, a statistically significant decline.[28] The results suggest that divided government does have a significant impact on legislative outcomes, even if Congress is still able in such times to muster large majorities for important legislation.

The Location of Gridlock

Because the editorial method for measuring legislative performance begins with issues on the agenda, rather than enacted laws, we can also

Table 3-1. *Impact of Divided Government on Legislative Performance,*
1947-2000

Party control of Congress and presidency	Number of landmark laws enacted (Mayhew)	Percent of agenda deadlocked (all issues)
Unified government	12.6	47.9
Divided government	11.1	53.8
Difference	1.5	-5.9*

Source: See text for tables in this chapter.
* Difference significant at p < .05.

use the data to pinpoint where in the legislative process salient issues have encountered stalemate.

House versus Senate

In table 3-2, I compare the two chambers' treatment of salient issues that failed to be enacted during the legislative process.[29] Most noticeably, neither the House nor Senate is disproportionately responsible for killing legislative measures during the past half-century. Although the framers argued that the Senate would serve as a restraint on a populous and potentially rash House, both the House and Senate are responsible for stopping legislation approved by the other chamber. Of the ninety-six measures passed by the House between 1947 and 2000, the Senate approved just over half. In comparison, of the eighty-seven measures passed by the Senate, thirty-eight were killed or ignored by the House. This suggests that the Senate is not the sole mechanism for checking legislative action in our bicameral system. Clearly the House takes on this role as well, a trend likely not anticipated by the framers given their focus on the Senate's ability to rein in the populist tendencies of the House.

Table 3-2 also shows that bicameral disagreements are important but hardly the most common source of legislative gridlock. Only 18 percent (49 of 280 total issues) of the salient, unsuccessful issues died after both chambers had passed versions of a bill. Of these 49 issues, just over half were killed when Congress failed to override the president's veto. Congress deadlocked on the remaining 22 salient issues when one or both of

Table 3-2. *Where Do Bills Die? 1947–2000*

Last formal action in House	Last formal action in Senate[a]					
	Passed chamber	Killed on chamber floor	Approved by committee	Committee hearing held	No action	Total
Passed chamber	49	21	13	11	2	96
Killed on chamber floor	16	19	3	4	2	44
Approved by committee	12	6	12	6	4	40
Committee hearing held	8	8	9	39	8	72
No action	2	8	4	6	8	28
Total	87	62	41	66	24	280

Note: N, 280.
a. Includes all salient legislative issues that ultimately ended in gridlock.

Figure 3-5. *Comparison of House and Senate Legislative Performance, 1947–2000*

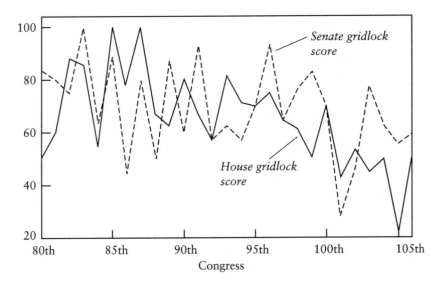

the chambers refused to go to conference or failed to agree to a conference report.

We can also compare the performance of the two chambers by calculating separate gridlock scores for each chamber. In figure 3-5, I compare each chamber's overall record each Congress on salient issues that were never enacted into law. The House series shows the percentage of such issues that ended in stalemate during House consideration, and the Senate series shows the Senate's performance on those same issues.[30] In thirteen of the twenty-seven Congresses, the Senate passed fewer of the salient issues than did the House; in ten Congresses, the performance of the two chambers flipped, with the House passing a lower percentage of salient issues than the Senate. The two chambers' performances in the remaining four Congresses were indistinguishable. On balance, this suggests that the Senate is not disproportionately to blame for inaction on major policy issues: both chambers over time have shown similar tendencies to prefer policy stability to policy change on important issues.

Notably, for most of the 1990s, the Senate was consistently a more frequent contributor to deadlock than the House. An assessment of the fate of salient issues that never became law shows that the House in the 103d Congress (1993–94) stalemated on 44 percent of those issues, and the Senate stalemated on 77 percent. That same gap in the two chambers' performance recurred in the 105th Congress, with 22 percent of salient issues never making it out of the House and 55 percent of those issues failing to be approved by the Senate. In the 104th and 106th Congresses too the Senate was more frequently the cause of stalemate than the House.

This recent pattern is striking, suggesting the limits of party control on legislative outcomes. If party control alone could account for what Congress and the president achieve, we would hardly expect to find the Senate exerting much restraint on the House during the unified 103d Congress in 1993 and 1994. Both chambers should have passed a similarly high percentage of the agenda. Instead, the Senate posed a significant and similar hurdle to legislative progress in both the unified 103d and divided 105th Congresses. Perhaps differences in the policy views of the two chambers—and not simply policy differences across the branches—may matter a lot in explaining the frequency of gridlock.

Bicameral Roadblocks

Another way to assess the impact of bicameral differences is to explore the fate of legislative measures after both chambers have passed an initial version of a bill. Although relatively few bills actually die after being passed by the two chambers, bicameral differences can occasionally prevent Congress from reaching final agreement on a bill. Procedurally, such differences manifest themselves when one or both chambers refuse to go to conference with the other (or when a filibuster prevents the Senate from going to conference), when a bill dies in conference, or when one chamber or the other kills a conference report. In these types of cases, bicameral differences prove impossible to resolve, either because irreconcilable disagreements emerge or because legislators lack sufficient incentive to resolve them.

The incidence of serious bicameral disagreement appears in table 3-3, column 1, showing the proportion of salient legislative issues that deadlock after initial passage by both chambers. This includes bills that pass both chambers but then die going to or during conference (or other means of resolving intrabranch disputes) or die when one chamber or the other defeats the conference report. In absolute terms, only a small fraction of the most salient issues encounters gridlock because of bicameral

Table 3-3. *Legislative Roadblocks after Initial Chamber Passage,*
1947–2000

Congress (years)	1 Percent killed by bicameral disagreement	2 Percent killed by presidential veto
80th (1947–48)	0	0
81st (1949–50)	0	0
82d (1951–52)	0	5.00
83d (1953–54)	0	0
84th (1955–56)	4.35	8.70
85th (1957–58)	0	0
86th (1959–60)	10.53	0
87th (1961–62)	0	0
88th (1963–64)	0	0
89th (1965–66)	3.57	0
90th (1967–68)	3.13	0
91st (1969–70)	0	2.56
92d (1971–72)	8.33	0
93d (1973–74)	0	5.41
94th (1975–76)	9.09	0
95th (1977–78)	2.94	2.94
96th (1979–80)	3.23	0
97th (1981–82)	0	8.00
98th (1983–84)	3.45	3.45
99th (1985–86)	0	5.56
100th (1987–88)	0	8.33
101st (1989–90)	10.53	5.26
102d (1991–92)	4.35	26.09
103d (1993–94)	12.5	0
104th (1995–96)	0	15.79
105th (1997–98)	26.67	20.00
106th (1999–2000)	21.43	7.14

disagreement following passage by the initial chamber. In just under half the Congresses, no salient issues were ever explicitly snagged by bicameral dispute. Even when bicameral disagreement is the overt cause of deadlock, the proportion of issues killed by such disagreement has been relatively low, ranging from a low of 2.9 percent of issues in 1977–78 to a high of 26.7 percent of issues in 1997–98.

Still, there are two striking trends in the incidence with which bicameral disputes are the overt cause of killing legislation. First is the surge in bicameral roadblocks at the end of the 1990s. A quarter of the agenda in the 105th Congress and a fifth of the agenda in the 106th ended in stalemate because of disagreements at the bicameral stage of negotiations. This suggests that even when the same party controls both chambers of Congress, we cannot simply assume that the two chambers hold a similar set of views on major policy issues. Second and related, there seems to be no relationship between party control and bicameral disagreement. The incidence of such disagreements is almost the same under unified and divided control. Under unified control in 1994, for example, bicameral disagreement prevented final enactment of numerous issues, including credit, lobbying, and mining reforms, even though both chambers had already passed initial versions of the bills. This suggests that bicameral disagreement may protect the status quo from major change—even during the periods of unified party control that we normally associate with major policy change. Same party control of both chambers and the presidency is insufficient to guarantee policy change in the face of differing policy views of the two chambers.

Interbranch Conflict

Deadlock also occurs when the president vetoes a measure, and Congress fails to muster the two-thirds majority required to override it. Table 3-3, column 2, shows the percentage of salient issues derailed when Congress fails to override presidential vetoes. Like bicameral roadblocks, veto problems are relatively rare. In thirteen Congresses, veto problems were never the direct cause of deadlock on a salient issue. In eleven of the remaining fourteen Congresses, under 10 percent of salient issues were killed by vetoes. Consistent with President Bush's extensive reliance on the veto to pursue his policy agenda, veto problems in the second half of Bush's term (1991–92) account for the death of more than a quarter of the salient issues in that Congress. Only Clinton's use of the veto against the Republican Congress in 1997 and 1998 compares, when presidential vetoes killed 20 percent of salient issues, for example, stalling measures to limit abortion and reduce payments to the United Nations.

There is some evidence that presidential vetoes are a more frequent cause of deadlock today than in previous decades. Vetoes become the proximate cause of deadlock starting in the 1970s, though at low levels.

Of course, Congress can fail to override a veto because of policy differences with the president or policy difference between the chambers. But in six of the thirteen Congresses where vetoes were never the direct cause of deadlock, neither was bicameral disagreement ever the cause of gridlock. And all six of these Congresses occurred before 1965.[31]

The emergence of veto politics as a more frequent cause of deadlock most likely reflects three concurrent developments across the decades. The first is a rise in both legislative and executive assertiveness, reflecting a decline in legislative deference and the rise of an activist presidency. As James Sundquist and others have argued, political conflicts between Richard M. Nixon and Democratic Congresses in the late 1960s and early 1970s helped make Congress more aggressive and assertive vis-à-vis the president, leading it to alter both policy (for example, the Congressional Budget and Impoundment Control Act of 1974) and organizations (creating the Congressional Budget Office, among others) to institutionalize its capacity to challenge the president.[32] Second is the recurrence of divided government, a governing pattern that probably encouraged presidents to expand their use of the veto as a tool for shaping legislative outcomes.[33] Third, and related, is the polarization of the two major parties after the 1970s. Coupled with the recurrence of divided government, partisan polarization also brought interbranch polarization as policy differences between Congress and the president increased across the broad array of issues on the agenda. Although we might attribute increased assertiveness of both branches to changing institutional norms of behavior, increased assertiveness probably also grew from the changing array of policy views between the two branches. The more the two branches disagreed on policy, the more sense it made for the president to use veto politics to affect policy outcomes.[34] It follows from all three of these trends that after the 1960s, vetoes became a more frequent cause of stalemate, as partisan, political, and institutional differences combined to encourage changes in the two branches' and parties' procedural tactics. This suggests that it may be difficult to disentangle the impact of divided government and policy differences on legislative performance: policy views in recent decades have become more polarized at precisely the same time as the two parties have tended to control opposite ends of Pennsylvania Avenue. In such times, policy, partisan, and institutional differences are intricately woven together.

Gridlock at Water's Edge: Foreign and Domestic Agendas

So far, I have treated all legislative issues alike. But there is good reason to consider foreign and domestic issues separately. First, as the old adage suggests, politics stops at the water's edge. Differences over domestic policy are often said to be put aside when the focus turns to international affairs. Even when political differences do emerge over foreign policy, one side inevitably implores its opponents to put aside differences lest American prestige and authority be diminished around the world. Second, many have argued that there are "two presidencies": one dominates the conduct of foreign affairs and the other competes with Congress for influence on domestic affairs.[35] Still, scholars have shown that the two-presidencies thesis may be timebound to the 1950s. We also know that politics today rarely stops at water's edge (witness legislative disagreement with the president over the NATO bombing campaign of the Serbians in Kosovo in 1999). New data on legislative gridlock allow us to revisit the received wisdom about Congress and foreign policy.

On balance, the legislative agenda is heavily tilted toward domestic affairs, with just 19 percent of the 3,152 agenda items during the past half-century addressing foreign policy, including just 22 percent of the most salient legislative issues and treaties.[36] The balance between foreign and domestic issues does vary somewhat over time, however, with the highest concentration of foreign policy issues appearing immediately after the end of World War II (table 3-4, column 1). Foreign affairs comprised 40 percent of the agenda in the three Congresses after 1946, with such issues as the creation of NATO, the Marshall Plan, selective service reform, and foreign military assistance dominating the agenda. Attention to foreign affairs waned during the 1950s, remaining relatively low until the 92d Congress (1971–72) when legislative activism on the Vietnam War and other foreign policy issues surged. Since then, foreign policy has taken up less than a fifth of the legislative agenda, although it increased slightly in the early 1990s when domestic attention to foreign policy peaked with American involvement in the Persian Gulf and other crises overseas. A similar pattern holds for the most salient agenda issues (column 2), with domestic attention to foreign affairs highest right after the war in the 1940s and surging again in the 1970s surrounding the war in Vietnam. Foreign affairs again rises in the 1990s, with debates over the Persian Gulf conflict and U.S. involvement in Kosovo and elsewhere.

Table 3-4. *Agenda Devoted to Foreign Policy, 1947–2000*
Percent

Congress (years)	1 All issues	2 Salient issues
80th (1947–48)	40.3	52.2
81st (1949–50)	40.0	44.4
82d (1951–52)	41.0	55.0
83d (1953–54)	22.6	30.0
84th (1955–56)	28.0	30.4
85th (1957–58)	21.7	32.0
86th (1959–60)	24.2	15.8
87th (1961–62)	20.8	13.5
88th (1963–64)	20.2	13.6
89th (1965–66)	11.6	3.6
90th (1967–68)	11.1	15.6
91th (1969–70)	12.4	25.6
92d (1971–72)	19.2	22.2
93d (1973–74)	13.3	16.2
94th (1975–76)	13.6	18.2
95th (1977–78)	14.5	17.6
96th (1979–80)	16.3	12.9
97th (1981–82)	16.2	12.0
98th (1983–84)	17.7	10.3
99th (1985–86)	14.9	22.2
100th (1987–88)	19.4	29.2
101st (1989–90)	20.0	5.3
102d (1991–92)	25.7	30.4
103d (1993–94)	19.2	12.5
104th (995–96)	21.3	15.8
105th (1997–98)	16.0	33.3
106th (1999–2000)	11.1	14.3

Are domestic policy proposals more likely to end in stalemate than foreign policy proposals? On average during the past fifty years, the answer is yes: Congress and the president deadlocked on 54 percent of domestic issues but only 44 percent of foreign policy matters.[37] This may help to explain why President George W. Bush encountered relatively little restraint even from congressional Democrats as he pursued a war on terrorism after the events of September 11, 2001. On foreign policy issues that arose because of the terrorist attacks, legislators were largely (although not entirely) willing to move swiftly to reach agreement among themselves and with the president.[38] No doubt, the framing of foreign policy issues as matters of national security makes it harder for opponents to derail foreign policy issues. This is particularly so when it appears that American lives may be at stake. Thus, it should not be too surprising to find lower levels of stalemate on foreign policy issues.

Still, there is a good degree of variation over time in how frequently Congress deadlocks on foreign policy. As shown in figure 3-6, the most productive Congresses, in terms of passing foreign policy proposals, occurred at the beginning of the cold war. In the 80th Congress (1947–48), only 29 percent of foreign policy proposals ended in stalemate; in the 82d Congress (1951–52), only 32 percent. Gridlock on foreign policy issues increased markedly in the 1960s with the rise of domestic conflict over the war in Vietnam, with Congress and the president deadlocking on more than half of the foreign policy issues in the late 1960s. Already by the 89th Congress (1965–66), stalemate on foreign policy issues had outstripped deadlock on domestic issues for the first time in the postwar era, with such measures as withdrawal of troops from Vietnam, draft reform, and reductions in troop commitments in Europe ending in deadlock.

The rise of domestic conflict over foreign policy accords neatly with the demise of the "two presidencies," as the two parties polarized across the period and legislators became increasingly assertive and less deferential to the president on foreign affairs.[39] Although conflict over foreign affairs has subsided somewhat since then, Congress has not returned to the pattern established before the Vietnam War. Deadlock on foreign issues surged again briefly in the early 1980s and again in the 1990s. In the mid- to late 1990s, Congress and the president stalemated on roughly half of all foreign policy issues, including measures to reform the United Nations, reorganize the State Department, and sell arms to Bosnia. Although much of the rise is likely attributable to the persistence of divided party control of government and the polarization of the parties across the issue spectrum, continued legislative assertiveness by Congress is probably the legacy of brawls over Vietnam, the Iran-contra affair, and other institutional and political disputes between Congress and the president. Finally, there is often a fine line between domestic and foreign policy issues in recent years, as new international issues have come to "blur the differences between domestic and foreign policy . . . [moving] the latter into the maelstrom of American politics."[40]

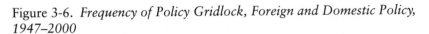

Figure 3-6. *Frequency of Policy Gridlock, Foreign and Domestic Policy, 1947–2000*

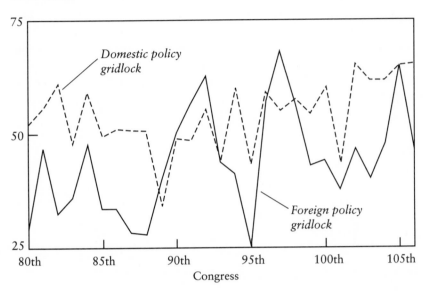

Although domestic gridlock still outstrips deadlock over foreign affairs, the gap between the two has shrunk considerably since the halcyon days of the cold war.

Conclusion

The measure of gridlock frequency developed here provides a way to gauge the legislative performance of Congress and the president over time, in light of the changing scope of the nation's policy agenda. Although such data cannot tell us whether any particular set of measures should have passed or not, they can reliably inform us of the frequency of policy change and stability during the past half-century.

Already we have a sense of the new perspective offered by a measure that incorporates information about the agenda in evaluating legislative performance. First, divided government seems to matter. A larger share of the agenda fails to be enacted during periods of divided party control than when a single party controls both branches of government. Second, the legislative records of the House and Senate do not mirror each other exactly, suggesting that policy differences between the two chambers may help to explain variation in legislative deadlock. Third, there seems to be a secular increase in legislative roadblocks caused by interchamber dynamics in recent years, suggesting that bicameral negotiations have become more critical in crafting major policy change. These bivariate trends suggest that divided government may have a significant effect on legislative outcomes but alone may not fully account for Congress's historical performance.

4 Institutional and Electoral Sources of Stalemate

W hen the 105th Congress adjourned in 1998, it could point to only a slim record of achievement. To its credit, it enacted a landmark package to balance the budget, streamlined federal procedures for moving new drugs and medical devices to market, and bolstered federal adoption laws. The Senate also ratified treaties to reduce chemical weapons and expand the North Atlantic Treaty Organization. But on numerous high-profile issues, Congress balked, deadlocking on campaign finance reform, overhaul of the financial services industry, regulatory reform, product liability, education reform, juvenile crime, missile defense systems, and other policy challenges.

Journalists, reflecting on the pileup of legislative road kill, largely stressed legislators' difficulty producing policy results under divided government during an election year. The approaching midterm congressional elections, according to the conventional account, lessened the parties' incentives to negotiate and bargain seriously to resolve major policy and political differences. As the *Washington Post*'s veteran Congress reporter concluded:

Republicans needed to fire up their conservative base—with issues such as tax cuts, abortion curbs and tax breaks for private schools—for what was otherwise likely to be a low-turnout election. Democrats needed broader issues such as curbing teenage smoking, protecting managed-care patients and hiring more teachers to give voters a reason to turn to them. There was little common ground here, and *many on both sides believed there was more to be gained politically by losing defiantly than by cutting a deal.*[1]

Legislators were seeking an "issue," rather than a "bill," a classic strategy in an election year.[2]

This electoral logic deserves a closer look, as it is often invoked to explain legislative deadlock. There are at least two foundations to the electoral logic. The first involves legislators' concerns about their long-term careers in the institution; the second, their long-term policy objectives. If legislators place a high value on re-election to Congress, then their behavior in office likely reflects their assessment of how they can maximize their chances of earning re-election. Maintaining the support of their partisan base probably often influences legislators' calculations of how best to ensure re-election. As such, the electoral logic would refer to legislators' tendencies to champion issues that rally the base (even if such issues are left on the agenda at the close of a Congress). Legislators' long-term policy goals might also be well served by holding onto issues, rather than seeking compromise to enact the relevant bills into law. In this case, the electoral logic refers to legislators' decisions to hold off acting on measures if they think the number of likeminded legislators will increase in the next Congress or if they expect a change in the party controlling the White House. In this scenario, legislators seek issues rather than bills not because of their party's immediate electoral need to distinguish itself from the opposition, but because of their party's long-term policy objectives. Both aspects of the electoral logic lead us to expect similar behavior and outcomes.

The question is whether electoral considerations will always produce an incentive for the parties to deadlock. Is an issue, rather than a bill, always preferred by legislators in the run-up to presidential and congressional elections? Many suggest so, arguing that the parties' desire to define their differences for the voters makes legislative compromise impossible as an election nears. As explained by one Republican senator, "As every week counts down [to the election], the partisan divisions are deepening, and both sides are trying to capture the issues for partisan gain—

we put the other guy on the defensive, force him into a corner and don't give anything we don't have to give."[3] The result, according to this account, is an increased chance of stalemate as fall campaigns approach. The "temptation to play politics with popular issues, rather than putting them into law," is too great to resist.[4]

The electoral logic, roughly sketched, holds some promise if we confine our view to the 105th and 106th Congresses, which deadlocked over a raft of salient issues with the approach of fall elections. But a look back to the 104th Congress in 1996 complicates this explanation. In that presidential election year, both parties ultimately sought bills, not issues. The result was a handsome record of legislative victories for both parties, including an increase in the minimum wage, a major overhaul of federal welfare programs, and a renewed drinking water law. The extreme gridlock in 1995 during the first year of Republican rule gave way to substantial and successful negotiation on salient legislative issues. Why? Pundits and journalists again pointed to the approaching elections, this time reversing the logic. Both parties wanted a record to run on, rather than a plate of issues to trumpet. That trend toward compromise in 1996, however, does not hold up more generally over the past half-century. Based on the measure of gridlock generated in chapter 3, deadlock increases only marginally in the Congresses leading up to presidential elections since 1946.[5]

Why do approaching elections sometimes bring deadlock and other times invite bargaining and compromise? The presence or absence of divided government fails to account for the differences: all three of the Republican Congresses of the 1990s just noted faced a Democratic president. Nor does another often-indicted culprit for gridlock, tough fiscal times, help explain Congress's uneven performance. True, in the 102d Congress, when deadlock reached close to its nadir for the postwar period, the federal deficit relative to outlays reached its worst level, reaching 20 percent of outlays. Legislative performance does seem to run loosely in tandem with sunnier fiscal times, but excess resources alone do not wipe out gridlock.[6] Despite the appearance of the first budget surplus in nearly thirty years, stalemate over how to spend the surplus in the 106th Congress seemed as prevalent as the deadlock was over how to create it.[7] Neither was the razor-thin Republican majority likely the central cause of deadlock in the 106th, as many observers suggested at the time.[8] During the past half-century, the size of the House majority party seems unrelated to the frequency of gridlock.[9]

My challenge in this chapter is to show the limits of analyzing legislative performance solely based on electoral dynamics. Instead, I show that institutional arrangements—interacting with elections—account for the uneven performance of Congress during the past half-century. Using the measure of gridlock developed in chapter 3, I explore aggregate changes in the frequency of stalemate as a function of the institutional and electoral forces outlined in chapter 2. Congressional structures—perhaps more so than electoral results—play a pivotal role in shaping the lawmaking capacity and promise of Congress.

Constructing an Empirical Test

Scholars and observers of Congress have long held that divided party control of government is the central obstacle to swift policy compromise on Capitol Hill. Political parties in this view facilitate the bridging of inevitable differences that emerge across constitutionally separated executive and legislative branches. Without shared policy and electoral interests, Congress and the president are unlikely to have sufficient incentive to seek compromise that suits their different electoral constituencies. Publication of David Mayhew's finding in 1991 that divided government failed to account for differences in Congress's legislative record in the post–World War II period not surprisingly rattled students of Congress and the presidency who had long targeted divided government as the central barrier to legislative action. In the years since Mayhew published *Divided We Govern*, numerous scholars have tackled the questions raised by Mayhew, with many of them seeking alternative empirical ways to test his key conjecture about the null effects of divided party control.

The limited impact of divided government on legislative performance can be seen in a simple bivariate test (table 4-1). The models in table 4-1 estimate the frequency of legislative stalemate as a function of party control—whether Congress and the White House were controlled by the same or different political parties.[10] I use the measure of stalemate developed in chapter 3, which taps the frequency with which issues on the agenda fail to be enacted into law. Because issues vary in salience and significance, we want to know how divided government affects legislative performance across different levels of salience. Thus the gridlock scores used in each of the columns of table 4-1 are calculated over different sets of issues, ranging from the broadest to strictest definition of issue salience.[11] Divided government registers only a limited effect on the frequency of legislative

Table 4-1. *Does Divided Government Increase Deadlock?* 1947–2000

Item	Gridlock 1	Gridlock 2	Gridlock 3	Gridlock 4	Gridlock 5
Divided government	.247* (.116)	.331* (.139)	.245 (.166)	.283* (.164)	.241 (.171)
Constant	–.083 (.095)	–.371** (.111)	–.433** (.130)	–.517*** (.129)	–.551*** (.133)
N	27	27	27	27	27
F	4.50*	5.65*	2.17	2.99	2.00
Adjusted R^2	.119	.152	.043	.071	.037

Source: See text for tables in this chapter.
Note: Dependent variables are the percentage of agenda items not enacted at the end of each Congress. Agenda issues increase in salience across the table from gridlock 1 (at least one *Times* editorial mention per issue) to gridlock 5 (at least 5 *Times* mentions per issue). Cell entries are estimated coefficients from a grouped logit model using Stata 7.0's *glogit* routine (standard errors in parentheses). * $p < .05$, ** $p < .01$, *** $p < .001$ (one-tailed t tests).

gridlock and alone fails to explain much of the variance in deadlock observed in the postwar period. Only for the broadest definition of the congressional agenda (columns 1 and 2) does the frequency of gridlock seem higher under divided government than under unified control. Once we narrow our focus to more salient issues, I find no evidence that divided government drives up the frequency of stalemate.[12]

We can perform similar bivariate tests to determine whether other electoral dynamics systematically affect the incidence of stalemate. I find that approaching presidential elections have only a limited impact on policy stalemate. With a presidential election on the horizon, the frequency of gridlock is just a couple of points higher than during the two years after a presidential election. Neither is Congress more prone to stalemate when presidential elections approach during periods of divided control—precisely when legislators might hold off acting on measures in anticipation of possibly gaining the White House.[13] Considered jointly, these several electoral forces explain little of the variation in the frequency of deadlock during the postwar period. Legislative performance is indistinguishable across these electoral contexts.

Such limited empirical evidence lends slim support for traditional notions about the impact of elections on legislative performance. The bivariate relationships suggested by those who argue that divided party control generates gridlock do not prove strong. Bivariate relationships, however, can be misleading. We need to consider the effects of each suspected factor, controlling for the influence of other factors and the joint effect of the several factors underpinning differences between unified and divided regimes. Next, I construct such multivariate tests, considering the effects of institutional structures and the joint effects of institutions and elections on legislative performance.

Explanatory Variables

In chapter 2, I argued that institutional developments after the founding of Congress altered the work ways of Congress in at least two ways. First, bicameralism took on a new cast with the emergence of a pro-active Senate. Second, the introduction of political parties altered the politics of constructing policy coalitions within Congress and between the branches. As a result, I expect policy differences between the chambers and partisan alignments within each chamber to affect legislative performance in predictable ways. In this section, my challenge is to devise a way to operationalize these institutional and electoral forces and to determine their impact on legislative outcomes.

BICAMERAL DIFFERENCES. As explored in chapter 2, we would expect legislators to more frequently encounter gridlock on major issues the greater the policy differences between the two chambers. In appendix B, I note that we might measure bicameral differences in a number of ways. For example, in a previous study of legislative stalemate, I used ideological scores derived from legislators' roll call records to array House and Senate legislators on a single policy continuum and then summarized differences in the policy dispositions of the two chamber medians.[14] As explained in detail in appendix B, the problem with this approach is that the House and Senate roll call records are composed of different sets of votes. Even when the two chambers vote on similar issues, the questions they vote on are often framed in different ways. The implication is that we cannot easily compare House and Senate voting records to detect the degree of policy differences between the chambers.

The solution is to isolate the set of policy issues on which both the House and Senate cast identical votes at roughly the same time. Up or down votes on conference reports provide precisely this set of votes.[15] Thus I assemble a database of every conference report brought to the floor of the House and Senate chambers between 1947 and 2000 and calculate the percentage of each chamber voting yea on each conference report. I can then measure the difference in policy views of the House and Senate median members by calculating the absolute difference between the two chambers' percentage approval for each report and averaging over all reports for each Congress to produce a mean disagreement score by Congress.[16]

On average in the postwar period, the two chambers differ by 7 percentage points. Bicameral differences were smallest in the 84th Congress (1955–56), with the two chambers differing on average by only 2 percent; bicameral differences were greatest in the 95th (1977–78), 96th (1979–80) and 103d (1993–94) Congresses when the two chambers differed on average by 11 percent.

DIVIDED GOVERNMENT. Assessing the impact of party control of government is more straightforward. I use a dummy variable to distinguish between periods of divided and unified control. Of the twenty-seven Congresses between 1947 and 2000, ten were periods of unified party control of Congress and the presidency, while seventeen featured split party control of Congress and the White House. I explore the impact of other specifications for divided government in appendix C.

PARTY POLARIZATION. To assess partisan polarization (or its opposite, partisan moderation), we need a way of gauging ideological differences among legislators and between the two parties. I begin by assuming that we can align legislators along a single liberal-conservative ideological dimension within each chamber. We can then use ideological scores derived from legislators' voting records to place each legislator spatially along the left-right spectrum.[17] We can think of legislators as moderate or not moderate, defining moderates as those legislators who are closer ideologically to the middle of the chamber than to their own party median.

We can represent the difference between moderates and nonmoderates graphically, as in the two panels of figure 4-1. Here, m is the ideological midpoint of the chamber (also the floor median's ideal point). The Democratic Party median lies at Pd and the Republican party median at Pr. The dotted lines on each side fall halfway between the party median and the ideological midpoint of the chamber. "Moderates" are thus those legislators whose ideal points place them between the two dotted lines (closer to the chamber median than to their party median). Having distinguished between moderates and nonmoderates, I count up the number of legislators in each party and chamber who are ideological moderates along the left-right spectrum. In practice, this amounts to a count of the number of

Figure 4-1. *Legislators' Ideal Points in a Stylized Chamber*

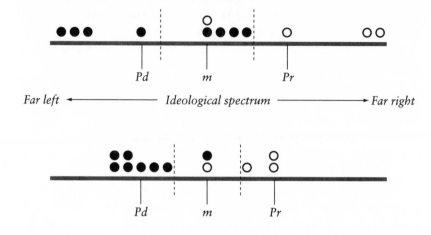

● Democrat   *Pd* Democratic Party median
○ Republican   *m* Chamber median
                  Pr Republican Party median

conservative Democrats (Democrats to the right of their party median *Pd*) and liberal Republicans (Republicans to the left of their party median *Pr*) in each chamber in each Congress.

The number or percentage of moderates, however, does not necessarily tell us how polarized the two parties are.[18] If we compare the two panels of figure 4-1, we would expect the bottom panel to represent the more moderate chamber, as legislators are distributed over a narrower and more central range of the ideological spectrum. In contrast, the top panel intuitively represents a more polarized chamber, as legislators and their party medians are further apart, and a good share of legislators are located at the extremes of the left-right dimension. If we calculate the percentage of moderates in each panel as discussed above, however, we would call the top panel more moderate: five out of twelve legislators are moderates in the top panel, compared with two out of twelve in the bottom panel. A better measure of partisan polarization would take account of the number of moderates relative to the distance between the two party medians. To gauge polarization in each Congress, I thus divide the number of moderates in each chamber by the distance between the two party medians. Because the House and Senate series are so highly correlated, I average the two series to produce a polarization score for each Congress.[19]

A word on interpreting the scores is in order. High scores mean low levels of polarization, and low scores mean high levels of polarization.[20] Thus, it makes more sense intuitively to think of the measure as tapping the level of partisan moderation in each Congress. The historical trajectory of partisan moderation appears in figure 4-2, showing separate histories for the House and Senate. Three patterns are striking: the close alignment of the House and Senate series; the duration of a sizable political center from the late 1950s well into the 1970s; and the precipitous decline—some say disappearance—of the political center since the 1980s. The quantitative portrait offered by the measure comports well with the conventional wisdom that the political center at the end of the 1990s had all but disappeared, as moderation ranged from a high score of 55 in the 92d Congress (1971–72) to a low score below 10 in the 105th (1997–99). For the percentage of moderates, similar differences emerge between the early 1970s and late 1990s: in the 92d Congress, moderates composed 32 percent of the chambers, in the 105th just 11 percent. The measure of partisan moderation thus nicely captures the received wisdom that today's parties are highly polarized, with a wide ideological gulf separating the two parties and few moderate legislators left in between.

PARTY MANDATE. To tap variation in the timing of major electoral change, I calculate the length of time a new congressional majority has been out of power. In practice, this means that I count the number of Congresses a new majority party (controlling both chambers) spent in the minority before gaining the majority, averaging the experiences of the House and Senate series.[21] When the new Republican majority took control in 1995, for example, Senate Republicans had been in the minority for four Congresses and House Republicans for twenty. This yields a mean time out of power of twelve Congresses.[22]

POLICY CONTEXT. We can tap the effect of the policy environment on legislative change in the following ways. First, I use Mayhew's approach for measuring the health of the budgetary climate, using the size of the federal budget surplus or deficit as a percentage of federal government outlays.[23] Second, to tap the national mood, I use an annual measure of domestic policy mood that James Stimson has derived from public opinion survey data.[24] Higher values reflect stronger preferences for a

Figure 4-2. *Partisan Moderation in the House and Senate, 1947–2000*

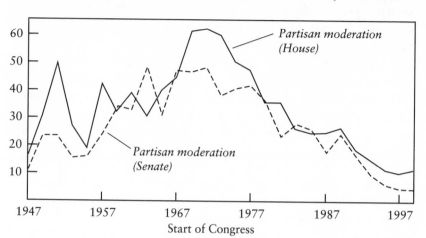

Start of Congress

more activist federal government.[25] As others have done, I lag the public mood variable by one Congress, to capture the idea that recent changes in public opinion are then registered in subsequent legislative deliberation.[26] As Stimson and colleagues have pointed out, "This cannot rule out the possibility that opinion responds to policy, but it definitively precludes the possibility of opinion responding to current policy."[27]

Dependent Variable

The dependent variable in the analysis that follows is the measure of gridlock introduced in chapter 3: the percentage of agenda items that end in stalemate at the close of each Congress. Because the salience of an agenda issue may affect the politics of its treatment in Congress, I create five versions of the gridlock measure, each tapping the frequency of stalemate over a different level of issue salience.[28] The broadest measure includes all legislative issues and treaties discussed by the *New York Times* during a Congress. By this measure, Congress encountered stalemate on average on just over half its agenda, with the frequency of deadlock ranging from 35 percent to 65 percent. The measure encompassing the most salient issues includes only those issues receiving five or more editorials during a Congress. By this measure, gridlock occurred on average on 40 percent of the agenda. The frequency of stalemate on these most salient issues was lowest in the 88th Congress in 1963 and 1964, occurring on only a fifth of the agenda; stalemate reached its peak of 70 percent in the 106th (1999–2000), Clinton's last years in office.

Explaining the Patterns

With a measure of gridlock in hand, we can now estimate the joint impact of the explanatory variables on the frequency of stalemate.[29] In table 4-2, I show the results for each of the five models.[30] Overall, the models perform well, explaining from 38 percent to 64 percent of the variance in the frequency of stalemate during the latter half of the twentieth century. Moreover, we can safely reject the null hypothesis that all the coefficients together are equal to zero, increasing confidence in the overall strength of the statistical model. These statistical results provide a firm foundation from which to interpret the impact of electoral and institutional forces on the frequency of deadlock.

Electoral Factors

A look at the impact of electoral forces shows some support for the idea that periods of divided government are likely to yield more frequent bouts of stalemate. In each of the models, deadlock is significantly higher in periods of divided party control than in periods of unified control.[31] Mayhew convincingly showed that divided and unified governments did not differ in the quantity of landmark laws enacted, but divided government does seem to affect the broader ability of the political system to address serious public problems. Once we incorporate a denominator measuring the overall issue agenda, our perspective on the impact of divided government changes. Split party control increases the likelihood that more issues on the agenda will end in stalemate. We can think of divided government as a force that erects another barrier in the legislative process: it traps bills that might have been enacted had control of government been unified in a single political party.[32] In this sense, the "party-government school" that advocated "responsible" parties is vindicated.[33] As Woodrow Wilson, V. O. Key, E. E. Schattschneider, James Sundquist, and many other party scholars argued during the past century, legislative deadlock grows more likely when the two major parties split control of government.[34]

Elections thus affect legislative performance when they allocate procedural control of the executive and legislative branches to opposing parties. But elections also matter by shaping the array of policy views within

Table 4-2. *Estimating the Frequency of Gridlock, 1953–2000*

Variable	Gridlock 1	Gridlock 2	Gridlock 3	Gridlock 4	Gridlock 5
Divided government	.306* (.122)	.432*** (.119)	.418** (.151)	.421** (.154)	.416* (.167)
Partisan moderation	−.006 (.004)	−.012** (.004)	−.012* (.006)	−.016** (.006)	−.014* (.006)
Bicameral differences	5.867* (2.750)	7.514** (2.739)	11.201** (3.570)	7.502* (3.626)	8.444* (3.954)
Time out of majority	.010 (.024)	−.009 (.025)	−.012 (.034)	−.050ᵃ (.035)	−.073* (.039)
Budgetary situation	.005 (.007)	.012 (.008)	.024 (.011)	.017 (.011)	.021 (.013)
Public mood (lagged)	−.007 (.012)	.001 (.011)	.005 (.015)	−.004 (.015)	−.011 (.016)
Constant	.100 (.790)	−.466 (.746)	−.973 (.975)	−.160 (.985)	.111 (1.052)
N	24	24	24	24	24
F	2.96*	5.81**	3.97**	3.64**	2.99*
Adjusted R^2	.339	.556	.437	.408	.341

Note: Cell entries are weighted least squares logit estimates for grouped data (standard errors in parentheses). * $p < .05$, ** $p < .01$, *** $p < .001$, ᵃ $p < .1$ (one-tailed t tests).

and between the two parties. Most striking is the impact of polarized parties. In four of the five models, rising levels of moderation (that is, decreasing polarization) make stalemate less likely. In the fifth model, the impact of polarization misses statistical significance by just a little, suggesting overall that policy moderation yields legislative dividends for Congress. This result is striking because it runs directly counter to the expectations of the party government school. Despite the faith of responsible party advocates in cohesive political parties, the results suggest that policy change is actually less likely as the parties become more polarized. Although single-party control of the branches may help to break deadlock, there are clearly limits to the power of political parties to smooth the way for legislative agreement. Intense polarization, in fact, seems counterproductive to fostering major policy change. Finally, there is only limited evidence that a party's electoral mandate matters. Only for the

Table 4-3. *Simulated Probabilities of Gridlock*

Variable	Change in X	Net change in expected probability of gridlock (percent)
Divided government	0 → 1	+11
Partisan moderation	17 → 44.58	–9
Bicameral differences	.04 → .096	+12

Note: Net change in the expected probability of gridlock is calculated as the independent variables change between the values in column 1 (that is, between one standard deviation below and above the mean value for each of the continuous variables and between 0 and 1 for the dichotomous variable). Simulated probabilities are based on the exponential linear predictions generated by the *adjust* routine in Stata 7.0 and are calculated assuming the presence of divided government (all other variables set at their mean values).

most salient issues does the time the new majority has been out of power seem to affect the incidence of deadlock. Potentially this influence reflects new majorities' efforts to prove their governing capacity on showcase items placed high on the agenda.

The substantive effect of these electoral forces can be seen by simulating the expected frequency of gridlock, given specified changes in the values of the explanatory variables.[35] The ranges of the independent variables appear in table 4-3, column 2, and the associated changes in gridlock appear in column 3. If we use the past half-century as our guide, we can expect divided control of government to increase the frequency of stalemate by roughly 11 percent. Given on average fifty-five issues on the agenda each Congress, the arrival of unified government should allow legislators to reach agreement on roughly six additional issues. Declines in polarization show similar effects, lowering the incidence of deadlock by roughly 9 percent, or an additional five issues. Such results confirm the claim that partisan polarization limits the legislative capacity of Congress.[36] The "incredible shrinking middle"—as Senator John Breaux called it in 1995—seems to substantially hamper the ability of Congress and the president to reach agreement on the issues before them.[37]

Institutional Effects

The bicameral context matters greatly. In all of the five models, the coefficient for bicameral differences is statistically significant. Substantively this means that even after accounting for the impact of elections through party control and partisan alignments, policy differences between the House and Senate still matter. Congress finds it tougher to reach final agreement on pressing policy issues as policy differences between the chambers grow more frequent. Bicameral differences have the greatest substantive impact of the frequency of deadlock: when the frequency of policy disagreement between the chambers doubles, the incidence of stalemate increases by 12 percent (table 4-3). This is probably why students of Congress may have been "overly optimistic" about the prospects for governance under unified government in the 103d Congress (1993–94).[38] Policy disagreement as measured through House and Senate differences on final conference reports reached 11 percent in the 103d, the highest level since the last period of unified control under the Democrats in the late 1970s. Given the high level of bicameral disagreement (and the intensely polarized parties), it is no wonder that seasoned observers concluded at the close of the 103d Congress: "The only good news as this mud fight finally winds down is that it's hard to imagine much worse."[39]

In contrast, I find no support for the idea that the policy environment affects the ability of legislators to secure major policy change. Improved fiscal discipline does not seem to make it easier to reach agreement on policy disputes. Nor does the liberalness of public opinion seem to matter. As the public's preference for activist government increases, we see little systematic response in Congress's legislative performance.

Additional Possibilities

How robust are the effects of these institutional and electoral factors? One way to determine our confidence in the models is to consider the impact of other potential forces, while controlling for the effects of the explanatory variables already considered. For example, several legislative scholars have recently suggested that the Senate's supermajority requirements imposed under its Rule 22 may help to shape legislative performance.[40] Given the hurdle imposed by the need to garner sixty votes to cut off debate under Senate rules, we might expect legislative deadlock to increase as the threat of the filibuster increases. The stronger the ideological disagreement between a filibustering senator and a Senate majority, the greater the threat posed by the filibuster: the obstructing senator is less likely to give way under such conditions as she stands to gain more in policy by withholding her consent. Still, it is possible that the obstructive impact of filibustering senators is washed away, as not every filibuster is motivated on ideological grounds and not every filibustering senator seeks to completely derail her legislative target.

There is no simple way to measure the threat of the filibuster. One way to roughly capture the frequency and severity of the threat is to count the number of filibusters that occurred in each Congress and then weight that number by the ideological distance between the pivotal "sixtieth" and "fifty-first" senators. The "sixtieth" senator is that senator who—along a left-right dimension—is the legislator whose vote is theoretically required to invoke cloture when an issue falls along the left-right spectrum.[41] Measured this way, the threat of the filibuster was lowest in the 82d and 84th Congresses (1951–52 and 1955–56, respectively), as there were no recorded filibusters in those Congresses; the filibuster threat peaked in the 102d Congress (1991–92), when Republicans filibustered numerous issues the Democratic Congress sought to pass. Regressing the frequency of deadlock on the threat of the filibuster yields a significant impact of the Senate's rules on legislative performance. As the severity of the threat goes up, the incidence of deadlock increases (table 4-4, column 1). However, when we control for the impact of our other explanatory variables, accounting for the filibuster threat does not appreciably alter the earlier results: the coefficients for divided government and partisan polarization remain statistically significant at conventional levels (table 4-4, column 2).[42] Only the significance of the parameter estimate for bicameral differences slips, suggesting a weaker effect of bicameral differences once we account for senators' exploitation of their chamber's rules. Although Senate filibustering considered alone does appear to drive up deadlock, there does not seem to be any broader connection between the two. The impact of supermajority rules appears to be challenged by other sources of variation in the legislative arena.

The impact of divided government also bears further scrutiny. To test whether control of the two branches by a single party significantly improves legislative performance, the conventional approach is to use a dummy variable denoting whether or not control of the branches is unified under a single party or divided between two. As shown, when we estimate the impact of divided government in this way, deadlock appears to rise significantly in periods of divided control. But a dummy variable distinguishing between periods of unified and divided control might also be demarking other factors that vary significantly under the two regimes of party control. One prominent alternative is that distinguishing between

Table 4-4. *Impact of the Filibuster Threat on the Frequency of Gridlock*

Variable	1 Coefficient	2 Coefficient
Filibuster threat	.121** (.036)	.009 (.088)
Divided government	. . .	.402* (.206)
Partisan moderation	. . .	−.012* (.006)
Bicameral differences	. . .	6.846[a] (4.922)
Time out of majority	. . .	−.008 (.032)
Budgetary situation	. . .	.009 (.015)
Public mood (lagged)	. . .	.000 (.018)
Constant	. . .	−.478 (1.207)
N	25	22
F	11.18**	2.73*
Adjusted R^2	.298	.366

Note: Cell entries weighted least squares logit estimates for grouped data (standard errors in parentheses). * $p < .05$, ** $p < .01$ (one-tailed t tests).

the two regimes may serve as a proxy for ideological differences between Congress and the president. If we assume that policy views are more distant in periods of divided control and closer under unified control, then using a dummy variable to demark the two regimes potentially masks the impact of ideological differences. If gridlock does rise as the two branches diverge ideologically, then our conclusions about the relevance of party control would be misplaced. Variation in party control would simply be a poorly measured proxy for ideological disagreement between the branches. Moreover, we might find that when we use a more direct measure of interbranch disagreement, interchamber disagreement no longer helps to account for the frequency of deadlock. Friction between the branches might be a stronger predictor of legislative gridlock than conflict between the chambers.

Table 4-5. *Does Ideological Disagreement between the Branches Matter?* 1953–2000

Variable	Gridlock 1	Gridlock 2	Gridlock 3	Gridlock 4	Gridlock 5
Divided government	.287*	.418**	.411*	.381*	.456*
	(.149)	(.142)	(.179)	(.179)	(.196)
Ideological disagreement between the branches	.103	.084	.045	.265	–.258
	(.435)	(.430)	(.551)	(.553)	(.621)
Partisan moderation	–.005	–.012**	–.012*	–.015**	–.014*
	(.005)	(.004)	(.006)	(.006)	(.006)
Bicameral differences	5.481ª	7.206*	11.043**	6.534ª	9.434*
	(3.261)	(3.226)	(4.147)	(4.223)	(4.701)
Time out of majority	.009	–.009	–.012	–.051ª	–.071*
	(.025)	(.026)	(.036)	(.036)	(.040)
Budgetary situation	.006	.013	.025	.018	.019
	(.008)	(.009)	(.012)	(.012)	(.013)
Public mood (lagged)	–.009	–.001	.004	–.008	–.007
	(.013)	(.013)	(.017)	(.017)	(.019)
Constant	.162	–.406	–.941	.039	–.103
	(.854)	(.828)	(1.079)	(1.090)	(1.195)
N	24	24	24	24	24
F	2.41ª	4.70**	3.21*	3.01*	2.46ª
Adjusted R^2	.300	.530	.334	.338	.308

Note: Cell entries weighted least squares logit estimates for grouped data (standard errors in parentheses). * $p < .05$, ** $p < .01$, ª$p < .1$ (one-tailed t tests).

Controlling for interbranch disagreement, however, does not shake our confidence in the earlier results (table 4-5).[43] For almost every level of issue salience, divided government remains a strong predictor of increased deadlock, as do increasing polarization and rising differences between the two chambers.[44] This suggests that it is more than just differences over policy that are at stake in leading Congress and the president to deadlock; ideological differences between the branches are insufficient on their own to make deadlock more likely. Instead, partisan control of the two branches matters a lot. Presidents who lack control over the agenda of the House and Senate during periods of divided government face an uphill battle securing passage of favored legislation. Once greater control of the agenda is secured during periods of unified government, the chances of stalemate decline. Party control alone, however, is insufficient for securing major policy change: bicameral differences and polarized parties make policy compromise hard even in periods of unified control.

We also need to consider whether the results are simply artifacts of time span and measurement of critical variables. David Mayhew, for example, found strong evidence that Congresses during the "activist era" from the early 1960s through the mid-1970s systematically produced greater numbers of landmark laws. It is worth re-estimating the models to see whether marking the activist era—rather than accounting for the liberalness of the public mood—produces substantively different results. Including a dummy variable to mark the era instead of using the measure of policy mood has the added advantage of allowing me to estimate the deadlock model reaching back to the 80th Congress, which started in 1947.[45] I find no evidence, however, that changing the time span or measures alters the previous findings.[46]

Why then did Mayhew find such an impact of the activist era on legislative performance, while I find none? One strong possibility is that activist era Congresses were so prolific legislatively because of the contours of partisan conflict at that time. Most noticeable was the strength of the political center during the activist era, a period with little of the partisan polarization that we see today. Remembering that the most polarized Congresses are those with the lowest scores on the polarization variable, the activist era Congresses were far more moderate than the other Congresses.[47] Activist era Congresses scored an average polarization score of 45 (meaning they were very moderate), while all other Congresses scored 23 on average (meaning they were quite polarized). We think of the activist era Congresses as highly productive most likely because the parties were moderate, a condition shown highly conducive to breaking deadlock.

We also need to consider more fine-grained measures to capture the politics of divided government. In the preceding analysis, I treated all types of divided government the same, regardless of whether control of Congress was unified or divided. We might wonder whether periods when the president's party controls at least one chamber are less prone to deadlock than periods of entirely divided control. I evaluate this possibility by demarking periods of "quasi-divided" control (when the Republicans controlled both the White House and the Senate from 1981 through

1986, but not the House) and "pure-divided" control (Congresses in which the parties controlled the White House, House, and Senate). When I replace the divided government variable with these two dummy variables in the earlier models, periods of pure-divided party control of government show significantly more frequent bouts of deadlock than periods of unified or quasi-divided control.[48] In contrast, frequency of stalemate during periods of quasi-divided control is indistinguishable from its frequency in other periods. The consistency in the results across each of these alternative specifications should increase our confidence in the original results: institutional factors rival the electoral environment in shaping legislative performance. The array of party preferences and control and the range of policy views between the chambers jointly affect the chances that Congress and the president will be able to compromise and thus produce major episodes of policy change.[49]

Budget Gridlock: An Additional Test

If elections and institutions together affect Congress's capacity to legislate, we should also see their effects on other aspects of the legislative process. One potential arena for a further test of the gridlock model is the world of budgetary politics. Given the centrality of budget politics in recent decades we should see familiar patterns recurring in battles over the budget as we have seen more broadly across the legislative agenda. Delving into budget politics, in other words, allows us to test conjectures about gridlock on an alternative indicator of stalemate.

According to the Congressional Budget Act enacted in 1974, Congress must pass a budget resolution every year that sets forth a fiscal framework for the coming fiscal year. Although the president lacks a formal role in the process of creating the resolution (it does not go to the president for his signature or veto), the incentives for presidential involvement are clear. First, presidents generally want budget resolutions to reflect the priorities set out in the version of the budget the president submits to Congress. Second, the resolution sets the framework for actual budgeting decisions to be made later in the year. The politics of the resolution thus reveals the capacity of Congress and the president to reach important legislative decisions. Budget resolution politics provides what budget expert Allen Schick calls a "barometer of budgetary conflict."[50]

Because the law sets an annual deadline for passage of the congressional budget resolution, Congress's record in meeting the deadline is a

Table 4-6. *Delay in Adoption of Congressional Budget Resolution,*
Fiscal Years 1976–2001

Fiscal year	Days past deadline	Fiscal year	Days past deadline
1976	1	1989	52
1977	0	1990	33
1978	2	1991	176
1979	2	1992	37
1980	9	1993	36
1981	28	1994	0
1982	6	1995	27
1983	39	1996	75
1984	39	1997	59
1985	139	1998	51
1986	78	1999	[a]
1987	73	2000	0
1988	70	2001	0

Source: Allen Schick, with Felix LoStracco, *The Federal Budget: Politics, Policy, Process* (Brookings, 2000), table 6-1, p. 109.
a. No budget resolution adopted.

marker for its performance in reaching tax and spending decisions.[51] For each fiscal year since the 1974 Budget Act was put into place, we can determine how late Congress was in passing the required resolution. The budget law now calls for adoption of the resolution by April 15, but the data in table 4-6 suggest that Congress often misses the deadline by weeks or months. Between the first budget resolution for fiscal year 1976 (adopted in 1975) and the resolution for fiscal year 2001 (adopted in 2000), Congress managed only four times to pass the resolution on time. On average, the resolution has been forty-one days late, although there is a lot of variation around that mean.

How well do electoral and institutional factors account for variation in budget delay? If the new wisdom on divided government is correct, patterns of party control should have no effect on adoption of the annual budget resolution. Neither Mayhew nor Krehbiel, for example, would expect to find much difference in budget delays across periods of unified and divided control. In contrast, if my alternative model of gridlock rings true, we would expect Congress to take longer to pass a budget resolution under divided government, all else equal. An initial survey of the data suggests that party control may strongly shape the timing of budget decisions. During the three periods of unified party control since the 1970s, Congress missed the budget deadline by just eleven days on average; during the ten episodes of divided control since 1976, Congress was on average almost two months late.[52]

Does divided government contribute to the budgetary slowdown once we control for the several other factors that are likely to affect budget politics? After all, since presidents do not sign congressional budget resolutions, interbranch conflict might be incidental to debates within Congress over the scope of the federal budget. Unfortunately, with such few cases it is difficult to conduct a multivariate test. As an alternative, I show the results of several bivariate tests, testing for the effect of each variable alone (table 4-7). As seen in table 4-7, column 1, when Congress and the White House are controlled by different parties, Congress is especially prone to miss the budget deadline by a significant margin—taking roughly forty days longer to reach agreement during periods of divided government. The lack of a formal role for the president in formulating the congressional budget blueprint does not preclude his involvement and influence in molding budgetary priorities, even controlling for the budgetary situation. Contrary to prominent political science models, unified party control of Congress and the White House does seem to facilitate agreement between the branches. Certainly the sharing of policy preferences within the party helps account for the speed of reconciling budgetary differences. But the electoral incentive shared by the congressional majority and the White House to show their party's capacity to budget and hence to govern may be equally important.

We can see the influence of the array of policy views by examining whether partisan polarization affects the speed of budget negotiations. As shown in column 2, more moderate Congresses take a shorter time to negotiate agreements, although sunnier fiscal times also speed up completion of budget resolutions. The model does not, however, detect a significant impact of bicameral differences on budget delay (column 3).[53] In sum, an additional test of the gridlock model serves its purpose well, as it suggests the broader fit of the model for other indicators of legislative delay. The distribution of policy views within the parties and the allocation of party control between the branches significantly affect the deadlock, a trend detectable even in the limited period inaugurated by the passage of a new federal budget law in 1974.

This alternative test also sheds some light on the consequences of the 1974 law itself. It is typically argued that the Budget Act was originally

Table 4-7. Impact of Elections and Institutions on Budget Conflict

Variable	Coefficient	Coefficient	Coefficient
Divided government	40.036** (20.302)	. . .	. . .
Partisan moderation	. . .	−1.515** (.793)	. . .
Bicameral differences	. . .	. . .	−799.445 (575.704)
Budgetary situation	−1.385[a] (.939)	−2.341** (1.080)	−1.370[a] (1.013)
Constant	−6.818 (21.636)	47.744** (19.199)	96.482[a] (54.235)
N	13	13	13
F	2.97[a]	2.84[a]	1.85
Adjusted R^2	.248	.235	.124

Note: Dependent variable is average delay (measured in days) in adoption of congressional budget resolution during each two-year Congress. The entries are OLS regression coefficients (standard errors in parentheses) generated from the *regress* routine in Stata 7.0. ** $p < .05$, [a] $p < .1$ (one-tailed t tests).

enacted to address recurring interbranch conflict over budget priorities: it was seen as a solution to Congress's frequent battles with President Richard M. Nixon over his authority to impound federal monies appropriated by Congress for federal programs.[54] Interbranch conflict over the budget has not disappeared, as the evidence showing a significant slowdown in the budgetary process during divided government illustrates. By institutionalizing a congressional role in formulating a budget, however, the budget law also encourages intra-Congress conflict to affect the character and timing of budget politics. Most likely this is an unintended consequence of a budget law written by Democrats eyeing an aggressive Republican president across town. Authors of the law no doubt failed to fully anticipate the sorts of budget politics that could now arise, such as the failure of the House and Senate to pass a budget resolution in 1998 and 2002. With bicameral differences over tax cuts and discretionary spending precluding compromise between House and Senate Republican leaders in 1998, appropriators simply went ahead on their own without a budget guideline and crafted their annual bills.[55] The budget process in short has created a venue for intrabranch disputes to color the shape and timing of the budget blueprint, regardless of the original intentions of the legislative authors of the act.

Institutions and Elections Revisited

Unified party control of government cannot guarantee the compromise necessary for breaking deadlock in American politics. As David Mayhew has argued, looking solely at the *structural* component of the American political system—the separation of powers between Congress and the president—tends to obscure important dynamics in American lawmaking.[56] As the analysis suggests, it is the *pluralist* component that deserves our more focused attention. The distributions of policy views within and across the two major political parties have predictable and important effects on the legislative performance of Congress and the president. The timing of party politics also matters. Long-frustrated congressional minorities often capitalize successfully on electoral mandates when their party gains unified control of Congress. Intrabranch politics, it seems, may be as important as the usual culprit of conflict between the branches.

So why did Mayhew and his critics reach such divergent conclusions about divided government? Although Mayhew found no effect of divided government on the production of important legislation, divided government clearly dampens the legislative performance of Congress and the president: a greater percentage of the agenda is killed under divided than under unified government. Focusing solely on what gets enacted—rather than on the agenda of problems facing Congress—risks understating the effects of divided government. George Edwards and his colleagues suggested as much in their analysis of the effect of divided government on the passage of legislation opposed by presidential administrations.[57] Still, as Edwards and his colleagues said—but did not pursue further—divided government is "only one of many obstacles that legislation faces on the path to enactment."[58] Mayhew, of course, reaches precisely the same conclusion after finding no unique effect for divided government: The effects of divided government are challenged by other realities of American politics.

Two of these other factors shaping Congress's policy performance command attention: the impact of parties and the consequences of bicameralism. First, consider party effects. My findings suggest that it is premature to reject the idea that political parties influence patterns of legislative outcomes. To be sure, the configuration of party control helps explain just a small portion of deadlock in contemporary politics. But as noted in earlier chapters, elections do more than divide control of the two major branches. Elections also determine the mix of ideologies within each major party. Such ideological divisions within the parties were decried in the 1950s by the "party government" school whose adherents believed that internal party divisions made it nearly impossible for the major parties to assemble and enact party agendas once they took office.

What is striking about the impact of parties in the latter half of the twentieth century is how strongly that impact differs from the expectations of the party government school. As the American Political Science Association's Committee on Political Parties argued in its often-cited 1950 report, cohesive political parties that offered distinctive choices to the electorate were critical for ensuring responsive and accountable government. The consequences of weak parties were steep: "The very heartbeat of democracy," the committee warned, was threatened by the state of the political parties.[59] Democracy was contingent on organizing and responding to majorities, and cohesive parties were deemed the only viable instrument for doing so.

As the two parties have polarized and the political center has stretched thin over the recent past, little evidence indicates that legislative performance has risen in lockstep. Paradoxically, far from ensuring that voters will be given meaningful choices between competing party programs, the polarization of the parties seems to encourage deadlock. Why should polarization have this effect? One prominent scholar of Congress and electoral politics observes that legislators' desire to be responsive to active constituencies affects the incentive to compromise. "I do not think that one must be overcome by nostalgia," notes Morris P. Fiorina, "to imagine that Everett Dirksen, Mike Mansfield, John McCormack, and Gerald Ford [House and Senate party leaders in the 1960s and 1970s] would have found some common ground and acted. Many of today's leaders, however, would rather have issues to use in the upcoming election than accomplishments to point to."[60] There may be a personal element to these temporal differences in leadership styles, but more likely the differences reflect changes in the makeup and activities of contemporary parties, as party organizations are increasingly defined by issue activists, constituency groups, and large-scale financial contributors with pointed policy and ideological agendas. With limited electoral ties to the mass and moderate middle, legislators have only limited and occasional incentive to craft moderate policy compromises to public problems. The statistical evidence presented in this chapter backs up this impression: the larger the political center and the less polarized the Congress, the greater the prospects for measurable policy compromise and change. Parties do affect Congress's capacity to legislate but not strictly according to whether their control is unified or divided.

Bicameralism is perhaps the most critical structural factor shaping the politics of gridlock. Bicameralism—rather than the separation of power between executive and legislative branches—seems most relevant in explaining stalemate in the postwar period. To be sure, both the separation of powers and bicameralism were central to the framers' late-eighteenth-century beliefs about the proper construction of political institutions.[61] Still, with important recent exceptions, the policy consequences of divided government, not bicameralism, feature prominently in theoretical and empirical treatments of legislative gridlock.

Bicameral differences arise of course because structural differences between House and Senate elections ensure that policy views will not be distributed and aggregated identically in the two chambers. Even when both chambers are controlled by the same party, we cannot assume that the two chambers desire the same policy outcomes. The impact of bicameral differences can be seen clearly in the fate of a patients' bill of rights measure in the 106th Congress (1999–2000). Although both chambers passed a version of the bill with the support of Republican majorities, no final agreement emerged from conference negotiations that took place over several months in mid- to late 2000. As one House Republican observed in trying to explain the bicameral impasse, "Just appreciate the fact that Republicans in the House and Senate sometimes have a gulf as large if not larger than some Republicans and Democrats."[62] The looming presence of a Democratic president ready to veto a bill deemed too responsive to the health insurance industry certainly influenced the Republicans' negotiating strategy, as they probably preferred no bill to the more moderate House bill that the president would have signed. But ideological differences between the two chambers also precluded policy compromise, no matter the views of the president. Given median Senate Republican preferences, Senate Republicans had little incentive to compromise with House Republicans in pursuit of a moderate agreement.

Some speculated that the chief Senate Republican negotiator, Don Nickles of Oklahoma, would move closer to the more moderate House bill if vulnerable Republican senators seeking re-election in 2000 could convince Nickles of the electoral imperative to compromise with the

House and pass a bill.[63] Despite some senators' efforts to persuade Nickles, no such compromise toward the House bill occurred. As it turned out, this mattered little to the Democrats, as bicameral negotiations were taking place in the run-up to the tightly contested 2000 presidential election. "For us, it's a win-win," explained Senator Minority Leader Tom Daschle (D-S.D.). "We win if we don't get a bill, politically. We win politically and legislatively if we do get a bill."[64] Not only did bicameral differences limit the feasibility of reaching a conference agreement, the polarization of the parties and the electoral rewards of doing nothing limited the incentive to compromise.[65]

The persistence of bicameral effects across the postwar period also sheds some light on the impact of divided and unified government on legislative performance. Spurred by Mayhew's unconventional finding about the limited impact of divided government, recent studies have re-examined "unified gridlock," stalemate that occurs when a single party controls both chambers of Congress and the White House. Most often fingered as potential causes of unified gridlock are supermajority institutions that limit the policymaking capacity of political parties: procedural rules that require three-fifths majorities to limit debate in the Senate in face of a filibuster and constitutional rules that require a two-thirds majority to override a presidential veto. Because presidential vetoes are rare under unified government, I focus on the impact of the Senate filibuster. A recent and compelling argument is that because a supermajority is needed to pass major policy change in the Senate, the majority party's ability to secure policy outcomes favored by its party median is limited.[66] Thus one can not predict major policy change based on the policy views of the median legislator of the chamber and the majority party. Instead, the views of the sixtieth senator—the senator whose assent is required to invoke cloture and break a filibuster—are pivotal.[67]

However, the severity of the filibuster threat showed little effect on the frequency of deadlock once bicameral differences and party polarization and control were taken into account. Are interchamber differences a more proximate cause of stalemate than supermajority Senate constraints? It is possible that senators are less likely to exploit their procedural rights to filibuster if they anticipate that House-Senate differences will be sufficient to kill major policy change. Or the threat of the filibuster—and thus the constraining effect of supermajority rules—might not be as uniform over time or issues as recent studies of gridlock suggest. Since the 1970s, Senate majority leaders have clearly had to contend with the strong possibility that any controversial issue might be filibustered, given senators' increasing willingness to exploit their procedural rights.[68] But even in recent years, senators are not always willing to push their floor rights to the extreme. Numerous factors raise the costs of excessive use of the filibuster: unrestrained filibustering may provoke the chamber to reform its rules, encourage other senators to retaliate against a filibustering senator at a later time, or may simply not be worth the time and energy involved. Senate leaders' recent efforts (starting in the early 1980s) to pack major policy issues into budget reconciliation bills likely also diminish the impact of filibusters, as filibusters are prohibited on reconciliation bills.

Gridlock under unified government may have more to do with differences between the majority party's House and Senate contingents than with supermajority constraints imposed by Senate rules. Still, such conclusions based on Congress's performance over such a time span leave open the possibility that supermajority constraints affect legislative progress on certain issues at certain times. By treating bicameral bodies as if they were unicameral, we underestimate how conflict between the House and Senate shapes the prospects for major policy change.

5 | What Drives Legislative Action?

E valuating Congress's capacity during the past half-century to reach policy consensus is one approach to unraveling the politics of legislative stalemate. This approach gives us a comparative feel for legislative performance over time and a general understanding of the forces that contribute to the frequency of gridlock in the modern Congress. Still, because the analysis is conducted at the aggregate level of Congress, it says little about the politics that propel individual bills toward enactment during a single Congress. In this chapter, I narrow my focus to a smaller set of agenda issues in a few recent Congresses, with an eye to explaining how institutions and electoral outcomes together shape the likelihood that bills will be enacted into law.

Methodological Challenges

One would think that explanations of bill passage would be a staple of legislative studies. Strangely enough, few published works have systematically explored why bills pass or fail. Numerous case studies examine the legislative journeys of prominent bills but rarely offer broader conclusions about the legislative process. Moreover, legislative scholars have often studied institutional arrangements and legislative behavior rather than the endeavor of making law.[1]

There are a host of reasons for this scarcity, all of which are essentially methodological in nature. Most problematic perhaps is capturing how contingency may move a bill toward passage. Had the *Exxon Valdez* not run aground off the Alaskan shore in 1989 would Congress have enacted major oil spill liability legislation the following year? Perhaps a crisis is necessary for generating the compromise necessary to drive legislative success. Of course, predicting which issues will be the subject of a crisis is impossible. Nor do crises always create opportunities that legislators take advantage of successfully. The shooting rampage at Columbine High School in Littleton, Colorado, in 1999, for example, did not facilitate passage of salient gun control measures in the 106th Congress (1999–2000), contrary to the expectations of many seasoned political observers.[2] Even the aftermath of the horrific attacks on Washington and New York on September 11, 2001, shows the limit of crisis for spurring legislative action. Although Congress responded swiftly to the president's requests for recovery funds, aviation security, and antiterrorism legal tools, the further the president's requests strayed from the war on terrorism and recovery efforts, the stronger was Congress's tendency to resist.[3]

More broadly, we might say that timing and sequence are immeasurably important in explaining legislative outcomes. As Richard Fenno has argued, "If we are to explain outcomes, who decides when may be as important to know as who decides what."[4] In a case study it is certainly possible to explore how timing and sequence affect legislative choices and outcomes, as several legislative studies have shown.[5] Still, beyond the individual case study, it quickly becomes very difficult to capture the consequences of timing in a systematic and theoretically relevant way. Context and contingency are extremely important, two concepts highly resistant to systematic measurement.

Asking which issues are more likely to end in stalemate, rather than which bills, also raises methodological obstacles. First, not all issues become subjects of introduced bills. If our analysis uses introduced bills as a vehicle for measuring characteristics of competing issues, then we automatically introduce selection bias into the analysis by limiting our attention to issues that attract the attention of legislative entrepreneurs.

Second, even when issues attract legislators' attention, several bills are often introduced—and only one usually becomes the vehicle for legislative action. Third, even when the major bill can be identified—for example, the Shays-Meehan bill on campaign finance considered in both the 106th and 107th Congresses—it is difficult to know just how to treat a major competing legislative bill. In the case of Shays-Meehan, a competing bill endorsed by the Republican leadership and introduced by Robert Ney (R-Ohio) would have had equal footing on the House floor had the chamber not moved to strike the bill from House floor consideration during initial consideration of the bill in the summer of 2001.[6]

Such methodological challenges have not entirely deterred scholars from attempting to build multivariate models of legislative action. Barbara Sinclair, for example, has shown how bill passage is shaped by committee and floor politics. Sinclair, studying legislative outcomes for selected Congresses between 1961 and 1998, finds that partisanship at the committee level significantly reduces a major bill's chance of enactment during periods of divided government.[7] Bills also face rougher sledding when they encounter filibuster problems in the Senate. Sinclair's approach is innovative because it tackles legislative outcomes for major bills, offering a detailed sense of why some bills tend toward stalemate and others sail more easily toward enactment.

Preliminary Expectations and Evidence

Can a simple empirical model help explain the fate of issues on the legislative agenda? Here I test whether and how electoral and institutional forces matter in driving the lawmaking process. In chapter 4, the analysis showed that legislative stalemate was less frequent in periods of low bicameral conflict and low partisan polarization. Now I look at the fate of individual issues on the agenda, trying to determine how partisanship and bicameral differences affect their likelihood of enactment.

Divided Government

As shown in chapter 4, electoral dynamics are often overcredited with shaping legislative outcomes. Although I find a stronger impact of divided party control on legislative performance than do others such as David Mayhew, my results suggest that divided government is just one of several factors affecting the incidence of deadlock. If party control is less important than might be expected, we should find that split party control has just a small impact on whether or not Congress and the president successfully enact legislation related to pending issues.

I concentrate on the fate of legislative agenda items between 1993 and 1996 (103d and 104th Congresses).[8] A cursory glance at the most salient legislative issues casts some doubt on the thesis that divided government significantly curtails legislative action. Under unified control in 1993 and 1994, efforts to enact lobbying reform and a congressional gift ban were stymied by a Senate filibuster. Under divided control in the following Congress, the reforms passed immediately as part of House Republicans' Contract with America. Health care reform experienced a similar fate. The Clinton administration's effort to enact major health reform foundered in the 103d Congress under unified control, but a more limited version providing for the portability of health insurance between jobs was enacted during the divided 104th Congress. This raises the more general question: when we look more broadly at the agendas of the two Congresses, does divided government make a difference in explaining which bills move toward enactment?

Partisan Polarization

As shown in chapter 4, polarized political parties are counterproductive in the making of major policy change. Instead, partisan moderation appears to pay off, as more moderate Congresses encounter stalemate less frequently. Far from promoting legislative action, polarization of the parties seems to stem the tide of forward motion.

We might expect then that polarized relations between the parties directly affect the fate of issues pending before Congress: as attitudes about an issue become more polarized, the chances that Congress will enact a bill addressing that issue should decline. But polarized views are not necessarily counterproductive to legislative motion. The more cohesive and ideologically extreme a majority coalition, the harder it might fight to pass favored measures. Polarization might then be helpful for pushing important measures through to passage. This is certainly an account that seems to ring true for the House, where bills with strong partisan support from within the majority party seem to routinely encounter smooth sailing on the floor. Consideration of President George W. Bush's tax cut and education bills upon taking office in 2001, for example, proceeded exceptionally fast in the House, compared with the multiweek amend-a-thon that characterized the Senate's consideration of the same bills. Because the House majority party leadership can use its dominance of the Rules Committee to structure floor voting procedures to its advantage, strong cohesive parties—no matter how strongly opposed by the minority—can usually work their way in the House.[9]

The impact of cohesive parties can also be seen in the fate of a few issues for which internal divisions plagued House majority parties. Fearing it would be defeated by a bipartisan coalition in favor of expanding patients' rights, the House leadership in 2001 refused to bring a bill to the floor until the leadership could secure sufficient votes for a purely Republican alternative. Similarly, House Republicans deferred consideration in 2001 of a measure to extend federal aid to faith-based charities when it became clear that a group of moderates would split off to defeat the Republicans' preferred bill. Had Republicans been assured of passage of a purely partisan alternative on both issues, both bills would surely have gone to the floor and been passed with little amendment or delay. House leaders, lacking a cohesive partisan coalition, preferred inaction.

Thus, conceivably, higher levels of partisan behavior on bills in the House help propel issues to final passage. Is such a dynamic likely in the Senate? No. Given the requirement that controversial bills today attract sixty votes to overcome filibusters—actual or threatened—majority parties rarely have sufficient votes within their ranks to force through to passage those bills with a partisan cast. As partisanship on an issue grows in the Senate, we might expect chances of enacting a related bill to decline. Only when bills are crafted in the Senate with an eye to securing bipartisan support should we expect to see a higher likelihood of final passage.

Presidential Support

Are presidents able to affect the fate of individual bills in Congress? Presidential support for a measure may spur Congress to act favorably. Up against the president's command of the bully pulpit, congressional opposition might fold in face of presidential attention. President Bush's full-court press in favor of fast-track trade negotiating powers in the summer of 2002, for example, helped to spur the two chambers to reach a conference agreement on a long-stalemated measure.[10] His call for action on a sweeping corporate accountability measure that week also yielded bicameral agreement.[11] Still, most studies show only a limited effect of the president on congressional outcomes, finding that presidential influence is exercised at the "margins" of the legislative arena.[12] Indeed, an alternative account of why the fast-track logjam was broken after eight years is that congressional Republicans felt the heat to act on measures enhancing economic security and thus caved in to Democrats' demands that the trade measure include a $12 billion expansion of benefits for trade-displaced workers. [13] Presidential pressure, in this account, had little independent impact on Congress's decision to compromise; the president simply rode the wave of legislative action spurred by the summer's spike in economic instability and erosion of consumer confidence.[14]

Most of what we know about presidential effects on lawmaking, however, is based on studies conducted at the aggregate level: over time, how successful has the president been in securing his policy objectives? Is presidential pressure necessary or sufficient to sway legislators to support particular measures? When the question is posed in this fashion, we might expect to find some evidence of presidential influence under certain conditions. During periods of unified control, if we assume that presidents and congressional leaders share a common agenda, then presidential attention is unlikely to have an independent impact on Congress's legislative record. But under divided control, we might find a presidential effect when the president favors legislative action. By calling on Congress to address issues at the top of the president's agenda, the president raises the stakes for opposition party leaders who might prefer to focus on their own agendas. Facing a Congress controlled by the other party might also give the president an incentive to seek legislative compromises that he would not pursue under unified government. Thus, the desire to shape legislative outcomes—whether for policy or electoral purposes or both— might be sufficient incentive for the president to use his agenda-setting powers to initiate and seriously pursue favorable congressional action on issues of importance.[15]

There is at least some anecdotal evidence from the 103d and 104th Congresses (1993–96) to support these conjectures. President Bill Clinton's major legislative push in the 103d Congress to enact landmark health care reform met with concerted opposition and ended in a resounding failure, despite Democratic control of both chambers. Although Democrats lost control of Congress in the 1994 elections, health care remained a presidential priority, with Clinton addressing several health care issues in his 1995 State of the Union address. In the 104th Congress, however, Clinton focused on a much narrower approach to health care reform—an issue known as health care portability.[16] With bipartisan support built by Senators Edward Kennedy (D-Mass.) and Nancy Kassebaum (R-Kans.), health care portability was signed into law in 1996 under divided party control. Although presidential attention may be insufficient under unified control to overcome legislative opposition, such attention during divided government may paradoxically prove more effective.

The Senate Filibuster

Do filibusters (actual or threatened) systematically derail legislative progress? The evidence is mixed. In chapter 4, I found only limited support for the idea that the increasingly severe filibuster threats make deadlock more likely. Other factors endemic to the legislative process seem to outweigh or mask the direct impact of filibustering senators when we look broadly at legislative performance during the past half-century.

Other evidence, however, points to a much stronger effect of the filibuster on the fate of individual issues. Sinclair, for example, finds that when bills encounter filibuster problems on the Senate floor they are less likely to be enacted into law. For individual issues, then, we might see a much stronger effect of the filibuster on legislative outcomes. Of course, senators do not always aim to kill the bill that is the target of their filibuster. At times, senators take bills hostage in their efforts to secure favorable treatment on tangential issues; other times, filibusters are intended to force the majority to amend the targeted legislation; and other times, filibusters are simply unsuccessful, as majorities marshal sufficient support to invoke cloture.[17]

Building a Model

Given the spate of methodological hurdles to studying bill passage politics with quantitative evidence, no empirical model of the legislative process can fully capture the dynamics of the legislative process. The problem is exacerbated if we want to track the fate of issues on the legislative agenda, rather than the fate of introduced bills. Although it is easy enough to create measures that tap factors such as media or presidential attention to an issue, for example, it is difficult to measure such things as the level of partisanship on an issue. Still, if we can construct a rudimentary model of legislative progress given myriad measurement constraints, it should offer some preliminary insights into how Congress successfully responds to pressing issues on the public's agenda.

My strategy for modeling the politics of issue passage follows:

DEPENDENT VARIABLE. The central question is whether or not a bill addressing a particular issue on the legislative agenda will be enacted into law. Thus, I start with the list of agenda items generated by the editorials written in the *New York Times* during the 103d (1993–94) and 104th (1995–96) Congresses. For each issue, I code whether it was successfully addressed in enacted legislation during the Congress in which it appeared in the *Times* (coding such issues as "1"). Issues that were not successfully addressed in legislation are coded 0. Considering the data in this way allows us to ask what factors shape the likelihood that a bill is successfully enacted into law and to determine the relative importance of each factor in shaping the fate of issues on the national agenda.

DIVIDED GOVERNMENT. To assess the impact of party control of government, I use a dummy variable to mark whether an issue appeared on the legislative agenda of the 103d Congress (unified government) or the 104th Congress (divided government). Agenda issues during the 104th Congress are coded 1, 0 otherwise.

PARTISAN POLARIZATION. Measuring partisan polarization on an issue is perhaps the most vexing challenge in constructing an empirical model. One option might be to measure the extent of opinion polarization along party lines through the use of public opinion polling. Given that the legislative agendas generated by the *Times* each Congress include more than a hundred issues, we lack polling data detailed enough to measure the extent of party differences on each issue. Pollsters simply do not ask questions about every issue that makes it onto the *New York Times* radar, no matter how pressing the issue might be to well-informed, avid observers in Washington. Nor is it possible to measure legislative polarization on such an extensive list of issues, as legislators rarely reveal their preferences until an issue garners attention during the legislative process.

Given these limitations, a reasonable proxy for issue partisanship can be built based on the characteristics of bills introduced in response to issues on the legislative agenda. In other words, I identify for each issue on the agenda what seems to be the major legislative vehicle for addressing it and then devise a measure that taps the extent of partisanship on the bill. As suggested earlier, this approach does have its drawbacks: not all issues generate a bill, some issues attract many bills, and some issues are folded into other legislative vehicles late in the legislative process (making it difficult to determine the extent of partisanship on the policy issue of interest). Such limitations, however, are unavoidable.

Matching issues and introduced bills during the 103d and 104th Congresses generates a rough sense of the costs of using bills as proxies for issues. Bills are certainly not generated on all issues: bills were introduced in the House on roughly 40 percent of the 213 issues on the legislative agenda during the 103d and 104th Congress, and senators introduced bills on just over 30 percent of the issues that attracted the attention of the *New York Times* in the same period. Not surprisingly, however, the issues most often incorporated into legislative bills tended to be the most salient issues. Nearly 80 percent of the most salient legislative issues were introduced as bills in the Senate, and 97 percent were the subject of bills introduced in the House during the 103d and 104th Congresses.[18] Thus the cost of using bills as proxies for issues might not be as steep as typically assumed.

Partisanship might be measured at any number of stages of a bill's introduction or consideration. Because not all bills come to the floor for a vote and not all are even afforded committee consideration, my measure of issue partisanship taps the first indication of partisan sentiment: the balance of cosponsors attracted to each bill. For each issue on which a bill (with cosponsors) is introduced in the House and Senate, I code bill partisanship as follows. First, I tally up the number of Democratic cosponsors and divide by the total number of cosponsors for each House or Senate bill.[19] Second, since perfect bipartisanship would be represented by a bill whose cosponsors were 50 percent Democratic and 50 percent Republican, I take the absolute value of the percentage Democratic cosponsors minus 50 percent. The distance from fifty thus represents the degree of partisanship on each bill. Purely partisan bills receive a score of 50; completely bipartisan bills score 0.[20] Thus, the Democrats' major campaign finance reform bill in the 103d Congress and the Republicans' term limits resolution from the Contract with America in the 104th Congress both receive a purely partisan score of 50.[21] A bill in the 103d Congress that would have required Congress to comply with federal laws, in contrast, is scored 0, reflecting the bipartisan support given to the bill. Partisanship scores are calculated separately for House and Senate bills on the legislative agendas of the two Congresses. Unfortunately, of the 185 legislative issues on the agendas of the two Congresses, there were only 43 issues for which partisanship scores could be calculated for bills in both chambers.[22] I calculate an overall level of issue partisanship as the mean partisanship score of the House and Senate bills introduced on the issue.[23]

PRESIDENTIAL ATTENTION. To measure the salience of an issue to the president, I code whether or not the president mentioned the issue in a State of the Union address during the Congress in which the issue was discussed in the *New York Times*. Issues appearing in a State of the Union address are coded 1, 0 otherwise. President Bill Clinton mentioned a fifth of the 185 issues on the legislative agenda between 1993 and 1996, and just under half of the 35 most salient issues on the agenda.[24] To indicate whether or not a bill attracted presidential attention during divided government, I interact the measure tapping divided government with the presidential attention dummy variable.

FILIBUSTER PROBLEM. Each issue is coded for the presence of a filibuster problem, meaning either that an issue attracted a filibuster on the Senate floor or the threat of a filibuster was apparent to Senate leaders. Evidence on the presence of a filibuster threat or actual filibuster is drawn from *Congressional Quarterly Almanac*'s treatment of each issue. Just under 20 percent of all legislative agenda items attracted a filibuster problem in the 103d and 104th Congress, with filibuster problems registered on nearly 40 percent of the most salient agenda items.

SALIENCE. As noted in chapter 3, the editorial method produces a long list of agenda items, some of which never attract legislators' attention. Issues receiving just a single mention by the *Times* over the course of a Congress most often fall into this category of minor issues. To weed out these issues, I control for issue salience. Because some major issues on occasion attract just a single editorial, I measure salience as a function of the attention given to an issue by both the *Times* and network evening news broadcasts.[25] Any issue receiving more than one *Times* editorial and at least one mention on a network news broadcast is coded 1 (meaning "salient"), 0 otherwise. Thirty percent of the 185 legislative agenda items merit consideration as salient. If we limit the analysis to the 43 issues for which partisanship scores can be calculated, 65 percent of the issues count as salient.

Impact of Electoral Dynamics

The variables used in the analysis are summarized in table 5-1. Although I have partisanship scores for 43 issues/bills, the number of cases in the analysis is 38 because of missing data on a few other variables. Of these thirty-eight cases, just under half were enacted into law.[26] By limiting the analysis to these thirty-eight cases, my sample of bills is weighted toward more salient bills, including issues more likely to have appeared in State of the Union addresses, and issues attracting filibuster problems.[27] Partisanship varies considerably over the issues. In the House, the balance

Table 5-1. *Summary of Variables Used in the Analysis*

Variable	Cases	Mean	Standard deviation	Minimum	Maximum
Enacted into law	38	.47	.51	0	1
Divided government	38	.50	.51	0	1
Issue partisanship	38	36.87	12.49	5	50
Filibuster problem	38	.37	.49	0	1
Presidential priority	38	.42	.50	0	1
Salient issue	38	.74	.45	0	1

Source: See text for all tables in this chapter.

is stacked heavily in favor of polarization, with nearly 40 percent of the issues attracting a purely partisan set of cosponsors. Although 37 percent of the relevant Senate bills attract a completely partisan set of cosponsors, the distribution of bill partisanship is not so heavily skewed in a partisan direction. The median Senate bill sports a partisanship score of 37, while the median House bill registers 44.

How important are electoral, partisan, and institutional factors in explaining the fortunes of legislative issues? A quick glance at the entire legislative agenda provides a few clues. First, 41 percent of the 78 issues discussed during the unified 103d Congress were enacted into law, while 40 percent of the 107 issues arising during the divided 104th Congress were enacted. This insignificant difference comports with the relatively minor effect we saw for the impact of divided government on gridlock more generally when assessed over time. Although legislative issues seem to fare worse during periods of divided control, the difference is not significant. Second, the data are suggestive that the partisan balance of an issue coalition strongly affects the likelihood of Senate passage of the bill but not House passage. Highly polarized coalitions in the Senate fared much worse in securing chamber passage of their bills than did more bipartisan coalitions. The difference is significant and striking: the parties were nearly twice as polarized on the issues that gridlocked in the Senate compared with the partisanship on issues that did pass the Senate.[28] Polarization of issue coalitions in the House, in contrast, seems to matter less, as the partisan balance of cosponsors is indistinguishable for bills that pass the House and bills that do not. Finally, there is some limited evidence that filibuster problems may pose insurmountable barriers to

Table 5-2. *Determinants of Legislative Success, 1993–96*

Explanation	Variable	1 Coefficient	2 Coefficient
Electoral	Divided government	−.272[a] (.187)	.108 (.140)
	Presidential priority	.079 (.400)	−.102 (.337)
	Presidential priority during divided government	1.673*** (.352)	1.126 *** (.228)
Institutional	Filibuster problem	−.533 (.881)	−.859[a] (.630)
	Issue partisanship	−.035** (.012)	...
	House issue partisanship	...	.043*** (.014)
	Senate issue partisanship	...	−.074*** (.003)
Policy	Issue salience	.794[a] (.566)	1.072* (.619)
	Constant	.709*** (.153)	.213 (.229)
	N	38	38
	Log likelihood	−23.326	−21.557

Note: The dependent variable is whether or not an issue is enacted into law through legislation. The entries in columns 1 and 2 are logit estimates (robust standard errors clustering on the Congress are in parentheses) * $p < .05$, ** $p < .01$; *** $p < .001$, [a] $p < .1$ (one-tailed t tests). Parameter estimates calculated via the *logit* routine in Stata 7.0.

enactment. When issues attract filibusters, 40 percent are eventually enacted into law; in contrast, 45 percent are enacted into law if no filibuster problem arises.

How do these trends hold up when subjected to multivariate controls? Table 5-2 presents results from two models, each exploring the effects of presidential, institutional, and electoral factors on the eventual fate of issues pending on the legislative agenda. The first model explores the general effect of polarized parties on legislative outcomes, averaging the partisan balance of House and Senate issue coalitions into a single measure of issue polarization. As expected, the higher the level of partisan polarization, the less likely issues are to be enacted into law. The impact of a polarized coalition is stark: the probability that the most partisan issue will be enacted is 37 percent, while the least partisan issue has a 77 percent chance of enactment.[29]

Divided party control of Congress and the presidency, in contrast, has little effect on an issue's fate, at best marginally decreasing the likelihood that an issue will be successfully addressed by legislation.[30] Assuming moderate partisanship, the arrival of unified government increases the chances of enactments 7 percent.[31] Presidential attention also seems to have little independent effect on outcomes, and filibuster activity registers a minimal impact on the eventual fate of legislative issues. In contrast, issue salience does seem to matter, with more visible issues more likely to secure passage than ones of marginal media and elite salience.

A final relationship is striking: the president appears to win more favorable legislative outcomes when he focuses on an issue during divided government, in comparison with his success under unified control. How might we explain this presidential impact? Perhaps presidents, confronted by an opposition Congress during divided government, scale back their priorities to make legislative success more likely. Presidents' strategic anticipation of legislative preferences, in short, might account for Congress's seemingly higher responsiveness to presidents and their agendas during periods of divided control.

Glancing at the issues that President Clinton favored under unified control—but did not see enacted into law until after Democrats lost control of Congress in 1994—lends some support for this interpretation. Broad-scale health care and welfare reform proposals were trumpeted by Clinton in the 103d Congress, but neither passed until the divided 104th. When health care legislation passed in 1996, it was a much more bipartisan and limited proposal that focused on the rights of individuals to health insurance when they lose or change their jobs. When welfare reform passed in 1996, it was indelibly marked by a Republican handprint, as evidenced by the defection of a handful of liberal Democrats when the bill came up for a final vote on the Senate floor. It may also be that the congressional opposition strategically alters its position on presidential initiatives after episodes of unified control, seeking to claim credit for resolving issue stalemate when it captures control of Congress. This would help account for the failure of lobbying reform in the unified 103d Congress, but its passage under the divided 104th—notwithstanding Clinton's attention to the issue in both Congresses.

A Closer Look at Bicameral Effects

In table 5-2, column 2, I take a closer look at the impact of bicameral differences on legislative outcomes. I evaluate separately the impact of partisan polarization in each chamber. Perhaps most striking is the different impact of issue partisanship in the two chambers. As suggested in the bivariate results just discussed, the greater the partisan skew of an issue coalition in the Senate, the less likely the issue will be enacted into law. Partisan skew in the House, in contrast, seems to have little effect on legislative outcomes. In fact, if anything, issues that attract highly polarized coalitions seem to fare better in the House, all else equal.

A different impact of partisanship in the two chambers should not be surprising, as it comports in many ways with the received wisdom about legislative dynamics in the two chambers. In the House, majority party leaders have procedural tools that can grant them great advantage in structuring the floor agenda. These advantages include control of the Rules Committee, as the majority party heavily stacks it in favor of their party, and the potential to set the floor agenda. With these procedural advantages available, House majority party leaders are reluctant to bring bills to the floor unless they have the support of a cohesive coalition—which usually means a coalition formed within the majority party. House leaders' initial reluctance to allow a bipartisan patients' bill of rights measure to come to the floor in summer of 2001—until sufficient votes had been secured to pass a preferred Republican version—illustrates why more partisan bills in the House may fare more successfully in the legislative process.[32] Using their control of the House schedule, House majority party leaders delayed consideration of a bipartisan version of the bill (the so-called Dingell-Norwood-Ganske bill) until President Bush had persuaded Rep. Charlie Norwood (R-Ga.) to endorse a version of the bill more palatable to Bush and to salient Republican constituencies. Once Bush locked up Norwood's support, House leaders scheduled the bipartisan version for floor consideration and secured passage of the Norwood amendment that embodied the more conservative Bush-Norwood deal. The impact of institutional rules is clear: given the majority party's procedural advantages (here, by dominating the Rules Committee it can structure the floor proceedings in its favor), a preferred partisan measure can be protected from amendment and challenge. Floor rules can be crafted that advantage majority party policy interests, and the floor agenda can be manipulated to delay consideration of measures until a preferred policy outcome is guaranteed. If majority party leaders routinely use their procedural control to secure policy outcomes favored by their caucus, then a pattern should emerge of more partisan bills being approved by the House.

In contrast, Senate rules and practices grant the majority party only limited procedural powers that enhance their leverage over the floor agenda. The lack of a Rules Committee to structure floor amendments to the majority party's advantage, the absence of a germaneness rule to keep unwanted amendments off the floor, and the need to secure a supermajority of sixty votes or unanimous consent of the body to limit debate—each of these procedural aspects of the Senate weakens party leaders' ability to manipulate the floor agenda. As a result, highly polarized issue coalitions face tough sledding in the Senate, as bill sponsors anticipate that chamber passage will require that provisions subject to cohesive partisan opposition be diluted before passage. This likelihood would lead us to suspect that the more polarized bills in the Senate are less likely to be enacted. Both of these expected House and Senate patterns are consistent with the results in column 2 of table 5-2.

We can estimate the precise impact of partisanship on Senate outcomes by looking more systematically at the relationship between Senate partisanship and floor outcomes in the 103d and 104th Congresses. As shown in table 5-3, column 1, the likelihood that a bill will be killed on the Senate floor rises significantly with the partisanship on the underlying bill. Bills are also more likely to be killed if they encounter a filibuster problem and when the president's party does not control the chamber.[33] Thus high levels of partisanship are lethal in the Senate because they limit a bill's probability of making it over to the House or into a bicameral conference.

Because filibusters are roughly 30 percent more likely during periods of divided control, I also assess the simple impact of partisanship and filibuster problems on Senate floor action (table 5-3, column 2). The impact of rising partisanship is dramatic, as the least partisan bills have an 11 percent chance of being killed on the Senate floor, while the most partisan bills face nearly a 65 percent chance of dying on the Senate floor.[34] Although a filibuster is not necessarily lethal to a bill of moderate partisanship, obstructionist tactics raise the chances of an issue dying on the Senate floor from under 3 percent to nearly 45 percent.

If highly partisan bills are unlikely to fare well in the Senate, then why does the House majority party exploit its influence over floor rules to push polarizing bills through the chamber? One possibility is that the

Table 5-3. *When Do Bills Die on the Senate Floor?*

Variable	1 Coefficient	2 Coefficient
Divided government	.294* (.155)	...
Filibuster problem	3.369* (1.693)	3.374* (1.675)
Issue partisanship	.051*** (.004)	.054*** (.002)
Constant	−5.532*** (1.245)	−5.500*** (1.098)
N	46	46
Log likelihood	−13.853	−13.894

Note: Dependent variable is whether or not a bill was killed on the Senate floor. The entries in columns 1 and 2 are logit estimates (robust standard errors clustering on the Congress in parentheses). * p < .05, ** p < .01, *** p < .001; (one-tailed *t* tests). Parameter estimates calculated via the *logit* routine in Stata 7.0.

House, lacking information on likely policy outcomes in the Senate, endeavors to set the agenda with a partisan bill. Thus, under periods of relatively cohesive Republican majorities, we might expect the House to pass bills with a strong conservative flavor and defeat efforts to dilute its provisions. If House leaders lack information on Senate preferences, it makes strong strategic sense for them to send the most conservative bill possible to the Senate or on to conference.

On most salient issues, however, the House leadership probably is able to anticipate Senate preferences. Oftentimes, the Senate acts before the House, leaving clear signals about its preferred outcomes. If so, a House preference for a more conservative bill probably reflects strategic calculation by the House leadership. If the House majority party anticipates that Senate conferees will prefer to moderate bill provisions passed by the House, it makes sound strategic sense for the party to seek to pass the most conservative bill possible given House preferences—all in an effort to protect its negotiating position in conference with the Senate. Moreover, more conservative bills are more likely to please Republican constituencies (just as more liberal bills would please Democratic constituencies), thus aligning Republicans' strategic interests with their policy interests. And finally, because the House Rules Committee exercises fairly strong discretion over the floor agenda on behalf of the majority party, it is difficult for alternative coalitions to strip out conservative elements of House bills. Dissenters have little recourse after offering an unsuccessful amendment, meaning that majority party interests will likely prevail unless a sizable cross-party alternative emerges.

Congressional consideration of a health care "portability" bill in 1996 illustrates nicely how bicameral differences affect legislative outcomes. After failure of Clinton's mammoth health care reform proposal in the 103d Congress, Senators Ted Kennedy (D-Mass.) and Nancy Kassebaum (R-Kans.) teamed up to propose a more targeted health care bill. Their proposal tackled the problem of employees losing their insurance when they lose or leave a job by guaranteeing insurance coverage to workers caught in such situations. The bill, introduced with a near balance of Democratic and Republican cosponsors (scoring 9.09 on the issue partisanship index introduced above),[35] was swiftly and unanimously approved in August of 1995 by the Senate Labor and Human Resources Committtee, a panel chaired by Kassebaum. Thus, when the House took up its own version of the bill seven months later in March of 1996, it had a reasonable sense of the bipartisan character of the Senate's preferences.

The version of the bill approved by Bill Archer's (R-Tex.) House Ways and Means Committee, however, added controversial—and more conservative—provisions, including the creation of "medical savings accounts" (MSAs). Given the partisan imbalance of the Archer bill, the addition of more conservative provisions is not surprising.[36] The MSAs allowed certain individuals to accrue tax-deductible savings to be used for medical expenses, accounts that critics at the time said would only serve the interests of high-income employees. Other provisions were intended to respond to the concerns of insurers that had arisen from the Kennedy-Kassebaum bill. The House vote was largely on party lines, with the Democratic alternative rejected in a straight party-line vote.[37]

Showdowns on the House and Senate floors help explain why the two chambers produced such starkly different bills on the same salient issue. In the House, the key vote occurred in March 1996 on a substitute amendment offered by John Dingell (D-Mich.). The amendment would have stripped the bill of provisions favored by conservatives, thus bringing the bill in line with the version by Kassebaum's Senate committee. The amendment was rejected by a vote of 192 to 226, with ten Republicans defecting to join Dingell and five Democrats defecting to join Archer and the Republicans. Party defectors were primarily from the wings of

Table 5-4. *House and Senate Votes to Moderate Health Care Bills, 104th Congress*

Variable	1 Dingell amendment Coefficient	2 Kassebaum amendment Coefficient
Republican	−8.983*** (1.123)	...
Democratic moderate	−2.970** (1.135)	...
Republican moderate	3.455*** (.722)	2.757** (1.052)
Constant	5.017*** (1.003)	−3.045*** (.724)
N	418	51
Log likelihood	−48.944	−12.916

Note: The entries in columns 1 and 2 are logit estimates (standard errors in parentheses). ** p < .01, *** p < .001; (one-tailed *t* tests). Parameter estimates calculated via the *logit* routine in Stata 7.0.

their parties. Conservative Democrats voted against the amendment, and moderate Republicans voted in favor.

We can examine the politics of the vote systematically by assessing the impact of members' party affiliation and centrist tendencies on their vote choice.[38] As shown in table 5-4, model 1, ideological moderation and party affiliation explain much of the variance in the vote. Republicans were markedly less likely to vote for the amendment, while Republican moderates were more likely to vote in favor. Democrats generally voted in favor of the amendment, but Democratic moderates (usually conservative Democrats) were strikingly less likely to vote for the amendment.[39] More generally, the probability that a Republican would vote for the amendment was less than 2 percent, but the probability that a Republican moderate would vote for the amendment was 37.5 percent. Ideology also tempered Democratic positions on the amendment. Democrats showed a 99 percent chance of voting for the amendment; conservative Democrats, 89 percent.[40] Despite the willingness of Republican moderates to cross party lines in favor of the Dingell amendment, there simply were not enough moderates for the bipartisan alternative to prevail.

Having failed to bring the House bill in line with expressed Senate preferences, Democrats and Republican moderates had no further procedural recourse for pushing the House to adopt the more moderate and bipartisan alternative.[41] On final passage, all Republicans except one voted in favor, joined by thirty-eight Democrats.[42] When the Senate considered the bill the next month, they knew full well the range of House preferences on health insurance portability. Senate Majority Leader Bob Dole (R-Kans.), seeking to send a more conservative bill to conference to match the House-passed version, introduced an amendment to the Kennedy-Kassebaum bipartisan bill that would have added MSAs and other provisions favored by Republican conservatives. The key vote occurred on a Kassebaum amendment to strip the Dole amendment from the bill, and Dole lost. Five Republicans voted against Dole's position, yielding a final tally of 52 to 46 (all Democrats sticking together to oppose the Dole provisions). Legislators' ideological tendencies again help to explain votes on the insurance provisions, as Republican moderates were far more likely to vote for the amendment than their colleagues in the Republican conference (table 5-4, column 2).[43] Republicans overall had less than a 10 percent chance of voting against Dole, but Republican centrists had more than a 40 percent chance of voting against their leader.

Why was the Senate able to secure a bipartisan outcome when the House had failed? First, the array of policy views in the Senate was sufficient to defeat a more conservative outcome. Second, and perhaps equally important, it was clear that had Dole prevailed, Dole's opponents were ready to filibuster the bill, precluding Dole from claiming victory on the issue.[44] (The vote by then had become a contest between the Republican presidential nominee Dole seeking to show his leadership qualities and incumbent president Clinton who strongly favored the Kassebaum version of the bill.) The threat of exploiting Senate rules was sufficient to help Democrats and more moderate Republicans secure a favorable Senate outcome, despite the more conservative preferences of the House and the preferences of the Senate majority leader. Any senator preferring passage of a bill to watching the bill die in a filibuster had an added incentive to vote against Dole's conservative provisions, a sufficient incentive to entice moderate Republicans to break with their leader.

The impact of bicameral policy differences does not stop, however, after the two chambers passed different versions of the bill. The House's strategy was clearly to send a more conservative bill to conference, with hopes of securing a final conference agreement more amenable to Republican conservatives. But the House strategy was foiled when Senator Kennedy exploited his procedural rights and successfully moved the final conference outcome closer to his liberal preferences. The conference agreement, in other words, did not simply split the difference between the House and Senate versions of the bill, but hewed close to the original Kennedy-Kassebaum bipartisan bill.

How did this come about? Before going to conference, Republicans Kassebaum and Archer had negotiated a compromise that dropped House provisions favored by the insurance industry on the pooling of insurance and medical malpractice. Those moderating changes, however, were not sufficient for Kennedy, who also wanted to eliminate MSAs from the bill. Exploiting his procedural right to block unanimous consent requests to appoint conferees and to go to conference, Kennedy delayed the meeting of House and Senate conferees until Archer had agreed to scale back MSAs into a very limited pilot program. As a result, in the end there was little for conferees to bargain over. The final conference agreement strongly resembled the original Kennedy-Kassebaum bill, and little resembled the conservative alternative favored by the House. President Clinton readily signed the bill into law in August of 1996, claiming credit for its expansion of health insurance guarantees to working Americans.

The health care portability case gives us a better sense of why policy differences institutionalized through bicameralism matter in shaping legislative outcomes. At the aggregate level assessed in chapter 4, we saw that the general ideological tendencies of the two chambers help to shape the overall frequency of deadlock: the higher the level of bicameral disagreement over all policies, the more frequently gridlock occurs. In predicting whether Congress will successfully legislate on an issue, however, we cannot simply rely on knowing something about the general ideological character of the two chambers. As the analysis in this chapter suggests, the partisanship of rival issue coalitions and the procedural context in which issues are considered both have great effects on legislative outcomes. Less polarized Senate coalitions seem to fare better in moving bills through to enactment, even as polarized issue coalitions are likely to succeed in pushing bills through the House and into conference. Because Senate rules grant considerable procedural rights to dissenting senators, it seems—at least from the case of health care portability—that senators are procedurally situated to extract additional concessions from the House when bipartisan coalitions exist in the Senate.

Do bicameral policy differences—reinforced by institutional rules of the two chambers—and partisan polarization alone help explain the fate of issues before the Congress? Although I have focused primarily on the impact of internal legislative conflict, interbranch pressures and electoral dynamics clearly contribute to shaping final legislative outcomes. To be sure, my accounting of the Kennedy-Kassebaum-Archer fight over health insurance portability suggests that the battle was shaped primarily by congressional dynamics. But elements of the electoral context surely made a difference in nudging the two sides toward final agreement. First, the bill was considered during a period of divided party control. The threat of a presidential veto on a popular issue likely increased House Republicans' incentive to give up favored provisions in face of bipartisan and sometimes partisan Senate pressures. Second, the two chambers considered the issue during a presidential election year, with the Republican presidential nominee assuming a high-profile role in trying to amend the Senate bill to better match the priorities of Republican constituencies. Third, in facing voters for the first time since winning control of the House in the 1994 elections, House Republicans had an extra incentive to reach a final agreement, even if the compromise significantly compromised their preferred policy outcomes. The fallout from the 1995 budget debacle and government showdown, many said at the time, gave Republicans added incentive to show that they could indeed govern as a majority party.[45] So certainly electoral motivations matter in shaping the fate of issues on the legislative agenda. But an exclusive focus on the electoral context fails to fully explain why some bills and not others are eventually signed into law by the president. Bicameral differences—coupled with varying patterns of partisan polarization—have a significant role to play in explaining when and why Congress seems to work effectively as a legislative body.

Conclusion

No statistical model can fully explain the myriad factors that affect legislative outcomes. Nor can a single case study offer strong grounds for broad generalizations about legislative dynamics. But the quantitative and qualitative evidence brought to bear in this chapter reinforce each other. The evidence suggests a similar story about the institutional and electoral determinants of stalemate and singles out bicameral politics as a potent influence on the fate of issues on the legislative agenda.

In chapter 4, I cast bicameral politics primarily in terms of the two chambers' ideological predispositions. When the two chambers converge in their policy views, legislating policy change becomes much easier; policy divergence leads us back to more frequent stalemate. When we shift our sights to the fate of individual bills, bicameral politics seems to matter in many ways. First, the distribution of policy views in the two chambers affects the likelihood of chamber passage, with less (more) polarized coalitions favored in the Senate (House). Second, differences in the two chambers' procedural rules shape the fate of issues on legislative and presidential agendas. The combination of these two forces—bicameral policy differences reinforced by different sets of institutional rules—affects the prognosis for issues on the agenda.

The interaction of institutions and preferences is seen most clearly in the impact of polarized parties in each chamber. The procedural tendencies of the Senate require party leaders to actively seek bipartisan solutions and may on occasion enhance senators' sway over the ideological tenor of conference agreements. The procedural tendencies of the House, in contrast, relieve party leaders of the task of seeking bipartisan compromise. The differing procedural landscapes of the two chambers also affect presidential strategies, as bipartisan solutions are rarely if ever sought in negotiating with the House in the currently polarized environment. To the extent that bipartisanship was sought in the first months of the Bush administration in 2001, it was seen in the courting of the Senate's more moderate Democrats in the formulation of the administration's tax cut plan, the top priority on its agenda. In contrast, venerable conservative Democrats in the House were passed over, as their involvement was calculated as incidental to the fate of the Bush tax package in the House.[46] When the tax package was signed into law in the summer of 2001, it bore the stamp of the new Republican administration and conservative allies in the House, but its overall size and makeup were significantly moderated by the involvement of the Senate's conservative Democrats, an impact felt even under the (brief) spell of unified Republican control. Institutions, as much if not more so than elections, indelibly shape the prospects for policy change in Congress.

6 Consequences of Stalemate

A rguments about gridlock took an interesting turn in the midst of a standoff between President Bill Clinton and the Republican Congress late in 1999.[1] Both sides had essentially fought to a draw in a debate over what to do with the new government budget surpluses: should they be saved, spent, or devoted to tax cuts? The sides were unable to reach consensus, and the result was essentially gridlock. No definitive action was taken to resolve the fate of the budget surplus. But owing to federal budgeting rules, excess revenues flowed automatically into reducing the nation's debt, which then stood at $3.6 trillion. "Neither party had debt reduction as its priority," one analyst observed, "but it ended up being the common denominator they could agree on through gridlock."[2] Given the salutary economic benefits of reducing the debt—including lowering interest rates and boosting savings—legislative deadlock was almost uniformly seen as a beneficial outcome.

This unintended consequence of gridlock raises a more fundamental issue. Although the causes of gridlock have often been explored, the consequences of legislative stalemate remain unexplored. As suggested by the 1999 standoff over the budget surplus, there may be strong consequences when Congress fails to act on pressing matters of public dispute. Moreover, the effects of gridlock might not be as rosy as the debt reduction that occurred in 1999. If gridlock produces consequences widely deemed undesirable, a case against legislative inaction might be made. Even those who believe the framers valued policy stability over policy change might decide that the negative effects of gridlock today outweigh the benefits of legislative inaction.

Several arenas may display the effects of gridlock: the collective electoral fortunes of the majority party and incumbents more generally, the personal electoral ambitions of incumbents, and the institutional reputations of Congress and the president. Studies of congressional elections do not typically finger gridlock as a force affecting electoral outcomes. But it is entirely plausible that voters' retrospective evaluations of legislative performance help to shape their choices at election time. By contrast, several scholars have evaluated whether legislative activity shapes public approval and disapproval of Congress. Paradoxically, a consensus is emerging that the more Congress attends to its legislative duties, the lower its public approval dips.

In this chapter, I introduce the possibility that gridlock affects legislators' electoral fortunes and ambitions and re-evaluate claims that stronger legislative performance is penalized by the public. I find mixed evidence of gridlock's electoral effects but strong evidence of institutional consequences. Such trends, I argue, produce a dilemma. The causes of gridlock clearly suggest several institutional reforms that might bolster Congress's lawmaking capacity. But the mixed effects of gridlock offer legislators little incentive to undertake reform.

The Electoral Impact of Gridlock

In the 1940s and 1950s an enduring belief that voters would use elections to hold the majority party responsible for what it achieved or failed to achieve as the governing party anchored the call for responsible political parties. Parties could be responsible and held accountable only if they presented alternative programs to voters at election time and if voters used elections to cast retrospective and prospective judgments about the two parties' achievements and promises. Implicit in this view is the idea that voters pay attention to what parties in power achieve, make judgments about their policy performance, and vote accordingly on policy and ideological grounds.

A long trajectory of research casts doubt on voters' capacity for such informed judgement.[3] Still another trajectory of work, however, has shown how retrospective evaluations of politicians' performance—in particular judgments about the president and his party—may be sufficient to help shape voting decisions in a seemingly rational way.[4] At least in theory voters should take account of legislative performance as they decide how to cast their votes. In evaluating incumbents, and majority party incumbents in particular, we might think that Congress's record would help shape constituents' voting decisions.

There are a number of ways in which we might explore the impact of legislative performance on legislators' electoral fortunes. First, we might consider whether the majority party's vote or seat share is affected by the frequency of deadlock in a Congress, under the hypothesis that voters are more likely to hold the majority party accountable for legislative outcomes than the minority party. Second, we might ask whether the level of stalemate affects incumbent margins more generally, under the hypothesis that voters are unlikely to blame only the majority party for congressional performance. Or we might explore electoral consequences at the individual level, asking whether legislative performance affects legislators' calculations about whether or not to run for re-election. If, as Richard Fenno has argued, the pursuit of good public policy motivates many members of Congress, then we might expect more frequent legislative gridlock to reduce the appeal of serving in Congress.

Collective Electoral Fortunes and Gridlock

There is, to be sure, good reason to be skeptical of claims about the impact of gridlock on legislators' collective electoral fortunes. Explanations of congressional elections point more often to the impact of factors closely associated with the candidates and the dynamics of the race, as well as to economic considerations. The activities of Congress are rarely, if ever, fingered as potential factors affecting voters' electoral choices.[5] Instead, prominent students of congressional elections such as Gary Jacobson have highlighted the strong influence of challenger quality in shaping electoral outcomes.[6] That scholars have typically not explored the relevance of legislative performance to congressional elections is not surprising, given the well-known "Fenno" paradox that constituents can love their member of Congress and yet still hate Congress.

Table 6-1. *Relationship of Gridlock to Collective Electoral Fortunes,*
House of Representatives, 1948–98

Electoral variable	Relationship to level of gridlock[a]
Majority party's share of all House votes[b]	–.03
Change in majority party's share of all House votes[b]	.0356
Change in majority party's share of House seats won[b]	.0308
Mean winning House incumbent electoral margin[c]	.0465
Incumbents' share of the major party vote[d]	.2261
Percent of incumbents re-elected with over 60% of the major party vote[b]	–.2332
Percent of incumbents re-elected (of those seeking re-election)[b]	.0665

a. Cell entries are pairwise correlations between the frequency of legislative gridlock and each electoral outcome variable. No entries are significant at p < .05.

b. Norman J. Ornstein, Thomas E. Mann, and Michael J. Malbin, *Vital Statistics on Congress 1999–2000* (Washington: AEI Press, 2000). Variable measuring percentage of incumbents re-elected with more than 60 percent of the major party vote limited to 1958–98.

c. Data from Gary King, *Elections to the United States House of Representatives, 1898–1992* (Ann Arbor, Mich.: Inter-University Consortium for Social Research, 1994), file 6311.

d. Data from replication dataset for Gary W. Cox and Jonathan N. Katz, "Why Did the Incumbency Advantage in U.S. House Elections Grow?" *American Journal of Political Science*, vol. 40 (May 1996), pp. 478–97. Data range is 1948–90.

Poor legislative performance by Congress in general, in other words, is unlikely to affect candidates' collective electoral fortunes.[7]

An initial glance at the evidence casts strong doubt on the hypothesis that legislative gridlock has a direct impact on legislators' electoral fortunes. In table 6-1, I show pairwise correlation coefficients between the level of gridlock for each Congress and several different indicators of House members' collective electoral fortunes.[8] None of the relationships is significant at standard levels of statistical significance, meaning that there seems to be no connection between legislative performance and standard measures of electoral outcomes. The strongest correlation detected—which suggests that as gridlock increases, fewer House members win with greater than 60 percent of the vote—still is not significant in a statistical sense.

Table 6-2. *Impact of Legislative Performance on House Members'*
Collective Electoral Fortunes, 1948–90

	1 Incumbents' average vote share coefficient	2 Mean electoral margin of winning incumbents coefficient
Variable		
Frequency of gridlock	.091 (.066)	.003 (.002)
State of economy	28.651* (14.802)	1.156** (.444)
Challenger quality	−17.627* (10.462)	.698 (.314)
Constant	61.930*** (3.515)	−.047 (.105)
N	22	22
F	2.60	4.43
Prob F	.084	.017
Adjusted R^2	.186	.329

Source: See text for this and following tables.
Note: * p < .05, ** p < .01, *** p <.001 (one-tailed *t* tests). Parameter estimates generated with *regress* routine in Stata 7.0.

We can further assess the impact of legislative performance on electoral outcomes by estimating a model of House incumbents' share of
votes each election. Guided by the national elections model proposed by
Gary Jacobson, I assess the extent to which legislative performance
affects incumbent vote shares between 1948 and 1990, controlling for
the effects of economic conditions and the presence of quality challengers (table 6-2, column 1).[9] In findings consistent with previous work
on congressional elections, incumbent vote shares increase as the economy improves and decrease as more incumbents face quality challengers.[10] As anticipated, however, legislative performance does not seem
to affect the electoral fortunes of incumbent House members. The frequency of stalemate also seems to have little effect on majority party
vote or seat shares, or on winning incumbents' average electoral margin
(table 6-2, column 2). Whether Congress does a better or worse job

addressing salient issues seems not to have any effect on legislators' collective electoral fortunes. Voters at election time hold neither the majority party nor incumbents individually accountable for the collective policy performance of Congress.

Why do members not pay an electoral price for gridlock? As Fenno explains, "We apply different standards of judgment, those that we apply to the individual being less demanding than those we apply to the institution."[11] Incumbents learn quickly the tricks of the trade for securing re-election, focusing on meeting constituents' service demands and maintaining contact with many constituencies. Moreover, as they perfect the art of incumbency advantage, they insulate themselves from voters' policy judgments. Even if voters were prone to judge their members on policy grounds, members work to develop what Fenno calls "leeway" and "trust." As long as members are able to explain themselves and their votes to constituents, Fenno argues, voters are likely to give their members sufficient leeway in the conduct of their Washington lives.[12] In the end, incumbents develop immunity from poor legislative performance, as voters divorce their judgments about Congress's record from their judgments about their own member.

Electoral Ambitions and Gridlock

Gridlock may have little direct effect on aggregate electoral outcomes. But the recurrence of legislative stalemate may take a toll on individual members' electoral calculations. True, if members are solely "single-minded seekers of re-election,"[13] then concerns about Congress's legislative capacity are unlikely to affect legislators' electoral ambitions. Knowing that there is little electoral cost for a poor legislative showing, members solely interested in being re-elected would have little reason to care about high or low levels of stalemate. Only if legislative gridlock curtailed members' ability to take credit, advertise themselves, and take positions—the activities suggested by David Mayhew as the staple of re-election minded legislators—would we expect legislators to take legislative performance into account when they consider their electoral options.

But legislators do sometimes care about re-election for more than just the sake of re-election. It may be that re-election for some is simply a *proximate* goal—it is necessary for anything else a legislator might want to achieve in office. Many years ago, Fenno suggested the related possibility that legislators have many goals: while some may be primarily motivated by gaining re-election, others are motivated by the pursuit of good policy or by the pursuit of power and prestige within the chamber.[14] In Fenno's study, variation in members' goals was critical to explaining differing patterns of committee politics and members' behavior on committees.

The pursuit of good policy is also prevalent in other theoretical treatments of Congress. Keith Krehbiel's informational model posits that Congress is organized to give members the incentive to develop and share policy expertise that redounds to the collective interests of the members, namely, the formulation of public policy.[15] If members cared only about their own re-election (or even about the provision of distributive goods to their constituencies), there would be little reason for them to invest in the costs of developing the expertise necessary to solve public problems. Even in more party-centric treatments of legislative organization, theoretical concerns about the production of good policy prevail. In Gary Cox and Mathew McCubbins's party-cartel model, for example, the majority party organizes the chamber and its committees with an eye to building the party's electoral reputation, as it seeks policy outcomes that serve the party's electoral agenda.[16] In the policy-focused party model of John Aldrich and David Rohde, policy goals are again dominant, as strong majority parties seek legislative outcomes that match the party's policy agenda.[17] Policy pursuits are also said to be critical to members seeking to climb leadership ladders in the House, as more active legislative "entrepreneurs" are more likely to advance to prestigious positions within the chamber.[18]

The production of public policy is thus central, though in varying degrees, to the individual and collective interests of legislators, parties, and chamber coalitions. Whether it serves legislators' policy goals or leadership aspirations, or parties' policy agendas or electoral reputations, Congress's policy performance can be critical to legislators even if its impact on incumbent electoral fortunes is tough to detect. One way in which Congress's collective performance might affect individual legislators is through members' electoral calculations. A simple conjecture is that episodes of stalemate directly affect the incentive to run for re-election. When Congress heads toward a dismal policy record, legislators' incentives to remain in office should decline. When Congress improves its legislative performance, incentives to run for re-election should rise.

Explanations of voluntary departures often explore what has been called the "no-fun" factor, a rising sense of job dissatisfaction.[19] "They [members] find practicing the basic politician's art of compromise more difficult. . . . The satisfactions members receive from realizing policy goals have declined as the difficulties of building majorities behind coherent and meaningful programs have increased," observed political scientists Joseph Cooper and William West two decades ago.[20] If anything, claims about job dissatisfaction have only increased since Cooper and West conducted their study. Former U.S. senator Warren Rudman reflected on life in the Senate in the 1980s and early 1990s.

> Why are outstanding people leaving who could serve in the Senate another decade or two? . . . Most [of the ones I've talked to] are leaving because the Senate has become so partisan, so frustrating and so little fun. . . . The number of votes that senators cast each year doubled between the 1960s and 1980s, and many of the extra votes are politically inspired and meaningless. Members serve on more committees . . . and cast more votes there. And it's not that more work means more results. More often it leads to posturing and partisan gridlock. . . . There's less time than ever for a social life or a family life, and the ever-increasing cost of running for election means that most senators must spend huge amounts of their time going with tin cup in hand to special interests for money.[21]

Such arguments implicitly assume that at least a sizable cohort of legislators is likely to care intensely about making public policy and thus individuals are moved to retire by recurring episodes of legislative stalemate.

To the extent that scholars have tried to explore the impact of the no-fun factor on legislators' electoral calculations, the analysis has been conducted at the individual level. The catch is that it is difficult to capture at that level the impact of legislative stalemate (as it varies by Congress, rather than across members). One study measures the impact of burnout by asking whether party mavericks are more likely to retire or whether stalled careers lead disproportionately to retirement. Another infers from patterns in retirees' partisanship and leadership status that job disaffection is likely a prime cause of the "broad or pervasive character" of the detected trends in retirements.[22] The advantage of looking at the individual level of course is that it comports with our sense that institutional experiences should matter in varying degrees across members of Congress. The disadvantages are essentially methodological: it is all but impossible to measure the impact of stalemate on a personal level in a satisfying way.

As an alternative approach, I move to the aggregate level to explore whether episodes of stalemate reduce the broad appeal of serving in

Congress. If so, as the level of deadlock in a Congress climbs, so should the number of voluntary departures. An initial glance at the evidence suggests such a relationship, at least for the House: as gridlock becomes more common, more House members retire.[23] The relationship holds when we examine the total numbers of retirees each Congress and the number of retirees who do not seek other public office. In contrast, legislative stalemate does not seem to drive up Senate retirements, suggesting that senators may derive job satisfaction from sources beyond Congress's collective legislative performance. Because Senate rules impart much broader parliamentary rights to individual senators, it may be that senators can achieve valuable policy and political goals short of seeing major policy packages enacted into law.

Does the relationship between gridlock and electoral calculation hold up once we apply multivariate controls? We can draw from the literature on congressional departures and consider whether the age of House members, the frequency of pay raises, and electoral vulnerability affect the number of retirements.[24] As shown in table 6-3, the frequency of stalemate shapes retirement decisions, even after controlling for the host of usual suspects indicted for driving up the number of retirements.[25] In column 1, the impact of gridlock is seen on the total number of retirees each Congress from the House. In column 2, I limit the analysis to explaining the number of members leaving public service altogether, dropping members who announce for other elective office. In both specifications, more frequent gridlock leads to higher numbers of retirees, as does an aging House membership and the decennial redrawing of electoral districts.[26] In the aggregate at least, members seem to respond to episodes of legislative stalemate by choosing to retire at higher rates than normal, suggesting some truth to the old wisdom that as Congress becomes increasingly less "fun," members are especially prone to retire.

Accounting for the impact of legislative performance helps shed some light on the puzzle in retirement trends across recent decades. Writing in the early 1980s, political scientists observed a near doubling of retirement rates in the 1970s, after a decade of fairly few retirees in the 1960s.[27] Hibbing attributes the increase in retirees to the lack of pay raises for members and the crumbling of the seniority system that would otherwise have given members an incentive to hang on till a committee or subcommittee chair was due to them. Job dissatisfaction, in contrast, was "overrated" as a cause of retirements.[28] But tracking the course of gridlock and retirement rates together helps to explain rising numbers of

Table 6-3. *Impact of Legislative Performance on House Retirement Rates, 1948–94*

Variable	1 All House retirees coefficient	2 House retirees not seeking other office coefficient
Frequency of gridlock	.009* (.004)	.013* (.006)
Mean age of members	.021 (.030)	.08* (.039)
Redistricting year	.222* (.096)	.329** (.119)
Pay raise year	.125 (.095)	.077 (.121)
Constant	1.905 (1.633)	–1.965 (2.114)
N	24	24
Log likelihood	–93.712	–90.563
LR Chi²	22.01	31.65
Prob. Chi²	.0002**	.0000**

Note: * $p < .05$, ** $p < .01$ (one-tailed t tests). Parameter estimates (standard errors in parentheses) generated with Stata 7.0's *poisson* routine.

retirees in the 1970s. After several productive Congresses in the 1960s (with Congress and the president deadlocking on just a third of the agenda), stalemate began to rise in the 1970s (as gridlock rose to greater than 40 percent of the agenda). The evidence, having controlled for monetary and electoral motivations, suggests that failure to resolve public problems may have increased members' incentives to call it quits. Not surprisingly then, the abrupt drop in retirement rates in the 1980s was matched by a marked decline in deadlock at the same time (falling twenty points between its high in the 97th Congress and low in the 101st).[29] Yet another reversal in retirement rates in the early 1990s then follows naturally from the prevalence of stalemate at that time.

Legislative performance thus affects the electoral lives of members in a limited, but consequential, way. Although I detect little collective electoral ramifications for members, legislative stalemate certainly helps to shape pivotal electoral choices made by legislators. Career decisions are indelibly shaped by legislators' experiences on the Hill, not surprising given how central the pursuit of good policy is to members' ambitions and goals in office. When Congress leaves a host of public problems unresolved (often year after year), we should not be surprised to find that such experiences lead more members to contemplate leaving Congress. Deadlock, it seems, has an electoral impact on the appeal of public service.

Institutional Impact

If gridlock's only consequence is to drive more House members to retire, one might counter that there is always a supply of candidates for congressional seats. None of the 435 House seats is after all empty. Even if legislative inaction were to lead the best members to retire out of frustration with their experiences on the Hill, newcomers would always be available to populate and rejuvenate the halls of Congress. Viewed in this light, a causal connection between deadlock and retirement rates would be of limited concern.

Such a conclusion would be premature, however, if legislative stalemate has ramifications beyond the electoral realm. We should be attentive to the possibility that legislative performance helps to shape public views about Congress. There may be enduring institutional, as well as electoral, consequences of gridlock. If policy stalemate does affect Congress's public standing and reputation, the legitimacy of the institution as a forum for resolving matters of public dispute may periodically be called into question. And if gridlock affects Congress's institutional standing, we might also expect legislative stalemate to affect public perceptions of the president.

Congressional Approval and Gridlock

A recent study of public approval of Congress by Robert Durr, John Gilmour, and Christina Wolbrecht ends with a provocative conclusion: enactment of important and consequential legislation drives down public approval of the institution. As the authors conclude, "When Congress acts as it was constitutionally designed to act—passing major legislation and debating the issues of the day– it is rewarded by the public with lower levels of approval."[30] After controlling for economic expectations and public views of the president, climbing levels of successful legislative activity (and rising levels of conflict in the chambers) drive down Congress's public standing. The conclusion is deemed ironic, and, as I argue, appropriately so. Others have argued that the public distrusts Congress because people dislike bargaining and conflict endemic in legislative politics.[31] But even proponents of that thesis argue that successful legislative agreement between Congress and the president can drive public approval back up. John Hibbing has attributed anecdotally the upturn in congressional approval in mid-1997 to the successful enactment that summer of a balanced budget agreement.[32]

That legislative performance would drive public views about Congress seems rational. An early Harris poll, conducted in December 1963, detected such a link when it asked a nationwide sample to rate the job performance of Congress. Thirty-five percent of respondents rated Congress's performance as "excellent" or "pretty good," while 65 percent considered it "only fair" or "poor."[33] Of those slapping Congress with the lower rating, fully two-thirds attributed their views to legislative inaction. Thirty-two percent said that Congress had "not done much"; 12 percent complained Congress had "avoided major bills," 11 percent felt that "everything stalled in committee," and 11 percent argued that Congress had simply been "too slow." Of those rating Congress more positively, a third praised Congress for its progress in passing legislation.[34]

Classic studies of the determinants of congressional approval, however, tend not to evaluate the impact of legislative performance on public views of the institution. Glenn Parker's work in the late 1970s focused on the impact of the economy and presidency-centered factors in explaining early trends in congressional approval.[35] A later study by Samuel Patterson and Gregory Caldeira also primarily examined forces external to Congress.[36] The Durr, Gilmour, Wolbrecht study is thus notable in part for its empirical effort to assess whether and to what degree congressional performance helps to shape public attitudes toward Congress. Given their ironic finding that higher levels of congressional activity drive down public approval, it pays to revisit the relationship between legislative performance and policy gridlock.

I start with the proposition that what Congress accomplishes—or fails to accomplish—strongly affects public evaluations of Congress. As deadlock becomes more frequent, we should expect congressional approval rates to go down. Unfortunately, there is no consistent time series of survey questions reaching back to the 1940s that asks respondents to evaluate Congress's job performance. Instead, I construct a series of survey responses for the period 1963 through 1998 based on surveys conducted by Gallup and by Louis Harris and Associates over that period.[37] Because I have a single measure of gridlock for each Congress, I use the survey results closest to the November elections in each Congress to measure congressional approval.[38] I can then assess the impact of legislative gridlock, presidential approval levels, and economic conditions on public approval of Congress.[39]

In table 6-4, I show the results of a model that explores the impact of legislative performance on public views of Congress.[40] Despite the small sample size, I detect a statistically meaningful relationship between legislative stalemate and congressional approval, as more frequent deadlock lowers the public's evaluation of Congress.[41] A 1 percent increase in gridlock lowers public approval by half a percentage point—perhaps not a huge effect, but certainly a noticeable one when stalemate fluctuates markedly over a short period. The nearly thirty-point jump in gridlock during the 102d Congress after a relatively productive 101st thus helped to provoke a marked decline in public approval by the time the 102d Congress concluded before the 1992 presidential election. In contrast, the connection between macroeconomic conditions and congressional approval is much weaker, though it heads in the expected direction: rising levels of inflation tend to lower Congress's standing in the public eye. Contrary to previous studies, however, congressional approval does not move in tandem with presidential popularity—perhaps a reflection of the predominance of divided government over the fourteen Congresses studied. Weakening political parties and the recurrence of divided government have likely combined to decouple citizens' evaluations of the president and Congress, links that were clearly visible several decades ago.[42]

The results are striking on several fronts. First, although there may be limited electoral consequence to legislative stalemate, institutional ramifications are clearly visible in the public's wavering esteem for Congress. Most important, the results put into perspective the ironic finding of recent research that the more Congress performs its constitutional duties, the worse its approval ratings.[43] By taking direct account of Congress's achievements as well as its failures, my analysis produces more palatable and intuitive results. It is safe to say that the public takes reasonable stock of Congress's overall legislative record and keeps that record at least partially in mind in evaluating its job performance. Legislative accomplishments are rewarded by the attentive public; legislative failures are not. Although this finding runs counter to the conclusions reached by Robert Durr and colleagues, it does comport with studies conducted many years

Table 6-4. *Impact of Legislative Performance on Congressional Approval, 1966–96*

Variable	Coefficient
Frequency of gridlock	−.528* (.250)
Presidential approval	−.550 (.273)
Inflation rate	−1.501[a] (.865)
Unemployment rate	−.618 (1.964)
Lagged congressional approval	.160 (.185)
Constant	86.676** 21.799
rho	.626
N	14
F	5.51
Prob F	.017*
Adjusted R^2	.634

Note: * $p < .05$, ** $p < .01$, [a] $p < .1$ (one-tailed *t* tests). Parameter estimates are corrected for first-order serially correlated residuals using the Prais-Winston estimator and are generated with the *prais* routine in Stata 7.0.

ago that concluded that public evaluations of Congress were based largely on perceptions of Congress's job performance.[44]

Second, the connection between gridlock and Congress's public standing lays to rest an alternative conjecture about the impact of deadlock on public approval of the institution. A reasonable hypothesis is that Congress's job performance should have little bearing on the public's approval of the institution, since citizens hold different views about the desirability of different policy outcomes. For example, if Congress passes a raft of liberal (or conservative) legislation, we would hardly expect voters with conservative (or liberal) policy views to approve of the institution's overall performance. However, because the public appears to reward Congresses that pass a greater proportion of their agendas with higher approval ratings, there seems to be little support for that conjecture. Variation in citizens' policy views seems not to matter in their estimation of the institution. A likely explanation lies in the moderating effects of our political institutions: given the institutional hurdles partisan majorities face in seeking major policy change, legislative outcomes are moderated to the extent that broad bipartisan majorities endorse them.[45] As such we would expect the public (usually lodged in the moderate middle) to reward legislative accomplishment and punish frequent bouts of stalemate—precisely the dynamic suggested by the empirical evidence marshaled here.[46]

Third, accounting directly for what Congress achieves or fails to achieve markedly improves our ability to explain fluctuations in congressional approval. Rather than attributing changes in public views to events and conditions external to Congress, the analysis suggests that Congress can have a direct and discernible impact on its public reputation—essentially eclipsing the impact of the economy on congressional popularity. This finding helps to put into perspective a recent argument that the inherent messiness of political debate, bargaining, and compromise inevitably lowers the public's view of Congress and thus puts real improvement in Congress's public standing out of reach of its members.[47] Although the messiness of democratic government may severely handicap Congress in the public's eye relative to other national institutions and players, the link between legislative performance and public approval suggests that Congress retains some ability to shape its popularity.[48] Finding ways to improve congressional capacity, in other words, may go a long way toward improving Congress's public standing and thus legitimacy in the eyes of the public.

Presidential Approval

Congress of course does not act alone in addressing the principal issues of the day. Final tallies of legislative performance also reflect the preferences and strategies of the president. Given the intricate involvement of the president and legislators in the fashioning of major policy change, it is reasonable to ask whether the public holds the president accountable for policy performance in Washington. Given the link between stalemate and congressional approval, we might expect to find a similar impact of stalemate on presidential popularity.

Studies of presidential popularity have in the past addressed the importance of the president's policy performance in shaping his public standing.[49] Most often, however, policy performance is measured indirectly—

for example, as a count of certain legislative roll call votes or by media coverage of salient policy issues.[50] In such studies, legislative performance is more often conceptualized as the president's legislative effectiveness, as scholars have primarily been interested in whether the public holds the president accountable for achieving his own policy agenda. Thus, studies of presidential approval have tended not to incorporate broader measures of legislative outcomes that would measure overall progress on the nation's agenda. Even so, scholars have shown through various indirect proxies for the president's policy performance that his legislative activities help to shape public perceptions of his presidency.

How and why might legislative outcomes affect the president's public standing? The simplest possibility is a direct effect. Just as congressional approval seems to run in tandem with Congress's overall legislative record, we might expect the public's perception of the president every two years to hinge in part on the overall policy record of each Congress. For the two to be tightly entwined, however, the public would have to associate Congress's legislative record with the president's agenda. If the two are seen as pursuing different sets of policy goals, then we might not expect the public to hold the president accountable for Congress's legislative work every two years. We can easily evaluate whether gridlock directly affects presidential popularity by examining the degree to which legislative performance drives changes in biennial approval ratings of the president.

There is good reason to be skeptical of finding a direct link between stalemate and presidential popularity. Most important, presidents tend to focus on a much narrower agenda than the fifteen to twenty salient issues that end up on the active agenda of each Congress. President Clinton's first-term agenda, for example, might easily be boiled down to health care and welfare reform, reducing the budget deficit, and securing a North American free trade agreement. President George W. Bush's first-term agenda might similarly be condensed to a thin slate: tax cuts, missile defense, Social Security, and education reform. If the president, and thus the media, focuses on a much narrower set of policy goals, public impressions of the president might not be colored by Congress's broader policy accomplishments or failures. Thus legislative performance might not register much of an effect on the president's popularity.

Another possibility is that presidential credit or blame for Congress's overall record hinges on whether or not his party controls Congress. During periods of divided control, a president might wisely distance himself from Congress's policy record, especially in times of considerable gridlock. Given his command of a bully pulpit and his ease of "going public," a president could easily blame Congress for its inability to act on matters of national importance. Given the division of party control of the White House and Congress, even an attentive public might have little means of deciding whether or not the president should be blamed for legislative inaction. Periods of split party government, in other words, might blunt the public's ability to reward or punish the president for legislative gridlock, insulating the president from being blamed for stalemate. In periods of unified control, in contrast, presidential and congressional fortunes should be tied more closely, as it is much tougher for the president to distance himself from the majority party's legislative record. We might expect then that during unified government, presidential approval would run closely in tandem with frequency of deadlock, as the president would be unable to escape blame for legislative inaction by his own party.

To evaluate whether and how stalemate might shape presidential approval, I build a simple model of presidential popularity. Such models typically suggest that economic conditions and dramatic international events or crises together shape public perceptions of the president.[51] Presidents are said to pay dearly for poor economic times and to be rewarded by the public in times of international crises, the so-called rally-around-the-flag phenomenon.[52] Thus I model changes in the aggregate level of presidential approval as a function of prevailing economic conditions, political crises, and the overall frequency of legislative stalemate each Congress.[53] I probe first for a direct effect of stalemate on popularity and then assess whether party control conditions the impact of gridlock on approval levels.

The results in table 6-5, column 1, largely confirm existing literature on presidential popularity.[54] Presidents are penalized as inflation rises, though in this specification are unaffected by crises abroad. Missing, however, is any direct effect of gridlock on the president's approval ratings. The public seems not to hold the president accountable for the general policy record of Congress, even though successful enactment of major legislation depends on the involvement and signature (barring a congressional override of a presidential veto) of the president.

The results in columns 2–6 suggest a more nuanced portrait of how legislative performance affects the president's standing. The direct impact of legislative stalemate on the president's standing is again muted. More important, the public appears to hold the president accountable for his party's legislative performance when his party controls both chambers of

Congress. Increases in gridlock during periods of unified control drive down the president's approval rating, even after controlling for changing economic conditions and dramatic political events. To be sure, the impact of gridlock on presidential popularity is slight compared with that of economic factors. But presidents clearly cannot escape blame for feeble legislative accomplishments, just as they are rewarded when their party is more successful on Capitol Hill. The president's public standing is marked by his party's legislative performance. Most striking, Congress's policy performance affects presidential approval at all levels of issue salience.

How important are these connections between gridlock and the public standing of Congress and the president? From one perspective, institutional effects of stalemate merit little additional thought. Given the limited electoral fallout of gridlock, politicians have little incentive to alter their ways of doing business, and citizens seem to have slight interest in holding legislators accountable for their broader policy records. But from another perspective, institutional consequences matter a lot. If the public standing of Congress and the president are driven down by legislative inaction, it follows that the legitimacy of the two as national policymaking institutions is inherently linked to their job performance. In other words, members of Congress and the president have some control over how the public views them and how highly they regard them. Some have argued that because the public is turned off by the messiness of legislative politics, institutional reforms alone are unlikely to improve Congress's public image.[55] But my results suggest the opposite. Because productive legislative periods are rewarded by the public, improvements in legislative mechanics may help to raise the public standing of Congress and the president.

The Dilemma of Gridlock

As noted earlier, considerable stalemate over budget priorities reigned in 1999 as Democrats and Republicans proved unable to decide what to do with a newly emerging budget surplus. Rather than decide affirmatively what to do with the surplus, the two sides essentially opted to do nothing. Excess revenues would go automatically into the general treasury, thereby reducing the nation's staggering national debt. Gridlock was hailed for its salutary economic effects: why push hard for policy agreement when stalemate was producing such positive results?

Table 6-5. *Impact of Legislative Performance on Presidential Approval, 1948–98*

Variable	Gridlock 1 coefficient	Gridlock 1 coefficient	Gridlock 2 coefficient	Gridlock 3 coefficient	Gridlock 4 coefficient	Gridlock 5 coefficient
Frequency of gridlock	-.064 (.307)	-.206 (.299)	-.000 (.273)	-.082 (.226)	-.119 (.213)	-.069 (.189)
Legislative gridlock during unified government	... (.097)	-.179* (.111)	-.158[a] (.110)	-.172[a] (.114)	-.195* (.115)	-.207* (.115)
Inflation	-2.369** (.765)	-2.306** (.722)	-2.345** (.754)	-2.253** (.737)	-2.224** (.727)	-2.271** (.722)
Unemployment	1.317 (1.711)	.242 (1.717)	.263 (1.814)	.437 (1.762)	.392 (1.720)	.271 (1.658)
International crisis	1.900 (4.230)	5.240 (4.386)	4.467 (4.471)	4.405 (4.517)	4.582 (4.392)	4.523 (4.266)
Lagged approval	.227 (.179)	.108 (.181)	.153 (.181)	.170 (.175)	.146 (.175)	.146 (.174)
Constant	45.803* (19.641)	67.130** (21.871)	53.759** (18.740)	55.182** (15.778)	58.124*** (15.871)	56.942*** (15.317)
N	25	25	25	25	25	25
F	3.12*	3.48*	3.10*	3.22*	3.40*	3.46**
Adjusted R^2	.306	.383	.344	.357	.375	.381

Note: * $p < .05$, ** $p < .01$, *** $p < .001$, [a] $p < .1$ (one-tailed t tests). Parameter estimates (standard errors in parentheses) generated with Stata 7.0's *regress* routine.

Despite the apparent economic benefits of gridlock during periods of budget surplus, neither party today likely sees gridlock as a long-term strategy for governing. First, the federal surplus has all but disappeared for now, with the war on terrorism and recovery efforts after the attacks of September 11 (as well as deteriorating economic conditions and tax cuts) eating into the surplus resting outside of Social Security accounts. Second, regardless of the health of the budget, both parties remain sufficiently committed to legislative agendas (whether conservative or liberal) that neither side will likely pursue gridlock simply for its economic effects. The costs of bolstering the nation's defenses against terrorism at this writing are at the top of both parties' agendas. Beyond that, Republicans keep tax cuts, education, and Social Security reform high on their agendas—all of which require serious legislative action and prowess to achieve. Democrats have their own slate of additional issues and are equally unlikely to settle for legislative inaction. And third, given the institutional consequences that accompany more frequent gridlock, such a strategy would be folly by the political parties. Members of Congress and the president might reap short-term gains from reducing the national debt through gridlock, but such gains would probably be washed out as their approval ratings sink with more frequent deadlock. The argument that gridlock has important and worthwhile economic effects is a two-edged sword: gridlock may help to reduce the national debt, but legislative inaction simultaneously drives down the public standing of Congress and the president.

Before leaping to the conclusion that presidents and Congress have important incentives to resolve pressing problems of public policy, a critical caveat remains. Although we can discern some institutional consequences of gridlock, there is only limited evidence that Congress pays an electoral cost for legislative stalemate. True, members' personal electoral ambitions seem to be tempered by periods of legislative gridlock, but there is little evidence that Congress or the majority party pays a collective electoral cost for its failures. Although gridlock may reduce Congress's standing in the public's eyes, voters seem not to let legislative performance systematically shape their choices at election time. So is there really an incentive for legislators to find ways of circumventing or reducing legislative stalemate?

This question raises what we might call the dilemma of gridlock. Despite the harm it does to institutional reputations, there is little electoral incentive for legislators to address it. Granted, legislators have other motivations that may impel them to work hard to resolve gridlock, be it the goal of making good policy, an electoral inducement or reward from interested outside groups, or some other motivation. But there is probably limited incentive for legislators to invest the time in institutional reforms that might help to alleviate the excesses of gridlock. Legislative scholars have repeatedly found that congressional reforms are more likely to be undertaken when sufficient numbers determine that their own interests would be best served by altering the institution.[56] Without such immediate benefits of reform, legislators will be unlikely to invest the time in devising reforms or to succeed in securing them.

This then is the dilemma: gridlock has harmful effects on institutional reputations, but there is little electoral incentive for legislators to do anything about it. In a sense, the dilemma is a corollary to Fenno's paradox, that the public loves their member while hating Congress. Because incumbents work so hard at securing their re-election by keeping constituents content, incumbents make themselves immune from electoral defeat, as well as from broader assessments of Congress as an institution. Congress bashing by members themselves helps to reinforce the distinction between Congress as an institution and its individual members. The dilemma of gridlock thus follows naturally from Fenno's paradox. Gridlock does not affect collective electoral fortunes because voters' electoral judgments are rarely colored by their institutional assessments of Congress. They can love their member while hating the institution (and thus its policy record).

Should we be worried about this dilemma? Only if we think there may be institutional changes that might help to alleviate the excesses of gridlock and if we think such changes are desirable. If gridlock is simply and inevitably a consequence of our political system, or it could be reduced if legislators simply tried harder to reduce their differences with one another, then there is little reason for concern. Eventually legislators will find it in their interest to reach policy compromises on salient issues, and stalemate will take care of itself.

This is a reasonable view. If the frequency of deadlock is largely a function of bicameral differences and polarization of the parties, then Congress's legislative performance is a simple function of electoral outcomes and the evolution of constitutional design. There is little that legislators can do to reduce the barriers to legislative stalemate they typically encounter. Legislators can only wait out electoral change that bolsters the presence of moderates and accept the reality of bicameralism. We cannot engineer electoral outcomes, so we should learn to live with gridlock. In a sense, this perspective commits us to accepting the conventional wisdom about the intentions of the framers: legislative inaction was one of their key goals, and thus they designed a political system of checks and balances that would slow down and often thwart efforts to enact major changes in public law.

I think there is some value to interpreting the causes of stalemate in another way. To be sure, there is little that congressional observers, scholars, and members can do to engineer electoral results that would rebuild the political center—short of intensive (and probably unrealistic) change in American political parties that would reduce party elites' dependence on the activist (and usually more extreme) wings of their parties.[57] Neither is constitutional reform plausible or likely to eliminate the bicameral structure of Congress. Interestingly, former governor Jesse Ventura of Minnesota advocated such a change at the state level, when he realized how bicameralism was thwarting his policy and political agendas. Ventura, commenting on the impact of conference committee obstruction, argued, "You go to unicameral, [and] it's [obstruction] out. You go to unicameral, that's [obstruction] dead meat."[58] Not surprisingly given the difficulty of state constitutional reform and institutional intransigence, bicameralism has not been replaced in Minnesota—a failure certain to recur at the federal level. But, arguably, a more limited set of institutional steps might be taken to reduce some of the barriers to legislative change in Congress.

Negotiating Differences

It is fair to say that legislators today toil in somewhat unusual political times. The decline of the political center has produced a political environment that more often than not gives legislators every incentive not to reach agreement. There are steady partisan and ideological pressures on members not to compromise on firmly held positions. Legislators also work in a remarkably public environment, are followed by an intensely negative media, and face a revolution in communications technology that grants little time or space for methodical deliberation. Legislators also often face an agenda that requires imposing losses rather than distributing benefits, as the promise of budget surpluses has given way to economic downturns, tax cuts, and politicians' unwillingness to spend from Social Security reserves.[59]

Atypical political times justify consideration of atypical institutional reforms. One idea is for both chambers to experiment with some new methods of reaching agreement in committee. If members were given the time and chance to develop reasonable compromises at the committee level, there would be fewer challenges from the leadership, the Rules Committee, and noncommittee members before bills reached the floor and during floor consideration itself. And most important, because more partisan deliberations in committee reduce the likelihood of bill passage, encouraging policy compromise at the committee level would probably bolster legislative performance overall.

One way to foster such constructive discussion at the committee level would be to try what is known as "facilitated consensus" methods.[60] This tactic is an increasingly popular innovation at the state level. At least seventeen states have established offices to promote the use of conflict mediation in government. As one North Dakota state senator noted about his legislature's experience with the use of mediators, "A consensus approach provides a great substitute for gridlock."[61]

In this method of conflict resolution a neutral mediator helps legislators to build agreements. The inclusion of a neutral mediator usually entails getting participants to clarify their basic interests and then helping them identify overlapping interests and discuss options for accommodating those interests. Mediation would help make the goal of committee markups to reach a compromise, rather than score political points. The mediator is simply a facilitator—a neutral third party who does not express substantive views on the issue and cannot impose a solution. In other words, members of Congress would not cede any of their authority or jurisdiction over an issue by allowing a facilitator into the committee room. Legislators are free to accept, modify, or reject proposals that result from the process. And the process could be used by members themselves, their staffs, or both—whether open to media coverage or not. In fact, allowing television coverage might help to educate the public about the need for compromise in crafting legislation—and to illustrate that bargaining is not a sign of weakness or mere politics but a necessary part of the legislative process.

Not every issue would necessarily be amenable to facilitated consensus. State legislatures have had the most success with facilitators when communication between parties was at an impasse, when the issue was a recurring one that had gone unresolved for several sessions, when the issue was a negotiable one, and when the heavy influence of certain interest groups had made it difficult to reach agreement in the past. Strongly ideologically charged issues—such as much of the debate surrounding abortion—are less likely to be negotiable issues. Moreover, the process is unlikely to work well if there are unreasonable time constraints or if broad public concern about reaching a solution is absent.

Most important, members of these state legislatures say that the use of mediators measurably helped improve working relationships among members. It gave them a cooperative history of working together that they could then try to apply by themselves to other issues. Given the intense partisanship prevailing in recent Congresses, an environment that fosters constructive bargaining and compromise might measurably improve the chances for major policy change.

Bicameral Adjustments

If bicameral disagreements systematically lead to more frequent stalemate, some consideration of bicameral reform makes sense. To be sure, bicameral hurdles arise because of policy differences between the two chambers. But adjusting congressional routines may reduce the impediment that bicameralism often poses to negotiating policy differences. Building from the idea of facilitating consensus in committee, Congress might be well served by adopting a procedure it authorized for executive branch agencies and departments: negotiated rulemaking, more commonly known as "reg-neg." Formalized by the Negotiated Rulemaking Act of 1990, reg-neg is an alternative method for developing federal rules. Instead of the usual process of publishing a draft rule, inviting public comment from interested parties, and then publishing a final rule, the use of reg-neg brings together agency staff, regulated entities, and others with a substantial interest in a federal rule to negotiate a rule before the normal rulemaking process takes place. The aim (and claim of its supporters) is that negotiating consensus among interested parties improves the efficiency of the regulatory process and reduces the risk of litigation over the final rule.[62] Just as in facilitated consensus, impartial mediators are used to facilitate agreement among negotiating parties.

Using a process resembling reg-neg in Congress might reduce conflict and stalemate at the bicameral stage. One way of applying a so-called bill-neg might be to institutionalize joint committees or task forces on major policy issues that would convene in a reg-neg style to negotiate differences likely to emerge between the House and Senate. Because House rules tend to produce more partisan bills, while more bipartisan bills are given a greater chance of survival in the Senate, some effort to reduce the extent of bicameral differences in the stage of drafting legislation might be especially worthwhile. Most important, it might head off inevitable bicameral and partisan conflict before it has time to deepen and develop, conflict fueled by outside interests who have a stake in escalating differences over measures they oppose.

Some procedural inducements would undoubtedly be required to encourage legislators to adopt bill-neg early in the legislative process (or at the conference stage). A key procedural protection might be offered to the final negotiated bill, such as limiting the right of senators to filibuster the three separate motions required in the Senate to send a bill to conference. In effect, bill-neg negotiators would be promised a fast track into conference (including the naming of conferees), requiring simply a majority vote (rather than a supermajority vote or unanimous consent). The Senate might go yet a step further and promise that a final conference agreement stemming from bill-neg would be entitled to fast-track protection, making conference agreements immune from Senate filibusters.

In a sense, Congress has adopted such procedural strategies in the past when it has authorized an independent commission to negotiate a policy agreement and afforded its final recommendations procedural protections in the House and Senate. The several rounds of base-closing commissions that recommended military base closings starting in the late 1980s and continuing into the 1990s are one such example. Not only did Congress delegate authority to an external group to devise the list, the final recommendations were granted fast-track protection in the House and Senate. The only way for Congress to defeat any of the recommended closings was through a joint resolution of disapproval that had to be passed by both chambers within forty-five days. Otherwise, the Defense Department would implement the closings.[63] Although bill-neg would also entail delegation and procedural protection, bill-neg would be unique in that legislators rather than outsiders would be the ones to negotiate differences. Legislators' typical objections to delegating away their authority would be moot. Undoubtedly, bill-neg would hardly be a cure-all (just as reg-neg is relatively infrequently used and not always successful),[64] but it could conceivably reduce several institutional obstacles that systematically lead to stalemate.

September 11 and Congress's Future

Not every reform that improves public approval of Congress will necessarily make it work better. Congressional term limits, banning contributions from political action committees, further cuts in congressional perks and staff—these types of reforms fall into this category. Such reforms would certainly meet public demand that members of Congress be less insulated and less beholden to organized interests, but they would be unlikely to help bridge policy differences in Congress and thus produce policy compromise and change. Similarly, some reforms might make Congress work better, but would not help to boost the public's impression of Congress. Relaxing sunshine requirements that require open legislative meetings and reducing television coverage might very well help members to reach agreement without the scrutiny of the press and lobbyists. But such reforms would likely further raise the ire of constituents who think members of Congress are already too insulated from the public and its concerns.

That said, if Congress did work better—forging compromise in a manner that the public perceives as efficient and equitable—public perceptions of Congress would undoubtedly improve. The challenge for legislators is to come up with new ways of addressing institutional stalemate by devising means of getting around stubborn obstacles to compromise. The reforms suggested are simply a down payment on such a list, and they are intended to make it easier for opposing sides to air differences, resolve conflicting interests, and secure compromise on pressing matters of public import.

To be sure, the notion of "fixing gridlock" can be troubling. One person's stalemate is another's preferred legislative outcome. In the polarized and polarizing era that legislators inhabit today, it is doubtful that true differences over desirable ends and means can or should always be negotiated away.[65] But neither can we depend on the emergence of cohesive political parties to resolve recurring episodes of gridlock, as we see now that the faith of party government scholars in disciplined parties was misplaced: gridlock only increases as the political center recedes.

Nor, one might argue, can the nation afford to wait for electoral change to bring conditions more favorable for major lawmaking. The events of September 11 forced Congress and the president to act with urgency. Notably, they enacted major war and recovery measures within days of the attacks, despite the presence of divided government and the slimmest of margins in both chambers.[66] Congress acquiesced quickly to President Bush's demands for financial support for New York and for the airline industry, although it did not give in completely to his requests. Congress refused, for example, to give the administration a blank check and authority over how appropriated funds would be spent, and Congress narrowed a use-of-force resolution requested by the administration to conduct a war against terrorism. [67] But in comparison to the partisan deadlock over Social Security, health care, and other issues before September 11, Congress made a concerted effort to ensure swift legislative action on the president's requests—completing action on major war and recovery measures within days of the attacks.

One explanation is simply the horrendous nature of the attacks and the unifying effect it had on legislators—indeed on millions of Americans. A complementary explanation is that the enormity of the crisis encouraged President Bush to alter his strategies for building coalitions on Capitol Hill. What was striking about the bipartisanship that emerged was Bush's central role and willingness to reach out to the Democratic leadership, with Bush meeting weekly with House and Senate leaders from both parties. This strategic approach was far different from his usual mode before September 11, when he was more likely to start with a base of Republican support and then work to attract the support of a few conservative Democrats to secure a winning coalition—the tax cut package of 2001 being a prime example.[68] Reaching out to both party leaderships after September 11 seems to have made a different kind of bipartisanship far easier to achieve, as opposition party leaders were brought in at the formative stage of the legislative process. Bush's flexibility on the details of several issues (such as the use of federal workers in an overhaul of airport security) seems to have made bicameral agreement easier to reach as well.[69]

By many accounts, however, the bipartisanship immediately after the attacks did not last long. To be sure, on measures directly related to the recovery, Democrats went along with the president's priorities. But in spite of September 11, the conditions that encouraged legislators to deadlock on major issues before the attacks were still in place. First, there were strong differences between the House and Senate on a slew of domestic policy issues, including bankruptcy reform, patients' rights, accounting standards, energy development, faith-based initiatives, tax cuts, and more.[70] Second, the political parties were highly polarized, holding slim margins of control in each chamber. And third, the two parties still divided up control of the White House and Senate. As the issues raised by the terrorist attacks continue to grow, improving Congress and the president's abilities to negotiate policy compromise—even under conditions that normally foster stalemate—will become even more important. The list of such debates is already long (restructuring the intelligence agencies and border control, bolstering homeland security defense, changing military doctrine and strategy, preparing against bioterrorism, to name just a few).

I conclude that even without the events of September 11, some modest retooling of Congress to improve its legislative capacity would have been in order. With the events of September 11, ensuring that legislators can readily reach agreement on vexing issues becomes even more important. Enhancing legislative capacity would hardly be out of keeping with the founding framers' intentions to build a more energetic and capable government. And having identified recurring institutional and electoral sources of legislative gridlock, reforms might be narrowly crafted to increase their probability of adoption. Institutional reputations ride on the ups and downs of legislative performance. How successful Congress and the president are in making law has deep and broad ramifications not only for the state of public policy but also for the character and legitimacy of the two branches.

APPENDIX A

Measuring Stalemate

This appendix contains further details about the measurement of gridlock.

Recreating the Legislative Agenda

To measure gridlock, I generate a list of agenda items each Congress between 1947 and 2000 and determine whether or not each agenda item was resolved by enactment of legislation in that Congress. The frequency of gridlock for each Congress is thus calculated as the number of failed agenda items each Congress divided by the total number of items on the agenda for that Congress.

I use daily editorials from the *New York Times* between 1947 and 2000 to identify issues that constitute the legislative agenda for each Congress, selecting every editorial that mentioned Congress, the House, or the Senate (editorials retrieved from microfilm 1947–80 and from Lexis-Nexis 1981–2000). The editorials were coded to identify only those issues for which the *New York Times* mentioned, advocated, or opposed legislative consideration. This coding rule eliminated editorials that only incidentally mentioned

Congress, the House, or the Senate (for example, editorials discussing Supreme Court rulings overturning laws enacted by Congress and editorials endorsing congressional candidates).

Editorials were then coded to determine the legislative issue at stake and the number of editorials written that Congress on the issue. Like Mayhew, I dropped routine appropriations bills. Although the politics of appropriations can be used to study gridlock, making judgments about their legislative fate in this context is problematic, as it is impossible to code objectively whether the final level of funding constitutes success or failure. To maintain consistency with Mayhew's approach, I also dropped agenda items about executive and judicial nominations, internal congressional procedures, and foreign aid appropriations with no major statutory changes. Like Mayhew, I included treaties and constitutional amendments. In all, nearly 15,000 editorials were collected and coded by a team of five college interns, a research assistant, and the author. To ensure the reliability of the coding, editorials coded by interns were also coded independently by the research assistant or the author. Intercoder reliability averaged 87 percent. Coding discrepancies were reviewed and resolved by the research assistant or the author.

Coding Legislative Outcomes

Each agenda item was then coded as a legislative success or failure. For most cases, legislative fate was readily coded from the yearly editions of *Congressional Quarterly Almanac*. If the *Almanac* provided no or ambiguous coverage, numerous sources were consulted, including the Library of Congress's Thomas website, Legi-Slate's on-line bill retrieval service, the U.S. Congressional Hearings Data Set maintained by the Center for American Politics and Public Policy at the University of Washington, and other sources. In most cases, it was relatively easy to match the *New York Times*'s discussion of an issue with its legislative fate. In the 104th Congress, for example, the *Times* called for passage of campaign finance reform, and no such legislation was enacted. Similarly, the *Times* opposed enactment of a bill making English the official language of the United States, and no legislation was enacted. In contrast, the *Times* advocated telecommunications, welfare, and immigration reform, and broad legislative packages were enacted on each.

More difficult coding decisions arise when Congress and the president enact a piece of legislation that addresses only a small portion of a larger issue. Many of these cases are not difficult to code, however, because the *Times* tends to adjust its editorials over the course of a Congress to discuss legislative realities (small bills) and larger unresolved issues. In the 104th Congress, for example, Congress enacted a health care bill, the so-called Kennedy-Kassebaum health care portability act. Congress did not, however, address broader issues of medical insurance reform that have been on the agenda in recent Congresses. In this case, the *Times* ran separate editorials on health insurance reform (eight editorials) and Kennedy-Kassebaum (six editorials). The former issue was coded as a failure; the latter, success. Similarly, in the 101st Congress (1989–90), Congress enacted a tax package that addressed only some of the broad tax issues on the agenda. In this case, however, the *Times* ran separate editorials on both a capital gains tax cut (twelve editorials) that was excluded from the final package and expansion of the earned income tax credit (four editorials) that was included. Thus, although Congress addressed only a portion of the tax issues, the two issues are easily coded as failure and success respectively.

Posing more difficult coding decisions are cases for which a legislative package was enacted that significantly amended the original proposal. For example, in the 103d Congress (1993–94), Clinton proposed a major economic stimulus package that was later whittled down to a minor extension of unemployment benefits after a prolonged Senate filibuster. The legislative outcome for the stimulus package was coded as failure, guided by analysis of the issue by *Congressional Quarterly Almanac*. When the *Almanac* proved inconclusive about the credibility of a final legislative enactment, news stories in the *New York Times* and *Washington Post* were consulted. If the legislative fate was still ambiguous, I erred on the side of coding the outcome a success if elite opinion suggested that Congress had made a substantial effort to address the underlying issue. Erring toward success minimizes the risk of penalizing Congress and the president for compromising on legislation. Moreover, since I am interested in the relative, rather than absolute, frequency of gridlock, my primary concern was consistency in determining legislative success or failure.

Determining Issue Salience

A critical distinction between Mayhew's focus on landmark laws and my focus on legislative agendas is that Mayhew's method allows him to isolate highly salient legislative measures. In contrast, the editorial-based method generates legislative agendas of uneven salience. Given this wide range of issue salience, it is helpful to have a means of partitioning the data into varying degrees of salience.

Fortunately, the number of *New York Times* editorials in each issue provides a proxy for issue salience.[1] This is readily established by correlating the number of editorials in each issue with a number of different indicators of policy salience. First, using a Pew Research Center database on public attentiveness to major news stories, the percentage of the public following an issue "very closely" rises with the number of editorials written on that issue by the *New York Times*. For 1993–96, Pearson's r = .341 ($p < .05$, one-tailed test).[2] Second, issues that receive greater numbers of *Times* editorials also generate more network news stories. For 1993–96, Pearson's r = .446 ($p < .01$, one-tailed test).[3] Third, as the number of editorials in each issue increases, the length of network news coverage for that issue increases. For 1993–96, Pearson's r = .437 ($p < .01$ one-tailed test).[4] Fourth, the *Times* wrote on average 8.5 editorials on issues that became landmark enactments, but wrote only 2.7 on average on all others. Finally, issues attracting only one or two editorials frequently had minimal national importance. The *Times*, for example, wrote one editorial on creation of Dinosaur National Monument in the 84th Congress (1955–56) and on zip code reform in the 97th (1981–82). More recently, establishing uniform poll closings was discussed once during the 103d Congress (1993–94). The relationship between salience and number of editorials, however, is not perfect. The *Times* wrote just one editorial about roughly thirty of Mayhew's landmark laws.

Because the number of *Times* editorials is a reasonable indicator of issue salience, I can divide up the legislative agenda using different numbers of editorials on each issue as a cut-off point for determining whether or not to include an issue in calculating gridlock scores. In chapters 3 and 4, for example, I divide up the agenda depending on whether the *Times* wrote one or more editorials (that is, all the legislative issues culled from the editorials), two or more editorials, three or more editorials, four or more editorials, or five or more editorials on an issue. I then calculate separate gridlock scores for each of the different sets of legislative issues. I refer to these variables in the statistical analyses as gridlock 1, gridlock 2, gridlock 3, gridlock 4, and gridlock 5. Gridlock 1 represents the frequency of deadlock based on issues receiving at least one editorial and thus includes the widest range of issue salience; gridlock 5 represents the frequency of deadlock on issues receiving five or more editorials and thus is limited to the most salient issues.

In most of the analysis in this book, I estimate five different versions of the model, re-estimating the model for each of the five different sets of gridlock scores.[5] In several places in chapter 6, however, I want to limit the analysis to more salient issues. There is no obvious standard for determining which threshold is the best proxy for highly salient issues. Because Mayhew's method clearly generates extremely salient measures, I choose a threshold that generates the closest approximation to Mayhew's series, which is the gridlock 4 series.[6]

Measuring Bicameral Differences

Bicameral policy differences are central to this book's treatment of legislative deadlock. Establishing a robust indicator of bicameral differences is thus critical to the persuasiveness of my account. This appendix discusses several potential ways of measuring House and Senate policy differences and demonstrates why the approach used in this book is superior to the alternatives.

A Debate Over Measures

In an earlier work on legislative gridlock,[1] I measured bicameral differences using a set of ideological scores generated by Keith Poole and Howard Rosenthal dubbed W-NOMINATE.[2] These scores are a measure of legislators' preferences estimated from a spatial model of voting. To measure differences in policy views between the two chambers, I calculated the absolute distance in W-NOMINATE scores between the House and Senate median members for each Congress between 1947 and 1996. This action produced for each Congress a score that indicates the distance between the median chamber members, which I inferred to be a measure of their general policy disagreement in each Congress. I then used the measure in empirical analysis as a measure of bicameral differences during the past half-century.[3]

In a reanalysis of my work, Fang-Yi Chiou and Lawrence Rothenberg suggest that my earlier empirical results linking increases in bicameral differences to a rise in legislative gridlock are likely the function of using "potentially inappropriate" preference measures.[4] When Chiou and Rothenberg substitute an alternative measure of interchamber differences in my original model, they get null results. Thus Chiou and Rothenberg conclude that my earlier work on gridlock lacks "much empirical foundation."[5] Chiou and Rothenberg argue that W-NOMINATE scores were not meant to be compared across chambers or over time. As an alternative, they substitute a recently developed variant of W-NOMINATE known as "common space coordinates."[6] Because common space scores were designed to travel across time and chambers, Chiou and Rothenberg argue that the scores are preferable for measuring bicameral differences.

Are common space coordinates truly a better measure of legislators' ideologies and superior for tapping bicameral differences? If so, Chiou and Rothenberg's new analysis offers a valuable improvement to existing empirical work on legislative gridlock. If not, little is gained by invoking the new scores to estimate the correlates of deadlock. And if neither W-NOMINATE nor common space scores are acceptable for measuring bicameral differences over time, we are still left with the challenge of developing a suitable measure.

The Assumptions of Common Space

Common space coordinates, close siblings to Poole and Rosenthal's more well-known NOMINATE scores, are said to place members of the House and Senate onto a single ideological space. In Poole's methodology, he makes the assumption that legislators' ideologies remain the same over time and, for those who served in both the House and Senate, across chambers.[7] This assumption allows him to use the voting behavior of members who served in both the House and Senate (he uses legislators' W-NOMINATE scores) as a " 'glue' to tie the House and Senate together in a single [rank] ordering [ideologically]."[8] In contrast, the methodology underlying other versions of NOMINATE (those known as "D" and "DW" variants) allows legislators' ideologies to change in a linear fashion over time. The assumption of fixed ideologies for common space coordinates is the first assumption that bears consideration in judging the validity of common space coordinates.

The second assumption relates to the relative importance of the two dimensions identified by Poole and Rosenthal as central to mapping the ideological landscape of Congress over time.[9] The first dimension taps the standard left-right ideological space; the substance of the second dimension has varied over time, most often capturing issues of racial politics and civil rights. According to Poole and Rosenthal, the first dimension today captures roughly 90 percent of the roll call votes, while adding a second dimension accounts for only an additional 1 percent. In contrast, in calculating common space scores, the coordinates are "adjusted so that the two dimensions are *equally salient and lie within a unit circle.*"[10] Because of these two strong assumptions, Poole warns that "these coordinates should be used with caution."[11]

These assumptions require us to be cautious in using common space coordinates to measure bicameral differences in the 1947 to 2000 period. Consider first the assumption of fixed ideologies underlying the common space method. First, assuming that a member's voting patterns are static across the two chambers makes it harder to detect ideological differences between the two chambers; if ideologies do change, any measure of cross-chamber differences will understate the true level of bicameral differences.[12] Second, given what we know about the differences between House and Senate constituencies, it is reasonable to expect that legislators would exhibit different voting patterns if they move from one chamber to the other.[13] Procedural differences between the two chambers might also affect the stability of legislators' voting patterns in the two institutional settings. Consider, for example, the impact of House rules that endow House majority party leaders with considerable control of the House floor agenda compared with the limited procedural tools afforded to Senate party leaders.[14] If House majority party leaders use their procedural control to limit the frequency of roll call votes on issues that divide their party, we might expect a legislator's party loyalty to vary after he moves from the House to the Senate. [15]

Comparing the voting behavior of members who served in both chambers produces some evidence that ideological voting patterns do not remain fixed across chambers. First, we can compare the average party loyalty score of members in the House before their switch to their party loyalty scores after they move to the Senate.[16] When we do so, we find that legislators' party loyalty scores drop a statistically significant amount when they move from the House to the Senate.[17]

To control for agenda and other potential changes over time, I examine the voting behavior of legislators who served in both chambers in a single congress.[18] Table B-1 compares party loyalty scores for the eight legislators who moved between the two chambers in a single session sometime between the 83d and 104th Congresses. Robert Stafford (R-Vt.), for example, voted with his party 77 percent of the time when he served in the House in the 92d Congress. After moving to the Senate later in the Congress, his party loyalty score dropped to 71 percent. Overall, seven of the eight legislators showed some change in party loyalty. The 14 percent average change across these eight members raises doubts about the assumption that House and Senate members' voting patterns remain stable across the two chambers.

Next, consider the decision to treat the two major ideological dimensions as equally salient in calculating common space coordinates. Poole and Rosenthal are explicit about the changing relevance of the dimensions over time.[19] Although in early periods of congressional history issues falling on the second dimension may have appeared more frequently on the agenda, this is a troubling assumption once applied to the postwar period studied in this book. As Poole noted, "With the passage of the 1964 Civil Rights Act, the 1965 Voting Rights Act, and the 1967 Open Housing Act, this second dimension slowly declined in importance and is now almost totally absent. . . . Voting in Congress is almost purely one-dimensional."[20] The near absence of second-dimension issues is confirmed by scanning the issues addressed in *New York Times* editorials. Issues related to civil rights and racial politics constitute under 5 percent of salient issues on the legislative agenda between 1947 and 1996.[21] The equal weighting of the two dimensions seriously weakens the validity of a measure of bicameral differences for recent Congresses that relies on common space coordinates.[22]

The consequences of overweighting the second dimension are visible if we compare the two measures of bicameral differences, one based on common space scores and the other on W-NOMINATE scores. If Poole and Rosenthal are correct that the second dimension recedes in importance after the 1960s, we would expect the common space measure to move in tandem with the W-NOMINATE measure from the 1940s through the 1960s. After 1970, we would expect to see a sharp drop-off in the correlation of the two series. This is precisely what we see in comparing

Table B-1. *Change in Voting Behavior across Chambers*

Member	Congress	House party loyalty (percent)	Number of votes	Senate party loyalty (percent)	Number of votes	Difference
Quentin Burdick (D-N.D.)	86th	88	120	100	22	12
Norris Cotton (R-N.H.)	83d	89	84	88	8	1
Charles Goodell (R-N.Y.)	90th	80	273	50	26	30
Robert Griffin (R-Mich.)	89th	80	159	72	111	8
Roman Hruska (R-Neb.)	83rd	89	103	38	8	51
Robert Stafford (R-Vt.)	92d	77	123	71	551	6
James Broyhill (R-Neb.)	99th	76	511	83	165	7
Ron Wyden (D-Ore.)	104th	88	790	88	255	0

Source: See text.

correlation coefficients for the two series across the two time periods. Before the 1970s, the correlation between the two series is a respectable .64, a statistically significant relationship. After 1970, the correlation drops to .34 and is no longer statistically significant. Although this difference would be acceptable if civil rights issues were more prominent on the legislative agenda in the later period, the exact opposite is true. The overweighting of the second dimension calls into question the validity of the measure for comparing chamber preferences after the 1960s.

In sum, the common space method relies on two strong assumptions that are untenable across the fifty-some years analyzed in this book. First, it assumes that the voting patterns of members in the House are the same as their Senate behavior. Second, it assumes that civil rights and racial issues consistently made up half of the legislative agenda and the roll call record of the House and Senate. Together, these concerns raise serious doubts about the validity and reliability of measures based on common space coordinates for detecting bicameral differences during the postwar period. Both common space and W-NOMINATE ratings I used previously to measure bicameral distance are flawed measures for this purpose.

An Alternative Measure and Results

Establishing weaknesses in Chiou and Rothenberg's alternative measure does not answer the charge that my original results can be attributable to the choice of measures. To evaluate their broader claim, I devise an alternative measure of interchamber differences. If I could not replicate my original results, we would be right to question the robustness of my original analysis. As I show here and in chapter 4, however, substituting the new measure does not alter my original results: regardless of the measure used, bicameral conflict helps to shape the frequency of deadlock.

As I argue in chapter 4, a more valid and reliable measure of interchamber differences would control for the key charge against W-NOMINATE scores: that House and Senate members are not arrayed on a single ideological space and thus their overall voting records cannot be compared. This charge is akin to arguing that differences in the two chambers' floor agendas compromise comparisons of House and Senate behavior. The best solution to this problem is to isolate the set of policy issues on which both the House and Senate cast votes at roughly the same time. Up or down votes on conference reports provide precisely this set of votes.[23] Thus I assemble a database of every conference report brought to

Figure B-1. *Comparing Measures of Bicameral Differences, 1947–1970*

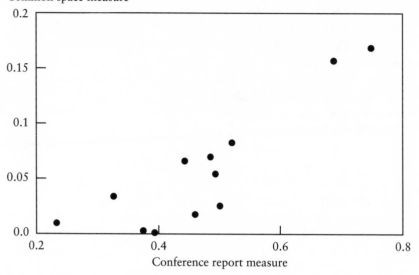

Common space measure

Conference report measure

the floor of both the House and Senate chambers between 1947 and 2000 and calculate the percentage of each chamber voting yea on each conference report. I can then measure the difference in policy views of the House and Senate median members by calculating the absolute difference between the two chambers' percentage approval for each report and averaging all reports for each Congress to produce a mean disagreement score by Congress.[24]

On average during the postwar period, the two chambers differ by 7 percentage points. Bicameral differences were smallest in the 84th Congress (1955–56), with the two chambers differing on average by only 2 percent; bicameral differences were greatest in the 95th (1977–78), 96th (1979–80), and 103d (1993–94) Congresses when the two chambers differed on average by 11 percent. Comparing the conference report measure of bicameral differences to the common space alternative is instructive. As shown in figure B-1, before the 1970s, the two series move in tandem with a correlation of .88. As shown in figure B-2, the two series show little relationship after 1970, and the correlation drops to –.43. This comparison confirms that common space coordinates are ill-suited for

Figure B-2. *Comparing Measures of Bicameral Differences, 1971–2000*

Common space measure

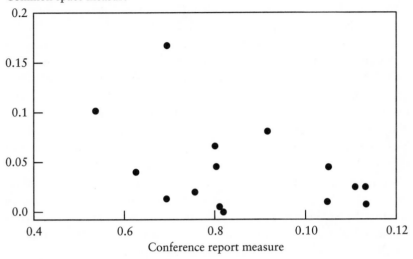

Conference report measure

detecting bicameral differences after the second dimension disappears after the 1960s.

In chapter 4, table 4-2, I used the new measure of bicameral differences in estimating the determinants of gridlock.[25] Substituting the new measure of House-Senate differences yields much different results than Chiou and Rothenberg lead us to expect.[26] Because I review the new results in detail in chapter 4, I limit my comments here to a few points relevant to Chiou and Rothenberg's argument. Although Chiou and Rothenberg find null results when the common space measure is used to tap bicameral conflict, using the more appropriate measure based on conference report votes yields considerable support for my conjectures. Of primary concern is the impact of House-Senate differences: the coefficient for bicameral differences reaches statistical significance in all of the five models. Even after accounting for the impact of elections through party control and partisan alignments, policy differences between the House and Senate still matter. The new analysis thus reconfirms my original conclusions: increasing polarization and strong bicameral disagreement drive up the frequency of deadlock.

Conclusions

Chiou and Rothenberg raise valuable questions about recent empirical work on the politics of gridlock. Given the reliance of many scholars on empirical estimates of legislators' ideologies, close scrutiny of measures is important. In this case, it is reasonable to raise doubts about using W-NOMINATE or common space coordinates to estimate bicameral differences. Both types of scores make comparisons of legislators' behavior over different sets of roll call votes, differences that make it difficult to place legislators along the same dimension. In contrast, the measure based on votes on conference reports that I use in this book overcomes the problem of differing agendas between the two chambers and thus offers a superior method of comparing policy views of the two chambers over time. My original empirical results are sustained regardless of whether W-NOMINATE scores or conference reports are used to detect bicameral differences, confirming that my perspective on intrabranch conflict and policy gridlock rests on a solid empirical foundation.

Appendix C
Alternative Specifications

Below are two alternative specifications of the gridlock model estimated in table 4-2. The first set of models (table C-1) shows the impact of an alternative way of operationalizing divided party control. The second set of models (table C-2) shows an alternative way of operationalizing public mood. Both specifications are discussed in chapter 4.

Table C-1. *Impact of Divided Government, Alternative Specification*

Variable	Gridlock 1	Gridlock 2	Gridlock 3	Gridlock 4	Gridlock 5
Quasi-divided government	.293 (.223)	.354 (.222)	.287 (.295)	.313 (.304)	.200 (.336)
Pure-divided government	.308 (.128)*	.443 (.125)**	.434 (.157)**	.435 (.161)**	.445 (.173)**
Partisan moderation	−.006 (.005)	−.013 (.005)**	−.013 (.006)*	-.016 (.006)**	−.015 (.006)*
Bicameral differences	5.828 (2.887)*	7.298 (2.855)**	10.800 (3.729)**	7.239 (3.771)*	7.929 (4.067)*
Time out of majority	.009 (.026)	−.011 (.026)	−.017 (.036)	-.054 (.037)	−.079 (.040)*
Budgetary situation	.005 (.009)	.010 (.010)	.021 (.013)	.014 (.013)	.015 (.015)
Public mood (lagged)	−.008 (.013)	−.002 (.012)	.002 (.016)	−.007 (.017)	−.016 (.018)
Constant	.126 (.894)	−.331 (.831)	−.754 (1.082)	.017 (1.096)	.425 (1.146)
N	24	24	24	24	24
F		2.39	4.76**	3.30*	3.00*	2.57*
Adjusted R^2	.298	.534	.412	.378	.324

Source: See text for tables in this appendix.

Note: Cell entries are weighted least squares logit estimates for grouped data (standard errors in parentheses). * $p < .05$, ** $p < .01$ (one-tailed t tests).

Table C-2. *Impact of Public Mood, Alternative Specification*

Variable	Gridlock 1	Gridlock 2	Gridlock 3	Gridlock 4	Gridlock 5
Divided government	.232 (.113)*	.338 (.117)**	.313 (.148)*	.333 (.145)*	.333 (.152)*
Partisan moderation	−.010 (.006)*	−.019 (.006)**	−.020 (.008)*	−.019 (.008)*	−.018 (.009)*
Bicameral differences	4.316 (2.630)*	5.415 (2.772)*	8.513 (3.571)*	4.874 (3.497)ᵃ	5.880 (3.661)ᵃ
Time out of majority	−.008 (.023)	−.034 (.026)ᵃ	−.047 (.035)*	−.080 (.035)*	−.100 (.037)**
Budgetary situation	−.002 (.006)	−.001 (.007)	.006 (.009)	.002 (.009)	.005 (.010)
Activist era	.120 (.166)	.199 (.172)	.259 (.215)	.085 (.214)	.111 (.228)
Constant	−.129 (.288)	−.206 (.288)	−.434 (.360)	−.227 (.353)	−.342 (.364)
N	27	27	27	27	27
F	2.51*	4.66**	3.05*	3.13*	2.82*
Adjusted R^2	.258	.458	.321	.329	.296

Note: Cell entries are weighted least squares logit estimates for grouped data (standard errors in parentheses). * $p < .05$, ** $p < .01$, ᵃ $p < .1$ (one-tailed t tests).

APPENDIX D

Comparison to Mayhew,
Divided We Govern

In this appendix I provide an explicit comparison of my
results with David Mayhew's 1991 analysis in *Divided We
Govern*.

Comparison of Dependent Variables
Mayhew uses a two-stage process to determine the number
of truly major laws enacted each Congress. His method
generates a total of 314 landmark laws enacted between
1947 and 2000. Notably, my method of using *Times* editorials to recover the legislative agenda for each of the
twenty-seven Congresses in that period captures over
90 percent of Mayhew's landmark laws; in ten of those
twenty-seven Congresses, the editorials discuss 100 percent
of the Mayhew laws. Of the fifteen landmark laws that
received no editorial mention by the *Times* between 1947
and 1986, eleven were identified by Mayhew from retrospective judgments of policy experts during his Sweep Two
(such evaluations were not yet available for the period after
1986 when Mayhew published his work). To some extent
then, our lists differ because of Mayhew's use of retrospec-

Table D-1. *Comparing the Correlates of Legislative Gridlock and Productivity, 1953–2000*

Variable	Gridlock 2 (Binder)	Number of laws enacted (Mayhew)
Divided government	.432***	−.977
	(.119)	(1.575)
Partisan moderation	−.013**	.276***
	(.004)	(.059)
Bicameral differences	(7.514**	8.867
	(2.739)	(35.320)
Time out of majority	−.009	.788
	(.025)	(.318)
Budgetary situation	.012	.111
	(.008)	(.101)
Public mood (lagged)	.001	.288*
	(.011)	(.147)
Constant	−.466	−13.384
	(.746)	(9.571)
N	24	24
F	5.81**	5.59**
Adjusted R^2	.556	.545

Source: See text.
Note: Cell entries in column 1 are weighted least squares logit estimates for grouped data (standard errors in parentheses). * $p < .05$, ** $p < .01$, *** $p < .001$, [a] $p < .1$ (one-tailed *t*-tests).

tive policy judgments. Still, the editorials do mention numerous laws identified by Mayhew during his Sweep Two, such as ratification of the Nuclear Nonproliferation Treaty in 1969, the National Forest Management Act of 1976, and the Job Training Partnership Act of 1982.

Comparison of Results

In column 1 of table D-1, I display the results from table 4-2 (using the results from table 4-2, column 2). This model estimates the impact of electoral and institutional forces on the frequency of deadlock (based on issues receiving two or more *Times* editorials in a Congress). In column 2 of table D-1, I substitute Mayhew's count of landmark laws per Congress as the dependent variable. This comparison allows us to determine whether the determinants of gridlock (failed issues as a proportion of the total number of issues on the agenda) differ significantly from the determinants of legislative productivity (the total number of landmark laws enacted).

Both models explain roughly 55 percent of the variance in the dependent variables. In the model predicting the number of landmark laws enacted, a number of results are noteworthy. First, extending the model through the 106th Congress (1999–2000) confirms Mayhew's finding that divided government does not affect the level of lawmaking. Second, the model shows support for the centrality of partisan polarization in shaping legislative performance: As legislators' moderation rises, more landmark laws are enacted.[1] Third, stronger party mandates lead to heavier legislative records, and a more activist public mood drives up legislative performance (as Mayhew argued). Fourth, and most important, bicameral conflict and divided government help to explain the frequency of issues stalemating in Congress but poorly explain successful legislative action.

This suggests that considering the broader universe of "potential enactments" significantly alters our view of legislative dynamics. Although divided party control of government, bicameral differences, and other factors may have little effect on the quantity of landmark laws enacted, these forces do significantly enhance the ability of legislators to block salient legislative proposals they oppose. The comparison of the two models suggests strongly that different dynamics underlie the blockage and passage of legislative measures.

APPENDIX E
Data for Replication

This appendix provides the data necessary for replicating the central analysis of the book (table 4-2; data can also be downloaded as a Stata 7.0 file from http://home .gwu.edu/~binder/replication.html).

Dependent Variable

The dependent variable presented in table E-1 shows the frequency of gridlock each Congress between 1947 and 2000. As explained in chapter 3, the frequency of gridlock is calculated as the number of failed agenda items each Congress divided by the total number of issues on the agenda each Congress. Because the equations in table 4-2 are estimated as grouped logit models, I also provide the component parts of the gridlock variable necessary for estimating the models (table E-2). I provide the gridlock data for each of five levels of policy salience, ranging from gridlock 1 (includes the widest range of issues) to gridlock 5 (includes only the most salient issues). I discuss in detail the method of determining issue salience in chapters 3 and 4 and appendix A.

Table E-1. *Frequency of Gridlock, 80th–106th Congresses*

Congress	Gridlock 1	Gridlock 2	Gridlock 3	Gridlock 4	Gridlock 5
80th (1947–48)	42.86	32.5	28.57	26.09	26.32
81st (1949–50)	52	44.68	41.18	37.04	39.13
82d (1951–52)	49.18	37.84	33.33	40	33.33
83d (1953–54)	45.16	43.9	36	35	35.29
84th (1955–56)	56	50	46.43	47.83	52.63
85th (1957–58)	45.78	40.82	36.36	36	35
86th (1959–60)	46.77	40	40.91	47.37	35.71
87th (1961–62)	45.83	38.89	36.73	40.54	35.71
88th (1963–64)	46.07	40.82	36.67	27.27	22.22
89th (1965–66)	34.88	31.91	35	28.57	35
90th (1967–68)	49.07	33.93	34.21	31.25	30.43
91st (1969–70)	49.61	45.33	44	38.46	34.38
92d (1971–72)	56.8	48.65	42	38.89	44.83
93d (1973–74)	44.17	37.84	38.78	43.24	45.16
94th (1975–76)	57.6	51.67	46.51	42.42	36.84
95th (1977–78)	40.58	34.18	32	29.41	34.78
96th (1979–80)	58.91	49.28	54.55	51.61	46.15
97th (1981–82)	57.26	55	51.43	56	50
98th (1983–84)	57.69	47.06	43.59	44.83	45
99th (1985–86)	52.48	47.27	35.48	33.33	30.77
100th (1987–88)	57.36	51.79	42.86	41.67	26.67
101st (1989–90)	42.5	42.55	35.71	36.84	41.18
102d (1991–92)	60.55	64	69.7	65.22	68.75
103d (1993–94)	57.69	58.33	56	56.25	54.55
104th (1995–96)	58.88	54.17	52	42.11	33.33
105th (1997–98)	65.09	61.54	60.87	60	60
106th (1999–2000)	63.25	71.8	80	71.43	70

Source: See text for tables in this appendix.

Independent Variables

The explanatory variables for the analysis are included in table E-3. The variables are as follows. Details on measurement are discussed in the text of chapter 4.

—Column 1: Congress number;

—Column 2: Dichotomous variable indicating unified or divided party government;

Table E-2. Number of Failed and Total Agenda Issues in Each Congress

	Gridlock 1		Gridlock 2		Gridlock 3		Gridlock 4		Gridlock 5	
	Failed	Total	Failed	Total	Failed	Total	Failed	Total	Failed	Total
80th	33	77	13	40	8	28	6	23	5	19
81st	39	75	21	47	14	34	10	27	9	23
82d	30	61	14	37	9	27	8	20	5	15
83d	28	62	18	41	9	25	7	20	6	17
84th	42	75	22	44	13	28	11	23	10	19
85th	38	83	20	49	12	33	9	25	7	20
86th	29	62	14	35	9	22	9	19	5	14
87th	55	120	28	72	18	49	15	37	10	28
88th	41	89	20	49	11	30	6	22	4	18
89th	30	86	15	47	14	40	8	28	7	20
90th	53	108	19	56	13	38	10	32	7	23
91st	64	129	34	75	22	50	15	39	11	32
92d	71	125	36	74	21	50	14	36	13	29
93d	53	120	28	74	19	49	16	37	14	31
94th	72	125	31	60	20	43	14	33	7	19
95th	56	138	27	79	16	50	10	34	8	23
96th	76	129	34	69	24	44	16	31	12	26
97th	67	117	33	60	18	35	14	25	8	16
98th	75	130	32	68	17	39	13	29	9	20
99th	74	141	26	55	11	31	6	18	4	13
100th	74	129	29	56	12	28	10	24	4	15
101st	51	120	20	47	10	28	7	19	7	17
102d	66	109	32	50	23	33	15	23	11	16
103d	45	78	21	36	14	25	9	16	6	11
104th	63	107	26	48	13	25	8	19	5	15
105th	69	106	24	39	14	23	9	15	6	10
106th	74	120	28	39	16	20	10	14	7	10

Table E-3. Explanatory Variables

Congress	Party control	Moderation	Bicameral differences	Party mandate	Budgetary situation	Public mood (lagged)
80th	Divided	13.55457	.0458492	7.5	25.64	.
81st	Unified	26.84522	.0441141	1	−2.92	.
82d	Unified	36.28793	.037384	0	5.59	.
83d	Unified	21.01035	.0500065	2	−5.08	50.7
84th	Divided	17.35537	.0232398	1	.61	54.09
85th	Divided	33.04635	.0392357	0	.55	59.4
86th	Divided	32.88646	.0325372	0	−6.81	63.22
87th	Unified	35.64632	.0484777	0	−5.05	65.24
88th	Unified	39.33174	.0746793	0	−4.63	69.78
89th	Unified	35.27684	.0492815	0	−1.97	65.21
90th	Unified	45.68549	.0685734	0	−9.81	62.91
91st	Divided	53.6116	.0519875	0	.06	63.59
92d	Divided	55.09127	.0624868	0	−10.55	60.13
93d	Divided	48.95611	.0535795	0	−4.18	60.77
94th	Divided	45.4786	.0809884	0	−17.93	58.61
95th	Unified	44.55386	.1132298	0	−13.01	55.6
96th	Unified	35.74067	.1108192	0	−10.29	53.77
97th	Divided	29.49153	.0756016	0	−14.4	52.47
98th	Divided	26.84457	.0916699	0	−23.74	54.33
99th	Divided	25.23659	.0802183	0	−22.39	59.29
100th	Divided	21.275571	.0692127	1.5	−14.75	60.18
101st	Divided	25.55219	.0817081	0	−15.49	62.89
102d	Divided	17.5216	.1046876	0	−20.68	65.9
103d	Unified	12.45326	.1130351	0	−16.01	66.31
104th	Divided	8.762393	.0695045	12	−8.86	63.34
105th	Divided	7.440328	.1048438	0	1.41	63.61
106th	Divided	8.153021	.0802124	0	10.27	60.54

—Column 3: Degree of partisan moderation (number of moderates divided by distance between party medians), average of House and Senate series;

—Column 4: Bicameral disagreement (percentage difference in voting yea on conference reports voted on by both chambers);

—Column 5: Party mandate (average number of Congresses out of the majority when a new majority gains control of both chambers of Congress);

—Column 6: Budgetary situation (surplus or deficit/total federal outlays); and

—Column 7: Stimson policy mood indicator (lagged one Congress).

Notes

Chapter One

1. See William Safire, *Safire's New Political Dictionary* (Random House, 1993), p. 305. Safire identifies the political origins of gridlock in the *Chicago Sun-Times* following the 1980 elections: "The instant analysis of election night raised the possibility of political gridlock, a government unable to function because of the division between the Republican President-Senate and the Democratic House of Representatives."

2. *Federalist* 1, in Garry Wills, ed., *The Federalist Papers by Alexander Hamilton, James Madison, and John Jay* (Bantam Books, 1982). (Hereafter *The Federalist Papers*.)

3. James L. Sundquist, "Needed: A Political Theory for the New Era of Coalition Government in the United States," *Political Science Quarterly*, vol. 103 (Winter 1988–89), pp. 613–35, citation p. 629.

4. "The Hollow Branch," *Washington Post*, August 26, 1994, editorial, p. A24.

5. For a classic statement of the effects of divided government, see V. O. Key Jr., *Politics, Parties, and Pressure Groups*, 5th ed. (Crowell, 1964). More recently, studies showing a significant impact of divided party control on legislative performance include John J. Coleman, "Unified Government, Divided Government,

and Party Responsiveness," *American Political Science Review,* vol. 93, no. 4 (December 1999), pp. 821–35; George C. Edwards III, Andrew Barrett, and Jeffrey Peake, "The Legislative Impact of Divided Government," *American Journal of Political Science,* vol. 41 (April 1997), pp. 545–63; William Howell, Scott Adler, Charles Cameron, and Charles Riemann, "Divided Government and the Legislative Productivity of Congress, 1945–94," *Legislative Studies Quarterly,* vol. 25, no. 2 (May 2000), pp. 285–312; Sean Q. Kelly, "Divided We Govern? A Reassessment: The Effect of Unified vs. Divided Government," *Polity,* vol. 25 (Spring 1993), pp. 475–84; Bruce I. Oppenheimer, "The Importance of Elections in a Strong Congressional Party Era," in Benjamin Ginsberg and Alan Stone, eds., *Do Elections Matter?,* 3d ed. (M. E. Sharpe, 1996); Paul J. Quirk and Bruce Nesmith, "Divided Government and Policy Making: Negotiating the Laws," in Michael Nelson, ed., *The Presidency and the Political System,* 5th ed. (Washington: Congressional Quarterly Press, 1998); Sundquist, "Needed," pp. 613–35; Gregory Thorson, "Divided Government and the Passage of Partisan Legislation, 1947–1990," *Political Research Quarterly,* vol. 51 (September 1998), pp. 751–64.

6. See David Mayhew, *Divided We Govern: Party Control, Lawmaking, and Investigations, 1946–1990* (Yale University Press, 1991); David W. Brady and Craig Volden, *Revolving Gridlock: Politics and Policy from Carter to Clinton* (Westview Press, 1998); and Keith Krehbiel, *Pivotal Politics: A Theory of U.S. Lawmaking* (University of Chicago Press, 1998).

7. See Charles O. Jones, "A Way of Life and Law," *American Political Science Review,* vol. 89, no. 1 (March 1995), pp. 1–9. As evidence, Jones notes that the *Handbook of Legislative Research* includes sixteen chapters, none of which explicitly addresses lawmaking. Instead, the chapters are devoted to elections, voting, committees, leadership, and so on. See Gerhard Loewenberg, Samuel C. Patterson, Malcolm E. Jewell, eds., *Handbook of Legislative Research* (Harvard University Press, 1985).

8. Jones, "A Way of Life and Law," p. 1.

9. Ibid., p. 1.

10. Some might attribute the maxim to Henry David Thoreau. See *Bartlett's Familiar Quoations* (Internet).

11. Safire, *Safire's New Political Dictionary,* p. 305.

12. Bill Frenzel, "The System Is Self-Correcting," in James L. Sundquist, ed., *Back to Gridlock? Governance in the Clinton Years* (Brookings, 1995), p. 105.

13. Frenzel, "The System Is Self-Correcting," p. 105.

14. Robert Shogan, *The Fate of the Union* (Westview Press, 1998), p. 5.

15. James MacGregor Burns, *The Deadlock of Democracy: Four-Party Politics in America* (Prentice-Hall, Inc., 1963), p. 6.

16. Burns, *The Deadlock of Democracy,* p. 22.

17. Jones, "A Way of Life and Law," quotation on p. 3.

18. James A. Morone, *The Democratic Wish: Popular Participation and the Limits of American Government*, rev. ed. (Yale University Press, 1998), p. 336.

19. There is no shortage of work on the political and intellectual currents leading to the Constitutional Convention. For comprehensive treatments see, among others, Terence Ball and J. G. A. Pocock, eds., *Conceptual Change and the Constitution* (University Press of Kansas, 1988); Lance Banning, *The Sacred Fire of Liberty: James Madison and the Founding of the Federal Republic* (Cornell University Press, 1995); Forrest McDonald, *Novus Ordo Seclorum: The Intellectual Origins of the Constitution* (University of Kansas Press, 1985); Jack N. Rakove, *Original Meanings: Politics and Ideas in the Making of the Constitution* (Knopf, 1996), and Gordon S. Wood, *The Creation of the American Republic, 1776–1787* (W. W. Norton, 1969). On the institutional dilemmas engendered by the structure of the Confederational Congress, see Calvin C. Jillson and Rick K. Wilson, *Congressional Dynamics: Structure, Coordination, and Choice in the First American Congress, 1774–1789* (Stanford University Press, 1994).

20. See Rakove, *Original Meanings*, chaps. 1, 2.

21. John R. Roche, "The Founding Fathers: A Reform Caucus in Action," *American Political Science Review*, vol. 55, no. 4 (December, 1961); Isaac Kramnick, *Introduction to the Federalist Papers, By Alexander Hamilton, John Jay, and James Madison* (Penguin Books, 1987); and Frances E. Lee and Bruce Oppenheimer, *Sizing Up the Senate* (University of Chicago Press, 1999), chap. 2.

22. *Federalist 1*, in Wills, *The Federalist Papers*, p. 4.

23. Lee and Oppenheimer, *Sizing Up the Senate*, p. 38. Lee and Oppenheimer's reasoning is rooted in a range of earlier works, including Lance G. Banning, "The Constitutional Convention," in Leonard W. Levy and Dennis J. Mahoney, eds., *The Framing and Ratification of the Constitution* (Macmillan, 1987), Kramnick, *Introduction to the Federalist Papers*, and Roche, "The Founding Fathers: A Reform Caucus in Action."

24. Lee and Oppenheimer, *Sizing Up the Senate*, p. 38.

25. Max Farrand, ed. *The Records of the Federal Convention of 1787* (Yale University Press, 1966), vol. 1, p. 201.

26. Clinton Rossiter, *Parties and Politics in America* (Cornell University Press, 1960), as cited in Sundquist, "Needed: A Political Theory for the New Era of Coalition Government in the United States," p. 620.

27. *Federalist 51*, in Wills, *The Federalist Papers*, p. 262.

28. Wood, *Creation of the American Republic*, p. 157.

29. Similar interpretations of the separation of powers have been suggested by Louis Fisher, *President and Congress; Power and Policy* (Free Press, 1972), chap. 1 and appendix; and Hugh Heclo, "What Has Happened to the Separation of Powers?" in Bradford P. Wilson and Peter W. Schramm, eds., *Separation of Powers and Good Government* (Rowman and Littlefield, 1994); Michael Malbin, "Was Divided Government Really Such a Big Problem?" in Wilson and

Schramm, eds., *Separation of Powers and Good Government;* and Garry Wills, *A Necessary Evil: A History of American Distrust of Government* (Simon and Schuster, 1999).

30. The Hamilton and Jefferson quotes appear in Joseph M. Bessette, *The Mild Voice of Reason: Deliberative Democracy and American National Government* (University of Chicago Press, 1994), pp. 16–17.

31. Samuel Kernell, "The True Principles of Republican Government: Reassessing James Madison's Political Science," in Samuel Kernell, ed., *James Madison: The Theory and Practice of Republican Government* (Stanford University Press, forthcoming).

32. The following is drawn primarily from Kernell, "The True Principles of Republican Government."

33. On the preferences of a large majority of the framers for a strong nationalist government, see also William H. Riker, *The Strategy of Rhetoric: Campaigning for the American Constitution* (Yale University Press, 1996).

34. Not until 1806 was the "previous question motion" eliminated in the Senate, a rule that could have been used by a simple majority to cut off debate. That rule change made possible unlimited debate, or the filibuster as it became to be known later in the nineteenth century. On the origins of the filibuster, see Sarah A. Binder and Steven S. Smith, *Politics or Principle? Filibustering in the United States Senate* (Brookings, 1997).

35. *Federalist* 58, in Wills, *The Federalist Papers,* p. 298.

36. *Federalist* 22, ibid., p. 107.

37. Kernell, "The True Principles of Republican Government."

Chapter Two

1. James Sundquist, "Needed: A Political Theory for the New Era of Coalition Government in the United States," *Political Science Quarterly,* vol. 103 (Winter 1988–89), p. 620.

2. Robert Shogan, *The Fate of the Union: America's Rocky Road to Political Stalemate* (Westview Press, 1998), p. 5. An alternative interpretation of the separation of powers is offered by Robert E. Goodin, who argues that the separation of powers encourages "least-common-denominator" policy compromises, legislative outcomes that meet a limited notion of the public's interest. See Goodin, "Institutionalizing the Public Interest: The Defense of Deadlock and Beyond," *American Political Science Review,* vol. 90 (June 1996), pp. 331–43, especially p. 333.

3. See Sarah A. Binder and Steven S. Smith, *Politics or Principle? Filibustering in the United States Senate* (Brookings, 1997), pp. 37–39

4. Charles O. Jones, "A Way of Life and Law," *American Political Science Review,* vol. 89, no. 1 (March 1995), p. 3.

5. Edward McChesney Sait, *Political Institutions: A Preface* (New York: Appleton-Century-Crofts, 1938), p. 529.

6. See, among others, Sarah A. Binder, *Minority Rights, Majority Rule: Partisanship and the Development of Congress* (Cambridge University Press, 1997); Joseph Cooper, *Congress and Its Committees: A Historical Approach to the Role of Committees in the Legislative Process* (Garland Publishers, 1980 [1960]); Joseph Cooper and Cheryl Young, "Bill Introduction in the Nineteenth Century: A Study of Institutional Change, *Legislative Studies Quarterly,* vol. 14 (February 1989), pp. 67–105; Douglas Dion, *Turning the Legislative Thumbscrew: Minority Rights and Procedural Change in Legislative Politics* (University of Michigan Press, 1997); Gerald Gamm and Kenneth Shepsle, "Emergence of Legislative Institutions: Standing Committees in the House and Senate, 1810–1825," *Legislative Studies Quarterly,* vol. 14 (March 1996), pp. 39–66; Jonathan N. Katz and Brian R. Sala, "Careerism, Committee Assignments, and the Electoral Connection," *American Political Science Review,* vol. 90 (March 1996), pp. 21–33; Nelson W. Polsby, "The Institutionalization of the U.S. House of Representatives," *American Political Science Review,* vol. 62 (March 1968), pp. 144–68; and Gerald Gamm and Steven S. Smith, "The Senate without Leaders: Senate Parties in the Mid-19th Century," paper presented at the annual meeting of the American Political Science Association, 2001.

7. See Gordon S. Wood, *The Creation of the American Republic, 1776–1787* (University of North Carolina Press, 1969), p. 449.

8. See Frances E. Lee and Bruce I. Oppenheimer, *Sizing Up the Senate* (University of Chicago Press, 1999), especially chap. 2.

9. Examples of recent work explicitly modeling inter-branch dynamics as a function of a unicameral legislature facing a single executive include Charles M. Cameron, *Veto Bargaining* (Cambridge University Press, 2000); David Epstein and Sharyn O'Halloran, *Delegating Powers: A Transaction on Cost Politics Approach to Policy Making under Separate Powers* (Cambridge University Press, 1999); and Keith Krehbiel, *Pivotal Politics: A Theory of U.S. Lawmaking* (University of Chicago Press, 1998).

10. This section draws largely from Lee and Oppenheimer's recent exploration of constitutional choices affecting the structure of the Senate in *Sizing Up the Senate*, chap. 2.

11. See James G. March and Johan P. Olsen, *Rediscovering Institutions: The Organizational Basis of Politics* (Free Press, 1989), p. 18.

12. Gary Wills, ed., *The Federalist Papers by Alexander Hamilton, James Madison, and John Jay* (Bantam Books, 1982), p. 315. (Hereafter *The Federalist Papers.)*

13. James Madison, in Max Farrand, ed., *The Records of the Federal Convention of 1787*, vol. 1 (Yale University Press, 1966), p. 151.

14. Lee and Oppenheimer make this argument forcefully in *Sizing Up the Senate*, chap. 2.

15. On the origins of the Senate, see Elaine K. Swift, *The Making of an American Senate: Reconstitutive Change in Congress, 1787–1841* (University of Michigan Press, 1996).

16. Daniel Wirls offers a different characterization of the early Senate's workload, emphasizing the Senate's heavy load of nominations and foreign policy issues. See "The Institutionalization of the Early Senate," paper delivered at the annual meeting of the American Political Science Association, 2002. Both our accounts suggest a rapid transformation of the Senate into a pro-active upper chamber.

17. This figure compares House-originated measures to Senate-originated measures, as compiled in Sarah A. Binder, "Partisanship and Procedural Choice: Institutional Change in the Early Congress, 1789–1823," *Journal of Politics*, vol. 57 (November 1995), pp. 1093–118, especially p. 1113.

18. These trends are discussed in Binder and Smith, *Politics or Principle?* chap. 2; and Swift, *The Making of an American Senate*, chap. 5.

19. On the early transformation of the Senate, see in particular the account offered by Swift, *The Making of an American Senate*. See also Binder and Smith, *Politics or Principle?* chaps. 2 and 3.

20. Swift, *The Making of an American Senate*, p. 117.

21. See Lee and Oppenheimer, *Sizing Up the Senate*, on the effects of Senate malapportionment on policy content.

22. On the impact of agenda control on policy outcomes, see Richard McKelvey, "Intransitives in Multidimensional Voting Models and Some Implications for Agenda Control," *Journal of Economic Theory*, vol. 12 (June 1976), pp. 472–82.

23. See George Tsebelis and Jeannette Money, *Bicameralism* (Cambridge University Press, 1997); and George Tsebelis, "Decision Making in Political Systems: Veto Players in Presidentialism, Parliamentarism, Multicameralism and Multipartyism," *British Journal of Political Science*, vol. 25 (July 1995), pp. 289–325. See also Thomas H. Hammond and Gary J. Miller, "The Core of the Constitution," *American Political Science Review*, vol. 81 (December 1987), pp. 1155–74; and William H. Riker, "The Justification of Bicameralism," *International Political Science Review*, vol. 13 (January 1992), pp. 101–16.

24. See George Tsebelis, *Veto Players: How Political Institutions Work* (Princeton University Press, 2002); and Tsebelis and Money, *Bicameralism*, p. 74.

25. On the emergence of political parties, despite framers' antipathy toward them, see, among others, John Aldrich, *Why Parties?* (University of Chicago Press, 1995); Richard Hofstadter, *The Idea of a Party System: The Rise of Legitimate Oppostion in the United States, 1780–1840* (University of California Press, 1969); and Joel H. Silbey, *The American Political Nation, 1838–1893* (Stanford University Press, 1991).

26. For an overview of the emergence of party leadership in both the House and the Senate, see Gerald H. Gamm and Steven S. Smith, "The Dynamics of Party Government in Congress," in Lawrence C. Dodd and Bruce I. Oppenheimer, eds., *Congress Reconsidered*, 7th ed. (Washington: Congressional Quarterly Press, 2001).

27. "Mr. Cleveland's Cabinet," in R. S. Baker and W. E. Dodd, eds., *The Public Papers of Woodrow Wilson: College and State*, vol. 1 (Harper and Brothers, 1925), pp. 221–22, as cited in Austin Ranney, *The Doctrine of Responsible Party Government: Its Origins and Present State* (University of Illinois Press, 1954), pp. 31–32.

28. E. E. Schattschneider, *Party Government* (Holt, Rinehart, and Winston, 1942), p. 1.

29. Sundquist, "Needed," pp. 613–35, especially p. 614.

30. For a careful delineation of what party theorists meant by responsive government, and thus the relevance of unified party control, see John J. Coleman, "Unified Government, Divided Government, and Party Responsiveness," *American Political Science Review*, vol. 93 (December 1999), pp. 821–35.

31. V. O. Key Jr., *Politics, Parties, and Pressure Groups*, 5th ed. (Thomas Y. Crowell Company, 1964), p. 688.

32. The argument is summarized and critiqued in Morris Fiorina, *Divided Government*, 2d ed. (Allyn and Bacon, 1996), chap. 6.

33. For details, see David Mayhew, *Divided We Govern: Party Control, Lawmaking, and Investigations, 1946–1990* (Yale University Press, 1991), chap. 3.

34. Either a contemporary or a retrospective judgment of significance was sufficient for a law to be included on the final list. For an alternative approach, see Sean Q. Kelly, "Divided We Govern? A Reassessment," *Polity*, vol. 25 (Spring 1993), pp. 475–84. Mayhew has subsequently extended his series through 2000; see http://pantheon.yale.edu/~dmayhew/data3.html.

35. See, in particular, Mayhew's conclusion in *Divided We Govern*, chap. 7.

36. Mayhew, *Divided We Govern*, p. 199.

37. The scores used here are dubbed DW-NOMINATE and were developed by Nolan M. McCarty, Keith T. Poole, and Howard Rosenthal, *Income Redistribution and the Realignment of American Politics*, AEI Studies on Understanding Economic Inequality (Washington: AEI Press, 1997). Figures 2-1 and 2-2 are density plots, which are essentially smoothed histograms. They can be read as if they were histograms: the higher the plot, the greater the number of members assigned that ideological score.

38. The four Democrats are Gene Taylor of Mississippi, Jim Traficant of Ohio, Ralph Hall of Texas, and Virgil Goode of Virginia. Goode left the Democratic Party in January of 2000 to become an independent and subsequently decided to join the Republican conference and eventually switched parties. See online update to the *Almanac of American Politics 2000* (Washington: National Journal, 1999), pp. 1649–51.

39. John B. Gilmour, *Strategic Disagreement: Stalemate in American Politics* (University of Pittsburgh Press, 1995).

40. See Gary C. Jacobson, "Party Polarization in National Politics: The Electoral Connection," in Jon R. Bond and Richard Fleisher, eds., *Polarized Politics* (Washington: Congressional Quarterly Press, 2000). Jacobson defines activist constituencies as voters who engage in at least two political acts during a campaign (such as putting a bumper sticker on a car, donating money to a campaign, and so on), p. 22.

41. Michael Grunwald, "Gephardt's Tireless Quest: Put Democrats Atop House," *Washington Post*, July 12, 1999, p. A1.

42. See R. Douglas Arnold, *The Logic of Congressional Action* (Yale University Press, 1990); Mayhew, *Divided We Govern*; and Krehbiel, *Pivotal Politics*. See also David W. Brady and Craig Volden, *Revolving Gridlock* (Westview Press, 1998), pp. 25–26, for a discussion of the relationship between polarization and gridlock. Polarization in their account, however, is technically nonpartisan, as it is measured as the distance between the left-side "filibuster pivot" (the forty-first senator, along an assumed left-right dimension) and the right-side "veto pivot" (the sixty-seventh Senate or House member, again along an underlying left-right continuum) (p. 17).

43. See Coleman's discussion in "Unified Government, Divided Government, and Party Responsiveness."

44. See Jacobson, "Party Polarization in National Politics: The Electoral Connection," p. 29.

45. "Eightieth Congress: To Date," editorial, *New York Times*, June 20, 1948, p. E8.

46. There is, however, a countervailing force that works against policy success. A new, inexperienced majority may also face the countervailing difficulty of "learning to govern," lacking legislators with the pragmatism and experience necessary to master lawmaking in a complex congressional environment. See Richard F. Fenno Jr., *Learning to Govern: An Institutional View of the 104th Congress* (Brookings, 1997).

47. On the dueling responses to budget surpluses, see Charles Babington and Eric Pianin, "Clinton, Hill Leaders Agree on Budget Goals," *Washington Post*, July 13, 1999, p. A1.

48. Roger H. Davidson, "The Presidency and Congressional Time," in James A. Thurber, ed., *Rivals for Power* (Washington: Congressional Quarterly Press, 1996), p. 34.

49. See Mayhew's extensive discussion in *Divided We Govern*, chap. 6.

50. Arthur M. Schlesinger Jr., *The Cycles of American History* (Houghton Mifflin Company, 1986); Samuel P. Huntington, *American Politics: The Promise of Disharmony* (Harvard University Press, 1981).

51. Mayhew, *Divided We Govern*, p. 160.

52. John W. Kingdon, *Agendas, Alternatives, and Public Policies* (Little, Brown, 1984), p. 153.

53. See James A. Stimson, Michael B. MacKuen, and Robert S. Erikson, "Dynamic Representation," *American Political Science Review*, vol. 89 (September 1995), p. 548.

54. Ibid., p. 544.

55. Jonathan Rauch, *Demosclerosis: The Silent Killer of American Government* (Times Books, 1994).

56. See Jeffrey M. Berry, "Interest Groups and Gridlock," paper presented at the annual meeting of the American Political Science Association, Boston, 1998.

57. Such an informational theory of groups is presented in John R. Wright, *Interest Groups and Congress: Lobbying, Contributions, and Influence* (Allyn and Bacon, 1996).

58. Berry, "Interest Groups and Gridlock."

59. On the influence of the president, the media, and Congress on the construction of the agenda, see B. Dan Wood and Jeffrey S. Peake, "The Dynamics of Foreign Policy Agenda Setting," *American Political Science Review*, vol. 92 (March 1998), pp. 173–84; and George C. Edwards III and B. Dan Wood, "Who Influences Whom? The President, Congress, and the Media," *American Political Science Review*, vol. 93 (June 1999), pp. 327–44.

60. James MacGregor Burns, *The Deadlock of Democracy: Four-Party Politics in America* (Prentice-Hall, 1963), p. 6.

61. On the relevance of uncertainty to legislative organization, see Keith Krehbiel, *Information and Legislative Organization* (University of Michigan Press, 1991).

62. Both organizational and rational choice theories leave room for viewing institutions as endogenous. No single cite does justice to the literature, but for applications in a political context see Cooper and Young, "Bill Introduction in the Nineteenth Century"; and Aldrich, *Why Parties?*

Chapter Three

1. David R. Mayhew, *Divided We Govern: Party Control, Lawmaking, and Investigations, 1946–1990* (Yale University Press, 1991), table 4-1, pp. 58–59.

2. Charles O. Jones, *The Presidency in a Separated System* (Brookings, 1994), p. 196.

3. Mayhew, *Divided We Govern*, p. 34.

4. "The Sluggish 91st," editorial, *New York Times*, August 14, 1969, p. 34.

5. Mayhew, *Divided We Govern*, pp. 35–36.

6. Morris Fiorina, *Divided Government*, 2d ed. (Allyn and Bacon, 1996), p. 89. Emphasis in original.

7. John W. Kingdon, *Agendas, Alternatives, and Public Policies* (Little, Brown, 1984), p. 3.

8. Roger W. Cobb and Charles D. Elder, *Participation in American Politics: The Dynamics of Agenda-Building*, 2d ed. (Johns Hopkins University Press, 1983), p. 85.

9. Focusing on "agendas" rather than "public demands" is preferable because of the inherent difficulty of determining what constitutes a demand. Paul J. Quirk and Bruce Nesmith define deadlock as "a failure to act, for whatever the reason, in the face of a pressing need or demand for action"; Quirk and Nesmith, "Explaining Deadlock: Domestic Policy Making in the Bush Presidency," in Lawrence C. Dodd and Calvin Jillson, eds., *New Perspectives on American Politics* (Washington: Congressional Quarterly Press, 1994), p. 192. However, they also recognize that it is difficult to determine demand in face of "countervailing demands or interests of comparable magnitude" that may in fact be served by the status quo (p. 209n). Moreover, it is not clear that public demand exists independently of the policy process and media coverage of such activity. On the interplay of public opinion, media coverage, and political activity, see, among others, Shanto Iyengar and Donald R. Kinder, *News That Matters: Television and American Opinion* (University of Chicago Press, 1987).

10. In recent decades, the *New York Times* is widely considered as espousing relatively liberal views, but because the editorials both support and oppose issues, there is no need to balance the data with information from a more conservative newspaper, such as the *Wall Street Journal*. A regional newspaper such as the *Chicago Tribune* (also considered conservative) was also not a viable option: its attention to national issues competes with coverage of local, state, and regional issues to a much greater extent than is the case for the *Times,* and its decisions about which national issues to cover are often strongly shaped by regional considerations (interview with N. Don Wycliff, *Chicago Tribune* editorial page editor, Chicago, April 23, 1998). Moreover, Benjamin Page suggests that the *New York Times* is an agenda setter for other media outlets; Page, *Who Deliberates? Mass Media in Modern Democracy* (University of Chicago Press, 1996). Finally, the *Washington Post* proved unusable because it is so tightly focused on the daily life of Congress that almost no legislative activity escapes its notice. In 1997, for example, the *Washington Post* ran nearly 900 editorials mentioning Congress, the House or the Senate; in contrast, the *New York Times* ran about 500.

11. I make no claim that the agendas generated from the editorials are entirely independent of politics on Capitol Hill. Timothy E. Cook and others have observed that "the political agenda is set not by the media by themselves or by the members [of Congress] by themselves but by the two sides, whether working together or in competition"; Cook, *Governing with the News: The News Media as a Political Institution* (University of Chicago Press, 1998), p. 13. But neither do

agendas derived from editorials simply reflect the political interests of presidents and legislators. Neither presidents nor legislators can dictate the issues addressed by the *New York Times*.

12. Personal conversation, Washington, D.C., April 3, 1998.

13. Phone interview with Steven R. Weisman, member of the *New York Times* editorial board, Washington, D.C., April 1, 1998.

14. Both cites are from Mayhew, *Divided We Govern*, pp. 35–36.

15. Interview with Wycliff, Chicago, April 23, 1998.

16. The peak in the 99th Congress seems to result from a higher than average appearance of certain types of policy issues on the pages of the *Times* in 1985 and 1986. The *Times* editorialized more frequently than normal on energy and public lands issues and voiced opinion on a larger than usual number of executive and judicial nominations pending before the Senate.

17. Many issues reappear on the pages of the *Times* across several Congresses, so that the 3,152 count of agenda items is not a count of the number of *different* issues discussed by the *Times* over the fifty-four-year period. For example, the *Times* editorialized about motor voter registration in three different Congresses: the 101st and 102d (when the issue was mired in gridlock) and the 103rd (when it was enacted into law). In the count of 3152 issues, motor voter registration appears three times.

18. Mayhew, *Divided We Govern*, p. 41.

19. The editorials also pick up important regulatory statutes enacted during the early 1970s that Mayhew notes his method misses. Of the seven such laws mentioned by Mayhew, the editorials picked up five. See David Mayhew, "Let's Stick with the Longer List," *Polity*, vol. 25 (1993), pp. 485–88.

20. George C. Edwards III, Andrew Barrett, and Jeffrey Peake, "The Legislative Impact of Divided Government," *American Journal of Political Science*, vol. 41 (April 1997), p. 551.

21. "A Retrograde Congress," editorial, *Washington Post*, October 11, 1998, p. C6.

22. The *Washington Post*'s assessment again helps to establish the reliability of the *Times* editorials as a means of measuring gridlock. As a reporter observed at the close of the 102d Congress, "When the final gavel fell Friday, Congress left behind one of the thinnest records of legislative achievement within memory. . . . Lawmakers brought a heavy load of legislation on a wide variety of issues to the verge of enactment, only to be thwarted by Republican filibusters . . . or by presidential vetoes that could not be overridden"; Helen Dewar, "Between Gulf War and Political Sniping, Legislative Casualties; 102d Congress Often Was Thwarted," *Washington Post*, October 11, 1992, p. A33.

23. Any threshold of "salience" might be chosen for any number of reasons. My goal is simply to select a cutoff point that yields a data series most proximate to Mayhew's for comparability purposes. Mayhew's series runs from a low of

five to a high of twenty-two landmark laws enacted. By selecting those issues on which the *Times* wrote four or more editorials, the number of issues on the agenda enacted into law ranges from four to twenty-four. In the statistical analysis in chapter 4, I use multiple thresholds of editorials to ensure that my results are not an artifact of the salience filter chosen. Discussion of the salience filter appears in appendix A.

24. With typical bravado and remarkable foresight (just a mere percentage point off), Lyndon Johnson predicted in 1964 that "when the record of this [88th] Congress is completed, it will place the 88th Congress in the record books as the most constructive in the twentieth century"; "'Salute' to Congress," *New York Times*, August 20, 1964. Although President Harry Truman calls the 80th Congress the "do nothing" Congress, David McCullough, in his 1992 biography of Truman, argues that the legislative record of the 80th suggests otherwise. Legislation passed included the Marshall Plan, National Security Act, Taft-Hartley Labor Act, Reciprocal Trade Agreements, and Selective Service Reform. See David McCullough, *Truman* (Simon and Schuster, 1992), p. 696.

25. In figure 3-4 I show a measure of productivity (number of enactments divided by the total number of issues on the agenda), rather than a measure of gridlock (failures divided by total number of issues). (Productivity is simply 100 minus percent gridlock in each Congress.) I do this for purposes of comparability to Mayhew's measure. The comparison is thus between enactments and enactments as a proportion of the agenda. In the figure, I rescale the Mayhew series for graphical comparability.

26. Mayhew, *Divided We Govern*, p. 89.

27. Ibid., p. 90.

28. In this and all subsequent analysis of the gridlock scores, I drop issues concerning nominations, matters of internal legislative procedure, and foreign aid matters. Nominations and procedural issues are dropped because they are not strictly legislative in nature, and foreign aid issues are dropped because it is difficult to assess "success" or "failure" when the issue is primarily framed in terms of the amount of funds provided. This is similar to Mayhew's move to drop appropriations matters. Treaties are included as they directly involve policy issues. No salience filter is applied in table 3-1. Significant differences in the frequency of gridlock also occur when salience filters of 2, 3, 4, and 5 editorials are applied.

29. I refer to "issues" here, as some issues that die with no formal action taken were never introduced as bills.

30. When a chamber achieves a gridlock score of 100 percent (as the Senate did for example in the 83d Congress), this means that all of the salient issues on the agenda died short of Senate passage.

31. The six Congresses are the 80th, 81st, 83d, 85th, 87th, and 88th.

32. See James L. Sundquist, *The Decline and Resurgence of Congress* (Brookings, 1981).

33. On the relationship between divided government and use of the veto, see Charles M. Cameron, *Veto Bargaining: Presidents and the Politics of Negative Power* (Cambridge University Press, 2000).

34. But see Cameron's argument that the anticipation of a veto can have the effect of removing potentially contentious measures from the agenda; ibid., chap. 6.

35. The classic statement of the two-presidencies thesis is Aaron Wildavsky, "The Two Presidencies," *Trans-Action*, vol. 4 (December 1966), pp. 7–14. The literature challenging Wildavsky's thesis is compiled in Steven A. Shull, ed., *The Two Presidencies: A Quarter Century Assessment* (Nelson-Hall, 1991). See also Thomas E. Mann, ed., *A Question of Balance: The President, the Congress, and Foreign Policy* (Brookings, 1990); and James M. Lindsay, *Congress and the Politics of U.S. Foreign Policy* (Johns Hopkins University Press, 1994).

36. I distinguish between foreign and domestic policy issues by coding each issue according to the major issue categories developed by the Policy Agendas Project at the Center for American Politics and Public Policy located at the University of Washington. Issues falling in the International Affairs and Foreign Aid, Defense, and Foreign Trade categories are coded as foreign policy issues; all others are considered domestic policy. The full list of topic codes is available at http://depts.washington.edu/ampol/topicindex.shtml [May 22, 2002].

37. These figures are calculated for all legislative issues and treaties. The difference is significant at $p < .001$. Comparable figures for only salient issues are impracticable, as the sample sizes are too small. In many cases, only one or two salient issues concerned foreign policy.

38. On constraints imposed by legislators from both parties, see, for example, Helen Dewar and Juliet Eilperin, "Emergency Funding Deal Reached," *Washington Post*, September 14, 2001, p. A30.

39. However, we cannot tell whether the *president's* own initiatives were more likely to fail. Although I coded whether or not the president/administration supported or opposed each policy proposal, *Congressional Quarterly* did not report a presidential position for more than half of the agenda. Even on the most salient issues, presidential positions were available for just 53 percent of salient issues. On the demise of the two-presidencies thesis, see Shull, *The Two Presidencies*. On the rise of legislative activism on foreign policy more generally, see Lindsay, *Congress and the Politics of U.S. Foreign Policy*; and Mann, *A Question of Balance*.

40. Mann, *A Question of Balance*, p. 29.

Chapter Four

1. Helen Dewar, "As Congress Winds Up Work, Legislative Casualties Mount," *Washington Post*, October 5, 1998, p. A4.

2. See John B. Gilmour, *Strategies of Disagreement: Stalemate in American Politics* (University of Pittsburgh Press, 1995).

3. Senator Chuck Hagel (R-Nebr.), as quoted in Helen Dewar, "In Congress, It's Politics over Progress: Deepening Election-Year Partisanship Has Created a Legislative Logjam," *Washington Post*, May 6, 2000, p. A12.

4. Dewar, "In Congress, It's Politics over Progress."

5. I conclude this by estimating five grouped logit models that each test whether the frequency of gridlock is higher in Congresses that end with a presidential election. The dependent variable in each of the five models is the percentage of agenda issues that end in deadlock in each Congress, with the scores calculated over varying levels of issue salience. As explained in chapter 3 and appendix A, I use the number of *Times* editorials on an issue in a Congress as an indicator of issue salience. I then construct five different versions of the gridlock measure: the first one includes all issues, the second one includes issues receiving two or more editorials, the third one three or more editorials, and so on. I find an insignificant parameter estimate for the presidential election variable in four of the five models. Approaching presidential elections drive up stalemate by roughly 5 percent only for the measure of gridlock that includes issues of all salience levels.

6. The null result for the impact of the budget situation on gridlock holds for each of the five levels of issue salience.

7. See Charles Babington and Eric Pianin, "Clinton, Hill Agree on Budget Goals; Differences Remain on Use of Surplus," *Washington Post*, July 13, 1999, p. A1.

8. See, for example, Michael Grunwald, "With Eyes on 2000, Congress Creates Issues but Not Laws," *Washington Post*, September 16, 1999, p. A1.

9. Again, the null result holds across all five levels of issue salience.

10. Unless otherwise noted, in this chapter, I code the 97th, 98th, and 99th (1981–86) Congresses as episodes of divided control. Even though the Republicans controlled the White House and the Senate during this period, they faced Democratic control of the House.

11. Specifically, the dependent variable in column 1 includes all issues receiving at least one *Times* editorial, in column 2 those issues receiving 2 or more *Times* editorials, in column 3 three or more *Times* editorials, and so on.

12. As shown in table 4-1, we cannot reject the null hypothesis that frequency of gridlock is similar under the two types of party control when we include issues of moderate to high salience (that is, ranging from at least three to five *Times* editorials per measure) in the measure of gridlock. Although the parameter estimate for divided government is significant in column 4, the F test suggests that we cannot reject the null hypothesis that the model coefficients are jointly zero.

13. Gridlock does increase significantly when I include the broadest set of issues in the measurement of gridlock (issues receiving at least one or at least two editorials in a Congress).

14. See my use of W-NOMINATE scores in Sarah A. Binder, "The Dynamics of Legislative Gridlock, 1947–1996," *American Political Science Review,* vol. 93 (September 1999), pp. 519–33.

15. See Greg Adams, Michael Bailey, and Chris Fastnow, "Bicameralism— Redundancy or Grand Plan? Cross-Chamber Tests of Ideological Difference," paper presented at the annual meeting of the Midwest Political Science Association, Chicago, 2000.

16. I use the *House of Representatives' Final Calendar* published each Congress to identify every conference report brought to both chambers' floors each Congress, and then determine the floor roll call vote outcome for each report (votes for the 80th–101st Congresses are obtained from ICPSR roll call files, and for the 102d–106th Congresses from Thomas, http://thomas.loc.gov). Conference reports approved by voice vote are coded as 100 percent approval. Conference agreements approved by votes on receding from disagreement to the other chambers' amendments are dropped from the analysis as identical votes are not cast in the two chambers.

17. The single left-right dimension is defended theoretically and empirically in Keith T. Poole and Howard Rosenthal, *Congress: A Political-Economic History of Roll Call Voting* (Oxford University Press, 1997). To place legislators spatially along the dimension, I use Poole and Rosenthal's W-NOMINATE scores. Poole generously makes NOMINATE scores available at www.voteview.uh.edu.

18. I apppreciate improvements to this measure offered by an anonymous reviewer, as well as the helpful illustration.

19. In earlier versions of this work (see Binder, "The Dynamics of Legislative Gridlock") I used only the percentage of moderates as an indicator of partisan polarization. In practice, however, there is little difference between that measure and one that adjusts for the distance between the parties. The sharpest declines in the number of moderates have been accompanied by sharp increases in the distances between the parties.

20. High scores represent low levels of polarization because large numbers of moderates divided by a small distance between the parties yields a high score; small numbers of moderates divided by a large distance between the parties yields a low score (but a high level of polarization).

21. Averaging is again made necessary by the high correlation between the House and Senate series (Pearson's $r = .70$).

22. For the Congresses between 1981 and 1986, when the two parties split control of the House and Senate, the variable is coded 0, as no party had a majority in both chambers. When the Democrats assumed control of both chambers in 1987, the variable takes the value of 1.5 (averaging three Congresses spent in the minority by Senate Democrats and none spent in the minority for House Democrats).

23. Federal budget data available in "Historical Tables, Fiscal Year 2002," *Budget of the United States Government.*

24. See James A. Stimson, *Public Opinion in America: Moods, Cycles, and Swings,* 2d ed. (Westview Press, 1999); see www.unc.edu/~jstimson/mood2k.xls [March 11, 2002] for data for the mood variable.

25. In contrast, Mayhew, in *Divided We Govern* (Yale University Press, 1991), used a dummy variable to denote the Congresses between 1961 and 1976 as a period of particularly activist government.

26. See, for example, James A. Stimson, Michael B. MacKuen, and Robert S. Erikson, "Dynamic Representation," *American Political Science Review,* vol. 89 (September 1995), pp. 543–65; and Andrew J. Taylor, "Explaining Government Productivity," *American Politics Quarterly,* vol. 26 (October 1998), pp. 439–58. I average Stimson's annual mood scores to create a public mood score for each two-year Congress. Because the data start in 1952, the variable for the 82d Congress (1951–52) takes the value for 1952.

27. Stimson, MacKuen, and Erikson, "Dynamic Representation," p. 546.

28. The measures are fairly highly correlated, with an average correlation of about .8. Even the weakest correlation (between the gridlock scores covering the least and most salient issues) still reaches .62.

29. Because the dependent variable is constructed from grouped data (total number of failed legislative issues per Congress divided by the total number of policy issues on the agenda each Congress) with unequal size groups, the ordinary least squares assumption of uniform variance is violated. That is, given agendas of varying sizes over the twenty-seven Congresses, heteroskedasticity will be present across the disturbances. The solution in this case is to model variation in gridlock with weighted least squares estimates in a grouped logit equation. I estimate the models below using the *glogit* routine of Stata 7.0. *Glogit* estimates weighted least squares, accounting for the different-sized denominators (total number of agenda issues) and, in principle, different variances across Congresses. Because the percentage data are bounded between 0 and 1, the logit function is more appropriate than weighted least squares through OLS.

30. In table 4-2, the number of each dependent variable ("gridlock 1," "gridlock 2," and so forth) indicates the number of editorials used as the threshold for including an issue in the calculation of the frequency of gridlock. In calculating gridlock 1, for example, I include every legislative issue that received at least one mention in the *Times* in a Congress; gridlock 3 uses three editorials as the cutoff for including an issue in measuring gridlock. Thus the dependent variables move from the broadest to most salient set of issues as one moves across the table. The average size of the legislative agenda for each Congress in the first model is 105 issues; the average size of the agenda in model 5 is 19 issues. The *N* for the analysis is 24, covering the 83d (the first Congress for which a lagged policy mood variable is available) through the 106th Congresses.

31. All *p* values reported in the tables are from one-tailed *t* tests, given the direction of my conjectures about the impact of the variables.

32. See appendix D for an explicit comparison of my results with Mayhew's.

33. See Austin Ranney, *The Doctrine of Responsible Party Government: Its Origins and Present State* (University of Illinois Press, 1954).

34. The prominent works are Woodrow Wilson, *Constitutional Government in the United States* (Columbia University Press, 1911); V. O. Key, *Politics, Parties, and Pressure Groups* (Crowell, 1942); E. E. Schattschneider, *Party Government* (Farrar and Rinehart, 1942); and James Sundquist, "Needed: A Political Theory for the New Era of Coalition Government in the United States," *Political Science Quarterly*, vol. 103 (Winter 1988–89), pp. 613–35.

35. I calculate the expected impact based on the parameter estimates from the model that includes all issues receiving two or more *Times* editorials in a Congress (table 4-2, column 2). I choose this version of the model simply because it explains the greatest portion of the variance in legislative stalemate.

36. See, for example, William S. Cohen, "Why I Am Leaving," *Washington Post*, January 21, 1996, p. C7; Lloyd Grove, "The So-Long Senators," *Washington Post*, January 26, 1996, p. F1; and Marilyn Serafini, "Mr. In-Between," *National Journal*, December 16, 1995, pp. 3080–84.

37. Ibid., p. 3084.

38. See Thomas E. Mann, "President Clinton and the Democratic Congress: Promise and Performance," in James Sundquist, *Back to Gridlock* (Brookings, 1995), p. 10.

39. "Perhaps the Worst Congress," *Washington Post*, October 7, 1994, p. A24.

40. See, in particular, David W. Brady and Craig Volden, *Revolving Gridlock: Politics and Policy from Carter to Clinton* (Westview Press, 1998); and Keith Krehbiel, *Pivotal Politics: A Theory of U.S. Lawmaking* (University of Chicago Press, 1998). See also my previous work, Binder, "The Dynamics of Legislative Gridlock," *American Political Science Review*, vol. 93 (September 1999), pp. 519–33. For analysis of individual issues, see Barbara Sinclair, "Structure, Preferences, and Outcomes: When Bills Do—and Don't—Become Law," paper presented at the annual meeting of the American Political Science Association, 2001.

41. Similarly, the fifty-first senator is simply the median voter of the Senate. I use DW-NOMINATE scores to measure the ideological distance between the sixtieth and fifty-first senators. Before the 95th Congress (1995–96), the pivotal senator was the sixty-seventh percentile rather than the sixtieth. My data run from the 80th through 104th Congresses.

42. The dependent variable is the frequency of gridlock on all issues receiving two or more *Times* editorials. When I run the analysis for the other four levels of issue salience, the filibuster threat is statistically significant for the most salient issues (gridlock 5). Weaker parameter estimates for the explanatory variables obtain when I run the analysis with the dependent variables based on lower levels of issue salience.

43. To measure the ideological distance between the president and Congress, I use DW-NOMINATE scores devised by Nolan M. McCarty, Keith T. Poole, and Howard Rosenthal, "Income Redistribution and the Realignment of American Politics," AEI Studies on Understanding Economic Inequality (Washington: AEI Press, 1997). To calculate a single presidential ideology for each Congress, I average each president's House and Senate DW-NOMINATE scores for each Congress. To calculate Congress's ideology, I average the DW-NOMINATE scores for the House and Senate medians in each Congress. I then calculate the absolute difference between the two branches' scores. One caveat is in order: McCarty, Poole, and Rosenthal assign presidents identical scores in each of the Congresses during which they served as president. Because DW-NOMINATE scores are calculated for the presidents only starting in the 84th Congress, I use Eisenhower's 84th–86th Congress score as his 83d Congress score.

44. The only statistically different results between the two estimations (tables 4-2 and 4-5) are those for the gridlock 1 (issues of broadest salience) model. Polarization and bicameral disagreement miss standard levels of statistical significance. Note that the results in table 4-5 are not an artifact of high correlations between interbranch disagreement and the other explanatory variables: Interbranch disagreement is correlated with divided government at .36, with polarization at –.25, and bicameral disagreement at .54.

45. Because the Stimson policy mood data begin in 1952, including a lagged public mood variable in the previous models in this chapter necessarily limited those models to the period starting in the 83d Congress (1953–54).

46. Results appear in appendix C.

47. The correlation between the activist era and polarization variable is .72.

48. Results appear in appendix C.

49. Data to replicate the analysis appear in appendix E.

50. Allen Schick, with Felix LoStracco, *The Federal Budget: Politics, Policy, Process* (Brookings, 2000), p. 109.

51. Before fiscal year 1987, Congress was supposed to adopt the resolution by May 15; the scheduled adoption date since then has been April 15.

52. Because the independent variables vary by Congress, not year, I calculate the mean days late for each Congress in passing the two budget resolutions (that is, I average the delay for fiscal year 1996 and fiscal year 1997 to obtain the mean delay for the 104th Congress). The data series runs from the 94th Congress (1975–76) through the 106th (1999–2000), yielding the thirteen observations noted above.

53. Note that we cannot be certain that the coefficients are not jointly zero, given the insigificant F test.

54. On the origins of the 1974 Budget Act, see, among others, Schick, *The Federal Budget*, chap. 2.

55. On the politics of the failed fiscal year 1999 budget resolution in 1998, see ibid., pp. 110–11.

56. Mayhew, *Divided We Govern*, pp. 198–99.

57. See George C. Edwards III, Andrew Barrett, and Jeffrey Peake, "The Legislative Impact of Divided Government," *American Journal of Political Science,* vol. 41 (April 1997), pp. 545–63.

58. Ibid., p. 548.

59. See American Political Science Association, "Toward a More Responsible Two-Party System: A Report of the Committee on Political Parties: Foreword," *American Political Science Review,* vol. 44 (September 1950), p. v.

60. Morris P. Fiorina, "*Keystone* Revisited," in Lawrence C. Dodd and Bruce I. Oppenheimer, eds., *Congress Reconsidered,* 7th ed. (Washington: Congressional Quarterly Press, 2001).

61. Frances Lee and Bruce Oppenheimer, *Sizing Up the Senate* (University of Chicago Press, 1999).

62. Rep. Bill Thomas (R-Calif.), as quoted in Andrew Taylor, "GOP Looks to Nickles to Deliver on Patients' Rights," *Congressional Quarterly Weekly Report,* March 11, 2000.

63. Taylor, "GOP Looks to Nickles to Deliver on Patients' Rights."

64. Quoted in ibid.

65. More generally on the incentives to disagree, see Gilmour, *Strategies of Disagreement.*

66. On the effects of supermajority rules on unified gridlock, see Brady and Volden, *Revolving Gridlock*; David R. Jones, "Party Polarization and Legislative Gridlock," *Political Research Quarterly,* vol. 54 (March 2001), pp. 125–41; and Krehbiel, *Pivotal Politics.*

67. This assumes that pending issues are unidimensional, allowing one to identify the filibuster "pivot" as the senator occupying the sixtieth percentile of the Senate's ideological range (or the sixth-seventh percentile before 1975).

68. On the rise of the filibuster since the 1970s, see Sarah A. Binder and Steven S. Smith, *Politics or Principle? Filibustering in the United States Senate* (Brookings, 1997).

Chapter Five

1. Charles O. Jones, "A Way of Life and Law," *American Political Science Review,* vol. 89, no. 1 (March 1995), pp. 1–9, citation on p. 2.

2. See, for example, Dan Carney, "Colorado Rampage Impels a Search for New Methods to Combat Juvenile Crime," *Congressional Quarterly Weekly Report,* April 24, 1999, p. 959.

3. See, for example, Dana Milbank and Juliet Eilperin, "Democrats Eager to Tackle Bush on Domestic Issues," *Washington Post*, December 6, 2001, p. A24.

4. See Richard F. Fenno Jr. "Observation, Context, and Sequence in the Study of Politics," *American Political Science Review*, vol. 80 (March 1986), pp. 3–15, quotation on p. 9.

5. Besides the analysis of the sale of AWACs to Saudi Arabia in 1981 in Fenno, "Observation, Context, and Sequence in the Study of Politics," see also Janet M. Box-Steffensmeier, Laura W. Arnold, and Christopher J. W. Zorn, "The Strategic Timing of Position Taking in Congress: A Study of the North American Free Trade Agreement," *American Political Science Review*, vol. 91 (June 1997), pp. 324–38.

6. The Ney bill was subsequently considered as an amendment to the Shays-Meehan bill when the House resumed consideration of campaign finance reform early in 2002. On the battle over campaign finance bills in the 107th Congress, see, among others, Alison Mitchell, "Campaign Measure Shelved after Fierce Fight on Rules," *New York Times*, July 13, 2001, p. A1; and Karen Foerstel, "Opponents of Shays-Meehan Bet It All on a Conference," *Congressional Quarterly Weekly Report*, February 9, 2002, p. 393.

7. See Barbara Sinclair, "Structure, Preferences and Outcomes: Explaining When Bills Do—and Don't—Become Law," paper presented at the annual meeting of the American Political Science Association, San Francisco, August 30–September 2, 2001.

8. The issues are culled from the editorial pages of the *New York Times*, as discussed in chapter 3.

9. See Stanley Bach and Steven S. Smith, *Managing Uncertainty in the House of Representatives* (Brookings, 1988).

10. Presidential fast-track powers had lapsed since 1994, when the Republican Congress refused to renew such power for President Clinton. See Joseph J. Schatz and Jill Barshay, "Deal Puts Fast Track on Track," *Congressional Quarterly Weekly Report*, July 27, 2002, p. 2021.

11. See Keith Perine, "Regulation is Back in Vogue," *Congressional Quarterly Weekly Report*, July 27, 2002, p. 2018.

12. See, for example, George C. Edwards III, *At the Margins: Presidential Leadership of Congress* (Yale University Press, 1989); Mark Peterson, *Legislating Together: The White House and Capitol Hill from Eisenhower to Reagan* (Harvard University Press, 1990); Jon Bond and Richard Fleisher, *The President in the Legislative Arena* (University of Chicago Press, 1990); and Charles O. Jones, *The Presidency in a Separated System* (Brookings, 1994).

13. See Schatz and Barshay, "Deal Puts Fast Track on Track."

14. On the political impact of economic conditions that summer, see David Hawkings, "A Worried Congress Forced into Legislative Overdrive," *Congressional Quarterly Weekly Preport*, July 27, 2002, p. 2016.

15. But George Edwards and Andrew Barrett predict the opposite pattern: presidents are more likely to succeed in passing their initiatives during unified government than during divided government. Their analytical concern, however, is with the fate of agenda items initiated by the president. My units of analysis, in contrast, are individual issues that appear on the legislative agenda—regardless of whether they were initiated by Congress or the president. Thus, rather than asking when does the president succeed, the research question is whether or not presidential attention to an issue has demonstrable effects under different patterns of party control. See George C. Edwards III and Andrew Barrett, "Presidential Agenda Setting in Congress," in Jon R. Bond and Richard Fleisher, eds., *Polarized Politics: Congress and the President in a Partisan Era* (Washington: Congressional Quarterly Press, 2000).

16. Health care portability refers to the right of employees to take health care coverage with them when they lose their jobs or transfer to a new job.

17. On variation in senators' intent and filibuster outcomes, see Sarah A. Binder and Steven S. Smith, *Politics or Principle? Filibustering in the United States Senate* (Brookings, 1997).

18. I consider "salient" bills those with four or more *Times* editorials in a Congress.

19. Given Bernie Sanders's (I-Vt.) strong tendency to vote with a majority of the House Democratic caucus, I include him as a Democrat in scoring bill partisanship.

20. For example, to determine the partisanship score for a bill whose cosponsors are 100 percent Democrats, one would calculate $|100 - 50| = 50$. For a bill whose cosponsors are 50 percent Democratic and 50 percent Republican, the score would be $|50 - 50| = 0$. Thus, partisanship ranges from a low of 0 (purely bipartisan) to 50 (purely partisan).

21. Determining what constitutes the "major" bill associated with an issue is admittedly at times difficult. Some issues clearly have a single bill associated with them; others attract numerous bills. To the extent possible, I was guided by the treatment by the *New York Times* and *Congressional Quarterly Almanac* of the issue and corresponding bills. Despite the introduction of several bills on a subject, there is typically a major bill that attracts attention as the central legislative vehicle. On campaign finance in recent years, for example, this has clearly been the McCain-Feingold bill in the Senate and the Shays-Meehan bill in the House. In just six of sixty-one bills for which the partisanship of cosponsors could be calculated were there two bills that might have claimed major bill status, and the competing bills for two of those bills had a similar partisan distribution of cosponsors (a perfect 50).

22. As in chapter 3, I drop issues concerning foreign aid, nominations, and procedural matters. Because I drop any issues without both a House and Senate bill partisanship score, this also forces me to drop treaties. This leaves a legislative agenda for the two Congresses of 185 issues. I can create partisanship scores

for just a quarter of the overall legislative agenda (43 out of 185 legislative issues) because of the difficulties noted in the text of matching issues and bills. Also, as suggested above, not every bill attracts cosponsors, which is necessary for me to calculate bill partisanship. Also, I can calculate bill partisanship for some Senate bills but not necessarily for their House counterparts, and vice versa.

23. For the forty-three issues for which a mean House-Senate partisanship score can be calculated, the average partisanship is 36, and median partisanship 38.

24. Salient issues are those receiving four or more *Times* editorials in the Congress in which it was considered.

25. Network television news coverage is determined from the "Evening News Abstracts" database available through the Vanderbilt News Archives (http:// tvnews.vanderbilt.edu). Because the time dedicated to each issue by the network news shows is highly correlated with the number of stories run on each issue (Pearson's $r = .98$), I stick with the simpler indicator of the number of news stories.

26. For the 185 legislative agenda items mentioned between 1993 and 1996 by the *Times*, 41 percent were enacted into law.

27. The most salient issues to be excluded are welfare and telecommunications reform in the 104th.

28. On average, issues that failed to pass the Senate scored a partisanship score of 42 (out of 50), compared with a partisanship score of 25 for issues that eventually passed the Senate (difference is statistically significant at $p < .0001$).

29. In calculating the marginal effects of a large change in issue partisanship, I assume that the issue is salient, considered in a period of divided government, not a top priority of the president, and does not attract a filibuster. Marginal effects are calculated via the *mfx* routine in Stata 7.0.

30. The p value for a one-tailed t-test of the effect of divided government equals .098.

31. In calculating the marginal effect of the change in party control, I assume the bill is salient, off the president's agenda, and does not attract a filibuster.

32. On House passage of the patients' bill of rights measure, see Rebecca Adams, "House Sends Patients' Rights on to Last Critical Test," *Congressional Quarterly Weekly Report*, August 4, 2001, p. 1900.

33. The results are not contaminated by multicollinearity between the independent variables, as there seems to be no strong statistical relationship in these data between the level of partisanship and the incidence of a filibuster problem. The harmful impact of filibuster activity is consistent with the findings over a broader set of Congresses in Sinclair, "Structure, Preferences, and Outcomes: Explaining When Bills Do—and Don't—Become Law." Paper presented at the 2001 annual meeting of the American Political Science Association.

34. Marginal effects of changes in the level of partisanship are calculated assuming the presence of a filibuster problem. Effects calculated via the *mfx* routine in Stata 7.0.

35. Thirty-nine Democrats and twenty-seven Republicans cosponsored Kassebaum's bill, S1028.

36. The bill scored a perfect 50 on the issue partisanship index, reflecting its twenty-two Republican cosponsors and no Democrats.

37. CQ Bill Track, H.R. 3103, 104th Cong. (www.cq.com [August 7, 2001]).

38. Party affiliation is coded by designating Republicans as "1," Democrats as "0." A negative coefficient on the party variable indicates that Republicans were less likely to vote for the amendment than were Democrats. To measure legislators' centrist tendencies, I use two dummy variables to identify Democratic centrists and Republican centrists. Centrists are identified following the method outlined in chapter 4. Democratic and Republican centrists are coded 1, 0 otherwise. The positive coefficient on Republican moderates indicates that these centrists were significantly more likely to vote for the Dingell amendment; the negative coefficient for Democratic centrists indicates that these moderates were significantly less likely to vote for the Dingell amendment.

39. Because the dependent variable (one's vote on the amendment) is dichotomous, I use a logit analysis to determine the influence of ideology and party on the vote. Model is estimated via the *logit* routine in Stata 7.0. House Roll Call Vote 104, March 28, 1996 (104th Cong. 2d sess.).

40. Predicted probabilities calculated via the *mfx* routine in Stata 7.0.

41. Republican moderates fell in line with their party on a more partisan motion to recommit to the Ways and Means Committee.

42. The lone dissenting Republican was Marge Roukema of New Jersey, who had originally sponsored a bill identical to Kassebaum's Senate bill.

43. Because all Democrats voted against the motion, the logit analysis is limited to Republicans. Senate Roll Call Vote 72, April 18, 1996 (104th Cong. 2d sess.).

44. On the threat of a filibuster, see "Key Votes," *Congressional Quarterly Weekly Report*, December 14, 1996 (www.cq.com [August 6, 2001]).

45. On Republicans' dilemma in 1995 and 1996, see Richard F. Fenno Jr., *Learning to Govern: An Institutional View of the 104th Congress* (Brookings, 1997).

46. See Michael Crowley, "Wag the Dog," *New Republic*, August 20, 2001, pp. 10–12.

Chapter Six

1. See Richard W. Stevenson, "Standoff on Budget Yields An Unexpected Dividend," *New York Times*, October 25, 1999, p. 1.

2. Van Doorn Ooms, research director for the Committee for Economic Development, as quoted ibid.

3. One might start with the classic treatment of American voters offered by Angus Campbell, Philip E. Converse, Warren E. Miller, and Donald E. Stokes, *The American Voter* (John Wiley and Sons, 1960).

4. See, for example, Anthony Downs, *An Economic Theory of Democracy* (Harper and Row, 1957); Morris P. Fiorina, *Retrospective Voting in American National Elections* (Yale University Press, 1981); Michael S. Lewis-Beck and Tom W. Rice, *Forecasting Elections* (Washington: Congressional Quarterly Press, 1992); and Edward R. Tufte, *Political Control of the Economy* (Princeton University Press, 1978).

5. But see David R. Jones and Monika L. McDermott, "Electoral Effects of Congressional Job Performance on the Majority Party," paper presented at the annual meeting of the American Political Science Association, 2001.

6. See Gary C. Jacobson, *The Politics of Congressional Elections*, 4th ed. (New York: Longman, 1997).

7. For the original statement of the paradox, see Richard F. Fenno Jr., "If As Ralph Nader Says, Congress Is 'The Broken Branch,' How Come We Love Our Congressmen So Much?" in Norman J. Ornstein, ed., *Congress in Change: Evolution and Reform* (Praeger, 1975).

8. Here I use a measure of gridlock over salient issues (that is, those receiving four or more editorials). The results do not change appreciably if other salience levels are used to calculate the gridlock scores.

9. See Jacobson, *The Politics of Congressional Elections*, chap. 6.

10. Following Jacobson, *The Politics of Congressional Elections,* and Tufte, *Political Control of the Economy,* the state of the economy is measured as the percentage change in real disposable income per capita over the year ending in the second quarter of the election year. For per capita income data, see U.S. Department of Commerce, Bureau of Economic Analysis, *National Income and Product Accounts Tables,* table 8.7 (www.bea.doc.gov/bea/dn/nipaweb/tableviewfixed.asp#mid [August 24, 2001]). Challenger quality is measured as the percentage of incumbents facing challengers who have previously held elective office (challenger quality data available in the replication dataset for Gary W. Cox and Jonathan N. Katz, "Why Did the Incumbency Advantage in U.S. House Elections Grow?" *American Journal of Political Science,* vol. 40, no. 2 (1996), pp. 478–97.

11. Fenno, "If as Ralph Nader Says," p. 278.

12. See Richard F. Fenno Jr., *Homestyle: House Members in Their Districts* (Little, Brown, 1978), p. 151. On the contextual nature of constituent trust, see William T. Bianco, *Trust: Representatives and Constituents* (University of Michigan Press, 1994).

13. See David R. Mayhew, *Congress: The Electoral Connection* (Yale University Press, 1974).

14. Richard F. Fenno Jr., *Congressmen in Committees* (Little, Brown, 1973).

15. Keith Krehbiel, *Information and Legislative Organization* (University of Michigan Press, 1991).

16. See Gary W. Cox and Mathew D. McCubbins, *Legislative Leviathan: Party Government in the House* (University of California Press, 1993).

17. See, for example, John H. Aldrich and David W. Rohde, "The Consequences of Party Organization in the House: The Role of Majority and Minority Parties in Conditional Party Government," in Jon R. Bond and Richard Fleisher, eds., *Polarized Politics: Congress and the President in a Partisan Era* (Washington: Congressional Quarterly Press, 2000).

18. See Gregory Wawro, *Legislative Entrepreneurship in the U.S. House of Representatives* (University of Michigan Press, 2000).

19. For support of the no-fun thesis, see Stephen E. Frantzich, "Opting Out: Retirement from the House of Representatives 1966–1974," *American Politics Quarterly*, vol. 6 (July 1978), pp. 251–73; Joseph Cooper and William West, "Voluntary Retirement, Incumbency, and the Modern House," *Political Science Quarterly*, vol. 96 (Summer 1981), pp. 279–300; and Sean M. Theriault, "Moving Up or Moving Out: Career Ceilings and Congressional Retirement," *Legislative Studies Quarterly*, vol. 23 (August 1998), pp. 419–33. The no-fun thesis is rejected by Michael K. Moore and John R. Hibbing, "Is Serving in Congress Fun Again? Voluntary Retirements from the House since the 1970s," *American Journal of Political Science*, vol. 36 (August 1992), pp. 824–28; and Richard L. Hall and Robert P. Van Houweling, "Avarice and Ambition in Congress: Representatives' Decisions to Run or Retire from the U.S. House," *American Political Science Review*, vol. 89 (March 1995), pp. 121–36.

20. Cooper and West, "Voluntary Retirement, Incumbency, and the Modern House," pp. 289–90.

21. Warren B. Rudman, *Combat: Twelve Years in the U.S. Senate* (Random House, 1996), pp. 254–55.

22. The two studies are, respectively, Theriault, "Moving Up or Moving Out," and Cooper and West, "Voluntary Retirement, Incumbency, and the Modern House," p. 293.

23. For the 80th–104th Congresses, Pearson's $r = .419$, statistically significant at $p < .05$.

24. Age of the membership is measured as the mean age of serving members; the data are drawn from Inter-University Consortium for Political and Social Research and Carroll McKibbin, *Roster of United States Congressional Officeholders and Biographical Characteristics of Members of the United States Congress, 1789–1996*, 10th ed. (Ann Arbor: ICPSR, 1997). A dummy variable is used to denote whether or not House members received a pay raise during the Congress, and I tap electoral vulnerability with a dummy variable indicating whether or not decennial redistricting took place during the Congress. This measurement strategy follows John R. Hibbing, "Voluntary Retirements from the House in the Twentieth Century," *Journal of Politics*, vol. 44 (November 1982), pp. 1020–34.

25. Because the number of retirees can only be a nonnegative integer, I model the count of retirees as a poisson distribution.

26. In both columns, I use four or more *Times* editorials for the threshold for including an issue in the calculation of the gridlock score for each Congress. The results for both columns hold for all levels of salience (from 2 to 5 or more *Times* editorials), except the lowest level (all legislative issues).

27. See, for example, Cooper and West, "Voluntary Retirement, Incumbency, and the Modern House"; and Hibbing, "Voluntary Retirements from the House in the Twentieth Century."

28. See Moore and Hibbing, "Is Serving in Congress Fun Again?" p. 828.

29. The drop in retirement rates in the 1980s helps eliminate another potential cause of retirement rates: the cost of campaigns. Although campaign costs have increased steadily since 1980, the frequency of gridlock has varied more widely; see Norman J. Ornstein, Thomas E. Mann, Michael J. Malbin, *Vital Statistics on Congress 2001–2002* (Washington: AEI Press, 2002), pp. 87–88.

30. Robert H. Durr, John B. Gilmour, and Christina Wolbrecht, "Explaining Congressional Approval," *American Journal of Political Science,* vol. 41 (January 1997), p. 199.

31. See John R. Hibbing and Elizabeth Theiss-Morse, *Congress as Public Enemy: Public Attitudes toward American Political Institutions* (Cambridge University Press, 1995).

32. See John R. Hibbing, "Appreciating Congress," in Joseph Cooper, ed., *Congress and the Decline of Public Trust* (Westview Press, 1999).

33. These results and the ones that follow are from Louis Harris and Associates, *Harris Survey,* December 1963. Poll results available through Roper Center at University of Connecticut, *Public Opinion Online.*

34. More specifically, 17 percent of respondents noted that Congress had "passed some good bills," and 17 percent credited Congress with "making some progress." If we add in the 49 percent who were satisfied that Congress was "trying hard," more than 80 percent based their evaluation on Congress's legislative performance.

35. See Glenn R. Parker, "Some Themes in Congressional Unpopularity," *American Journal of Political Science,* vol. 21 (February 1977), pp. 93–109.

36. See Samuel C. Patterson and Gregory A. Caldeira, "Standing Up for Congress: Variations in Public Esteem since the 1960s," *Legislative Studies Quarterly,* vol. 15 (February 1990), pp. 25–47. The analysis examines legislative activity in a very limited way. Congressional action is measured by a dummy variable for the first session of each Congress (on the assumption that partisan activity is higher in that session than the second) and by a count of *New York Times* mentions of Congress as an institution, of members of Congress, and of ethics reports and investigations.

37. The data are compiled in Cooper, *Congress and the Decline of Public Trust*, table A.20. The question asked by Harris for 1963–70 and 1973 is "How would you rate the job Congress has been doing so far this year—excellent, pretty good, only fair, or poor?" Excellent and pretty good responses are considered as approval of Congress; only fair and poor responses are coded as disapproval. Gallup began asking a similar question in 1974, continuing to the present: "Do you approve or disapprove of the way the U.S. Congress is handling its job?" Neither organization appears to have asked the question in the 92d Congress (1971–72), forcing me to drop this observation in the analysis below (as well as the observation for the 88th and 93d Congresses since I lack lagged approval ratings for both Congresses).

38. Durr, Gilmour, and Wolbrecht, "Explaining Congressional Approval," in contrast, use a quarterly measure of congressional approval. Moving to that unit of analysis is impractical for this analysis, however, as my theoretical interest is in whether the sum of each Congress's legislative record affects the public's near final evaluation of each Congress.

39. Presidential approval is based on the president's average approval rating in each election year; see Lyn Ragsdale, *Vital Statistics on the Presidency: Washington to Clinton* (Washington: Congressional Quarterly Press, 1996), chap. 5. Macroeconomic conditions are measured by the average unemployment and inflation rates for each Congress. Annual unemployment rates and inflation rates available at U.S. Department of Labor, Bureau of Labor Statistics, ftp://ftp.bls .gov/pub/special .requests/lf/aat1.txt [August 24, 2001] and ftp://ftp.bls.gov/ pub/special.requests/ cpi/cpiai.txt [August 24, 2001], respectively. Following Durr, Gilmour, and Wolbrecht, "Explaining Congressional Approval," I also control for the lagged level of congressional approval (from the previous Congress).

40. We can safely reject the presence of a unit root in the congressional approval time series with a Dickey-Fuller test ($p = .05$). Running the analysis with an ordinary least squares (OLS) regression yields a Durbin-Watson statistic of 1.1. Thus, in table 6-4, I estimate the model using a Prais-Winston estimator to correct for possible first-order serially correlated residuals. Doing so, however, does not improve the Durbin-Watson statistic and produces substantively similar results. The Prais estimator does improve the overall fit of the model, so I present these results in lieu of the OLS estimates.

41. I calculate gridlock over salient legislative issues (those issues receiving four or more *Times* editorials). The results hold for gridlock measures based on three, four, and five or more *Times* editorials per issue.

42. On the link between congressional and presidential assessments, see Roger H. Davidson, David M. Kovenock, and Michael K. O'Leary, *Congress in Crisis: Politics and Congressional Reform* (Belmont, Calif.: Wadsworth, 1966), chap. 2. The effects of weakening parties on public evaluations of candidates, presidents,

and parties are discussed in detail in Martin Wattenberg, *The Decline of American Political Parties, 1952–1996* (Harvard University Press, 1998).

43. See Durr, Gilmour, and Wolbrecht, "Explaining Congressional Approval."

44. See, for example, Glenn R. Parker, and Roger H. Davison, "Why Do Americans Love Their Congressmen So Much More Than Their Congress?" *Legislative Studies Quarterly*, vol. 4 (February 1979), pp. 53–61.

45. On the tendency toward bipartisan supermajorities to support major legislation, see David R. Mayhew, *Divided We Govern* (Yale University Press, 1991); and Keith Krehbiel, *Pivotal Politics* (University of Chicago Press, 1998).

46. Unfortunately, we cannot tell whether the public is particularly likely to reward or to punish the majority party in its approval of the party's performance as we lack a survey question over a long enough time period that assesses citizens' views about the job performance of the congressional majority party.

47. See Hibbing, "Appreciating Congress," p. 62.

48. Whether the public holds the majority party especially accountable for Congress's legislative performance remains an unanswered question, owing to the lack of a coherent Gallup time series that asks respondents their views about the congressional majority party performance.

49. For a summary of the literature as of 1990, see George C. Edwards III, with Alec M. Gallup, *Presidential Approval: A Sourcebook* (Johns Hopkins University Press, 1990).

50. See, for example, Charles W. Ostrom Jr. and Dennis M. Simon, "Promise and Performance: A Dynamic Model of Presidential Popularity," *American Political Science Review*, vol. 79 (June 1985), pp. 334–58; Richard A. Brody, *Assessing the President: The Media, Elite Opinion, and Public Support* (Stanford University Press, 1991); and George C. Edwards III, William Mitchell, and Reed Welch, "Explaining Presidential Approval: The Significance of Issue Salience," *American Journal of Political Science*, vol. 39 (February 1995), pp. 108–34.

51. On the balance between the economy and crisis events, see Michael B. MacKuen, "Political Drama, Economic Conditions, and the Dynamics of Presidential Popularity," *American Journal of Political Science*, vol. 27 (May 1983), pp. 165–92.

52. See Brody, *Assessing the President*.

53. My dependent variable is the president's average approval rating in every even-numbered (election) year. I measure economic conditions with two variables: the rate of inflation and unemployment (see note 39). To account for the impact of international crises, I create a dummy variable denoting whether or not a noted crisis occurred in the election year during which presidential popularity is measured. For the period 1948–52, I use the list of rallying events in Brody, *Assessing the President*, table 3.1; for 1952–80, I use the list of crises that provoked or were created by U.S. involvement compiled by Ostrom and Simon, "Promise and Performance: A Dynamic Model of Presidential Popularity," table 2; for the period

1981–86, I use Brody's list; and for 1988–96, I code as international crises the Persian Gulf war in 1990 and the Haiti uprising in 1994. To test for the conditional effect of gridlock, I interact the measure of stalemate with a dummy variable indicating whether or not unified party control was in place during the Congress.

54. The models are estimated as ordinary least squares. The Durbin-Watson statistic for column 1 is 1.63; column 2, 1.66; column 3, 1.72; column 4, 1.71, column 5, 1.64, and column 6, 1.73. All are sufficiently close to 2.0 to eliminate the need to control for first-order autocorrelation of the residuals. A Dickey-Fuller test rejects the null hypothesis that a unit root exists in the presidential popularity data. I estimate the models with the *regress* routine in Stata 7.0.

55. See Hibbing and Theiss-Morse, *Congress as Public Enemy*, p. 155.

56. The list of relevant cites is lengthy, but a concise sampling would include Roger H. Davidson and Walter J. Oleszek, *Congress against Itself* (Indiana University Press, 1977); Steven S. Smith, *Call to Order: Floor Politics in the House and Senate* (Brookings, 1989); Barbara Sinclair, *The Transformation of the U.S. Senate* (Johns Hopkins University Press, 1989); Sarah A. Binder and Steven S. Smith, *Politics or Principle? Filibustering in the United States Senate* (Brookings, 1997); Douglas Dion, *Turning the Legislative Thumbscrew: Minority Rights and Procedural Change in Legislative Politics* (University of Michigan Press, 1997); C. Lawrence Evans and Walter J. Oleszek, *Congress under Fire: Reform Politics and the Republican Majority* (Houghton Mifflin, 1997); and Eric Schickler, *Disjointed Pluralism: Institutional Innovation and the Development of the U.S. Congress* (Princeton University Press, 2001).

57. On the emergence of polarized parties and the causes thereof, see Gary C. Jacobson, "Party Polarization in National Politics: The Electoral Connection," in Bond and Fleisher, *Polarized Politics: Congress and the President in a Partisan Era.* On the connection between activism and extremism, see Morris P. Fiorina, "Extreme Voices: A Dark Side of Civic Engagement," in Theda Skocpol and Morris P. Fiorina, eds., *Civic Engagement in American Democracy* (Brookings, 1999).

58. Interview with Governor Jesse Ventura, *St. Paul Legal Ledger*, September 10, 1999.

59. On declining surpluses in 2001, see Richard W. Stevenson, "Bush Projections Show Sharp Drop in Budget Surplus," *New York Times*, August 23, 2001.

60. On the use of facilitated consensus (and other dispute resolution methods), see Allan R. Talbot, *Settling Things: Six Case Studies in Environmental Mediation* (Washington: Conservation Foundation, 1983); Stephen C. Fehr, "Use of Third Party Now Second Nature," *Washington Post*, August 12, 1996, p. B1; Christine Carlson and Larry Spears, "Getting Past Gridlock," *State Legislatures*, vol. 22 (January 1996), pp. 30–33; and Sol Erdman and Lawrence Susskind, "To Solve Hard Problems, Congress Needs a New Method of Negotiating," *Roll Call*, September 22, 1997, p. 5. For broader theoretical treatments of negotiation and bargaining strategies in political settings, see, among others, John B.

Gilmour, *Strategic Disagreement: Stalemate in American Politics* (University of Pittsburgh Press, 1995); Marieke Kleiboer, "Understanding Success and Failure of International Mediation," *Journal of Conflict Resolution,* vol. 40 (June 1996), pp. 360–89; and Paul J. Quirk, "The Cooperative Resolution of Policy Conflict," *American Political Science Review,* vol. 83 (September 1989), pp. 905–21.

61. Quoted in Carlson and Spears, "Getting Past Gridlock," p. 33.

62. The classic statement in support of introducing reg-negs into the rule-making process is Philip J. Harter, "Negotiating Regulations: A Cure for Malaise," *Georgetown Law Journal,* vol. 1, no. 1 (1982), pp. 31–42. Harter's and others' claims in support of the benefits of reg-negs have not gone unchallenged. A case against reg-neg is made forcefully in Cary Coglianese, "Assessing Consensus: The Promise and Performance of Negotiated Rulemaking," *Duke Law Journal,* vol. 46 (April 1997), pp. 1255–349.

63. On the politics (and demise) of the base-closing commissions, see Kenneth R. Mayer, "The Limits of Delegation: The Rise and Fall of BRAC," *Regulation,* vol. 22 (Fall 1999), pp. 32–38; Kenneth R. Mayer, "Closing Military Bases (Finally): Solving Collective Dilemmas through Delegation," *Legislative Studies Quarterly,* vol. 20 (August 1995), pp. 393–413.

64. See Coglianese, "Assessing Consensus."

65. See, for example, Jonathan Chait, "Means of Consent," *New Republic,* January 15, 2001, pp. 17–19.

66. On Congress's swift and bipartisan response to the president's requests, see John Lancaster and Helen Dewar, "Congress Clears Use of Force, $40 Billion in Emergency Aid," *Washington Post,* September 15, 2001, p. A4.

67. Both Democrats and Republicans sought to scale back the spending and use-of-force resolutions originally sought by the president. See Helen Dewar and Juliet Eilperin, "Emergency Funding Deal Reached," *Washington Post,* September 14, 2001, p. A30.

68. The president's tax bill strategy is discussed in detail in Michael Crowley, "Wag the Dog," *New Republic,* August 20, 2001, pp. 10–12. The president's education package was a clear exception pre–September 11, as the administration worked from the outset with both liberal and conservative education leaders in Congress to craft an acceptable legislative package. See Lizette Alvarez, "On Way to Passage, Bush's Education Plan Gets a Makeover," *New York Times,* May 4, 2001, p. A16.

69. See Gebe Martinez and Karen Foerstel, "GOP Misjudged Public Sentiment with Hard Line on Aviation Bill," *Congressional Quarterly Weekly Report,* November 24, 2001, p. 2781.

70. See Dana Milbank and Juliet Eilperin, "Democrats Eager to Tackle Bush on Domestic Issues," *Washington Post,* December 6, 2001, p. A24. Granted, rapid deterioration of the economy and consumer confidence in the summer of 2002 was sufficient to break the logjam on issues most closely tied to the econ-

omy, such as trade promotion authority for the president and corporate account-ability standards. Even the president, though, seemed surprised by the rush of legislative action in one pivotal week in July 2002: "You know," the president observed, "it's been an amazing week"; as quoted in David Hawkings, "A Worried Congress Forced into Legislative Overdrive," *Congressional Quarterly Weekly Report*, July 27, 2002, p.2016.

Appendix A

1. For the 3,152 issues that appear on the editorial pages between 1947 and 2000, the mean number of *Times* editorials per issue is 3.26, with standard deviation 4.96; the number of editorials per issue ranges from 1 to 87. The issue receiving the 87 editorial mentions in a single Congress was campaign finance reform in the 105th Congress.

2. See "Pew Research Center Database: Public Attentiveness to Major News Stories (1986–1999)" (www. tvrundown.com/views/zstorint.html [September 18, 2002]).

3. See "Evening News Abstracts," http://tvnews.vanderbilt.edu/eveningnews .html [April 21, 1999].

4. Ibid.

5. On the consequences of varying levels of salience, see Charles M. Cameron, *Veto Bargaining: Presidents and the Politics of Negative Power* (Cambridge University Press, 2000), chaps. 6, 7; and William Howell and others, "Divided Government and the Legislative Productivity of Congress, 1945–94," *Legislative Studies Quarterly*, vol. 25, no. 2 (2000), pp. 285–312.

6. To determine the "closest approximation," I correlate the number of issues (that is, bills) enacted into law (from the different gridlock series) with the number of landmark laws enacted each Congress. When I limit the agenda to issues receiving four or more editorials per Congress, the correlation between the number of issues enacted into law and the number of Mayhew's landmark laws enacted is .727.

Appendix B

1. See Sarah A. Binder, "The Dynamics of Legislative Gridlock, 1947–1996," *American Political Science Review*, vol. 93 (September 1999), pp. 519–33.

2. See Keith T. Poole and Howard Rosenthal, *Congress: A Political-Economic History of Roll Call Voting* (Oxford University Press, 1997).

3. For others who have used W-NOMINATE scores to compare legislator ideologies between Congresses, see Charles Cameron, *Veto Bargaining: Presidents and the Politics of Negative Power* (Cambridge University Press, 2000), p. 249.

4. See Fang-Yi Chiou and Lawrence S. Rothenberg, "The Dynamics of Legislative Gridlock Reconsidered," typescript, Princeton University and University of Rochester, January 2002.

5. Ibid., p. 6.

6. Keith T. Poole, "Recovering a Basic Space from a Set of Issue Scales," *American Journal of Political Science*, vol. 42 (July 1998), pp. 954–93.

7. Keith T. Poole, "Changing Minds? Not in Congress!" GSIA Working Paper 1997-22 (Carnegie Mellon University, September 16, 1998).

8. Ibid., p. 10.

9. See Poole and Rosenthal, *Congress*.

10. Keith T. Poole, "Description of NOMINATE DATA," http://voteview .uh.edu/page2a.htm (October 23, 2001). Emphasis in the original.

11. Ibid. Also, in personal correspondence to me in 1997, Poole observed that treating legislators as fixed ideologically is "a strong assumption."

12. See Greg Adams, Michael Bailey, and Chris Fastnow, "Bicameralism—Redundancy or Grand Plan? Cross-Chamber Tests of Ideological Differences," paper presented at the annual meeting of the Midwest Political Science Association, 2000.

13. See, among others, Richard F. Fenno Jr., *Homestyle: House Members in Their Districts* (Little, Brown, 1978); Richard F. Fenno Jr., *The United States Senate: A Bicameral Perspective* (Washington: American Enterprise Institute for Public Policy Research, 1982); and Jonathan S. Krasno, *Challengers, Competition, and Reelection: Comparing House and Senate Elections* (Yale University Press, 1994). See also Adams, Bailey, and Fastnow, "Bicameralism," who show that House and Senate members respond differently to district-based characteristics.

14. On the procedural advantages of House majority party leaders, see John Aldrich and David R. Rohde, "The Consequences of Party Organization in the House," in Jon R. Bond and Richard Fleisher, eds., *Polarized Politics: Congress and the President in a Partisan Era* (Washington: Congressional Quarterly Press, 2000). On the limits of party rule in the Senate, see Eric D. Lawrence, Forrest Maltzman, and Steven S. Smith, "Party Effects in the Senate," paper presented at the annual meeting of the American Political Science Association, Washington, D.C., 2000.

15. McCarty, Poole, and Rosenthal's analysis of the ideological change of party switchers led them to acknowledge that NOMINATE scores incorporate some party pressure. Thus, it is not surprising that House and Senate scores are not comparable across the two chambers if party leaders have different sets of procedural tools. See Nolan McCarty, Keith T. Poole, and Howard Rosenthal, "The Hunt for Party Discipline in Congress," *American Political Science Review*, vol. 95 (September, 2001), pp. 673–88.

16. For every House and Senate member, I calculate their mean party loyalty score over all mildly contested roll call votes in each Congress, and then calculate an average score for their tenure in each chamber. Following Poole and Rosenthal,

Congress, I define mildly contested votes as those where more than 97.5 percent of the chamber voted on the same side.

17. Although the drop is statistically significant, the substantive drop is an average of 2 percent.

18. These are all sitting House members who were appointed to the Senate in mid-Congress and accumulated a voting record in both chambers in a single Congress.

19. See Poole and Rosenthal, *Congress,* pp. 230–32.

20. See Poole, "Changing Minds?" p. 4.

21. The percentage remains below 5 percent, regardless of how I code civil rights/racial issues after the 1960s. Poole, "Changing Minds?" p. 4, notes that voting on these racial issues today largely falls along the first, left-right, dimension.

22. The ability of southerners to use the filibuster to keep civil-rights–related issues from coming to the floor in the mid-twentieth century Senate also raises the possibility that second dimension issues are disproportionately underrepresented in senators' roll call behavior.

23. See Adams, Bailey, and Fastnow, "Bicameralism."

24. I use the *House of Representatives' Final Calendar,* published each Congress, to identify every conference report brought to both chambers' floors each Congress, and then determine the floor roll call vote outcome for each report (votes for the 80th–101st Congresses are obtained from ICPSR roll call files and for the 102d–106th Congresses from Thomas (http://thomas.loc.gov). Conference reports approved by voice vote are coded as 100 percent approval. Only up-or-down votes to approve a conference report are coded. Other votes related to conference reports (such as one chamber's motion to recede from disagreement with amendments added by the other chamber) are dropped since identical votes would not have been cast by the two chambers.

25. In the models in this book, I drop the measure of ideological diversity that I used in my 1999 analysis since it was obtained by averaging the mean House and Senate standard deviation around the first dimension W-NOMINATE scores for each Congress. As my theoretical interest is in the impact of bicameralism and party moderation on legislative outcomes, dropping these two variables is of little cost theoretically. Nor do my original results change appreciably with the new specification.

26. Note that in the estimations in this book, I use an improved measure of partisan moderation. Nearly identical results obtain when I use the simpler measure (percentage of moderates) from my original analysis (also used by Chiou and Rothenberg, "The Dynamics of Legislative Gridlock Revisited"). In other words, the results in chapter 4 are not an artifact of substituting one measure of moderation for another. Nor are the results an artifact of the estimation routine. Nearly identical results obtain when Prais-Winsten estimation is used as Chiou and Rothenberg advocate.

Appendix D

1. The sign of the coefficient for moderation is reversed across the two models because the direction of the hypothesis changes. In the gridlock model, the greater the degree of moderation, the lower the frequency of gridlock expected (thus the negative coefficient). In the productivity model, the greater the degree of moderation, the greater the number of landmark laws expected (thus the positive coefficient).

Index

₿ THE BROOKINGS INSTITUTION

The Brookings Institution is an independent organization devoted to nonpartisan research, education, and publication in economics, government, foreign policy, and the social sciences generally. Its principal purposes are to aid in the development of sound public policies and to promote public understanding of issues of national importance. The Institution was founded on December 8, 1927, to merge the activities of the Institute for Government Research, founded in 1916, the Institute of Economics, founded in 1922, and the Robert Brookings Graduate School of Economics and Government, founded in 1924. The Institution maintains a position of neutrality on issues of public policy to safeguard the intellectual freedom of the staff.